The Joy of CHINESE COOKING

The Joy of CHINESE COOKING

A step-by-step guide with 186 recipes

Lo Mei Hing, Giulia Marzotto Caotorta and Sun Tzi Hsi

GREENWICH HOUSE

Distributed by Crown Publishers, Inc.

New York

N.B. All recipes serve 4 unless otherwise indicated

Translated by Sara Harris
Copyright © 1981 Shogakukan Publishing Co. Ltd., Tokyo for the original edition
Copyright © 1982 Arnoldo Mondadori Editore, S.p.A., Milan for the international
edition
English translation copyright © 1983 Arnoldo Mondadori Editore, S.p.A., Milan

This 1983 edition is published by Greenwich House,
a division of Arlington House, Inc.,
distributed by Crown Publishers, Inc.

Library of Congress Cataloging in Publication Data
Lo, Mei Hing.
    The joy of Chinese cooking.
    Translation of: Cucina cinese.
    Includes index.
    1. Cookery, Chinese.   I. Marzotto Caotorta, Giulia.
II. Sun, Tzi Hsi.   III. Title.
TX724.5.C5L6513 1983   641.5951   83–1600
ISBN 0–517–41019–2

h g f

Printed and bound in Italy by Arnoldo Mondadori Editore, Verona

Contents

". . . there are few who know how to distinguish the true taste of food."
—Mencius (372–289 B.C.)

"From the moment I awake each morning I must occupy myself with seven things: fuel, rice, oil, salt, soy sauce, vinegar, and tea."
—Lines spoken by the wife in a Chinese play dating from the Yüan dynasty (1280–1368).

Author's Note

The recipes given in this book are accompanied by the following symbols:

 30′   Preparation and cooking time

        Classic Chinese dishes

       Memorable dishes for important occasions

Cooking methods

        Shallow-frying

        Stir-frying

        Steaming

        Pot roasting or casserole cooking

        Boiling and simmering

        Deep-frying

        Stewing

        Mongolian hot pot cooking

Harmony, Balance, and Joy: A Glimpse of Chinese Philosophy through Chinese Cooking

When I was a little girl in China the grown-ups used to say to me, "Eat this, it's Yang and it's good for you!" or "Drink this, it will give you energy!" From then on I realized that we should no more draw a distinction between food and medicine than try to separate the body and the soul; anything that is good for the body must be both therapeutic and nourishing at one and the same time.

Eating is one of the necessities of life, but it should be enjoyed and become as pleasurable as singing, talking to one another, inquiring into the meaning of life, breathing, painting . . . activities which are the very stuff of being. Good nutrition consists of eating only when you are hungry, rather like writing poetry only when inspired; it is not healthy to stuff yourself full of food until you feel your stomach may burst. Likewise, we should drink only when we feel thirsty and then preferably hot or cool drinks – iced drinks are not advisable. A good general rule is always get up from the table feeling as if you could eat a little more, and never get so hungry that you suffer from a feeling of malaise. In my youth, the grown-ups were echoing the words of the ancient philosophers when they told me, "This will keep you healthy because you will maintain the vital flow of energy and life force and the positive and negative forces of Yin and Yang will be evenly balanced."

Perhaps the best word to use when describing Chinese philosophy and the way it has inspired the art of Chinese cooking would be "harmony." There are no hard and fast rules, no fixed dogma, no arbitrary categories or immutable approved methods; the aim is to achieve balance.

This means that an hors d'oeuvre can equally well serve as a side dish or as part of a main course and that a particular ingredient can form a complete meal. It is all up to the individual; the important thing to remember is not to force yourself to eat something which you don't want, for this would only harm the body and mind. In China, our constant endeavor is to achieve the balance between the principles of Yin and Yang.

This underlying philosophy should be constantly borne in mind when learning about Chinese cooking; nor should we forget that the Chinese civilization is more than five thousand years old, and yet China's population is still growing and now represents one-third of the human race. China covers vast stretches of Asia, and climate and conditions therefore vary widely from region to region. The country is surrounded from the northeast to the southwest by high mountains, fertile plains, lakes, rivers, and seas; and all these have inevitably made their mark on the inhabitants, determining countless different ways of living and eating.

For long periods of time some regions were cut off from the rest of the country by natural barriers, so that China has been influenced by many different, often alien, cultural traditions. The people of the various regions share certain characteristics: lively imagination, creativity, and the ability to make the most of what nature has provided. In central and southern China rice is the staple food; in the north, maize and cereals are the staple, depending on whether a particular region's soil and climate are more suited to growing one or the other. The variations in each region's principal crop are reflected in the thousands of local dishes which for convenience are classified under four main "schools" of cooking: the North (Hebei, Shandong, and Henan); the South (Guangdong); the East (Fujian and Jiangxi); and the West (Sichuan and Yunnan).

One must remember that China has always been a poor country with only a small proportion of her enormous land area suitable for agriculture. Successive invasions by barbarians, famines caused by drought or floods, and the inexorably soaring population have meant that throughout her long history the problem of food has always been crucial. Anything and everything that can possibly be eaten has therefore found a place in the Chinese repertoire of cooking: such parts of the duck as the beak and feet are regarded as inedible and faintly repulsive in many countries of the world; the Chinese consider them a delicacy, and take as much care in their preparation as a Westerner would devote to the choicest ingredients at his disposal. When they do not form the basis of a meal, chicken blood, feet, and nearly every imaginable organ are used as additional ingredients in dishes, often inspired by necessity and enhanced by the imagination. There is a dish which is considered by the inhabitants of Shaoxing in Zhejiang province to be the epitome of refined cooking; it combines the tastes of chicken skin with the wing flesh, tendons, and feet – an example *par excellence* of the Chinese dictum, "Everything but the feathers."

THE COOKING OF NORTHERN CHINA: The cuisine of the Emperors

It is difficult to define the exact area which constitutes northern China. For simplicity's sake it can be said to be made up of the Yellow River basin, and more specifically of the provinces of Shandong and Hebei. These two provinces have played an important part in Chinese history: Shandong is the native province of the two greatest Chinese philosophers, Confucius and Mencius; Hebei is the province of Beijing (Peking), China's capital, from time immemorial. The two provinces are, in fact, so closely linked as almost to be considered one, and together are known as the cradle of Chinese civilization.

Shandong can reasonably take credit for being the main source of and having the greatest influence on northern Chinese cooking, although Hebei has certainly made a considerable contribution. Hebei, more specifically Beijing (Peking), has been the melting pot of regional traditions in cooking and the focal point that attracted the best and most original cooks from all over China.

A considerable external influence on northern Chinese cooking has come from Mongolia; for centuries a steady flow of emigrants from this region moved southward to settle in China. Later, there were several dynasties of Chinese rulers of Mongolian origin, and many Mongolian dishes were adopted by the people of northern China.

The Great Wall, that monumental barrier straddling the country, had kept out the Tatar hordes for hundreds of years; but eventually, in the early thirteenth century, China was invaded, and Kublai Khan, who enjoyed a very long reign, finally ruled over all the "Sons of Han" when he became Emperor of all China in 1280. Under his reign Mongolian influence reached its highest point and left behind a legacy which survives to this day. The fact that many of the invading hordes were Moslems accounts for the relative scarcity of pork dishes in this region's cuisine and for the abundance of recipes based on mutton and goat (whose strong flavor and smell are repugnant to the Chinese from other regions).

A long succession of emperors imprinted their customs and ways of living on the country, each bringing his own native region's usages and distinctive styles to be adopted and given the seal of the imperial court's approval.

The climate in northern China is too cold for the cultivation of rice, but the alluvial plains of the Yellow River and the windswept expanses of yellow earth in the provinces of Shanxi, Shaanxi, Ningxia, and Gansu have for thousands of years provided the fertile soil necessary for growing wheat, millet, barley, and other cereals (*kaoliang*). Flour is a basic ingredient in the cooking of these regions.

In addition to limiting the choice of ingredients, the extreme cold in this region has determined the cooking techniques used. The Mongolian hot pot of today is a modest, scaled-down version of the great braziers which were once used both to cook food and warm people's homes. A great deal of oil was used for this method of cooking and so it was necessary to include plenty of vinegar, garlic, and leeks to counteract the oily taste. The popularity of such starchy items as steamed breads, pancakes, and dumplings of many kinds, some stuffed with finely chopped meat or vegetables, can also be explained by the need to combat the rigors of the climate.

The long duration of the Qing (Ch'ing) dynasty (1644–1911), also known as the Manchu dynasty, provided the final impetus to the establishment of what is now recognized as a separate school of cooking in the north; under Manchu supremacy northern Chinese cuisine received its finishing touches.

Since the Manchus had no real school of cooking of their own, they were content to adopt the best of the other regions' cuisines (especially that of the south) and to absorb them into their own, less venerable culinary tradition. For this reason some purists maintain that there is no genuinely native school of northern China and that it has simply imported what is most outstanding from the rest of the country. Be that as it may, the originality and exquisite taste of many dishes from this area – Peking Duck, for example – are beyond question.

THE TASTE OF THE SOUTH: Where the sun is reflected in the paddy fields

Far beyond the borders of China, in restaurants scattered all over the world, the taste of the food of Guangdong (Canton) and, to a lesser extent, of Guangxi is certainly the most widely known and is usually referred to as Cantonese cuisine.

The main crop is rice; the subtropical climate makes possible three harvests a year. In addition, the region produces an almost inexhaustible quantity and variety of fruit and vegetables, a selection wide enough to satisfy the most demanding cooks; hence, the richness of taste, color, and aroma in Cantonese cuisine.

From the earliest days of their ancient history the people of Guangdong and Guangxi have derived a large part of their food from the sea, so seafood of all kinds figures largely on the menus of southern China. The freshness of these fish and shellfish is so highly prized that they are sold live in the markets. Nonetheless, the practice of preserving fish by drying or salting is popular, and therefore many sauces are made with seafoods of various kinds.

As for meat, pork and chicken are the most widely consumed; beef is not particularly popular, and mutton or lamb is very rarely encountered.

Despite the fact that as far back as the Qin (Ch'in) dynasty (255–207 B.C.) Chinese emperors sent troops to colonize this area, it became increasingly susceptible to foreign influence. The first Arab traders established trading settlements in southern China from A.D. 400 onward, acting as middlemen in commerce with the West. The Portuguese were the first Europeans to trade with the Chinese, and they only entered the scene in the sixteenth century.

The nineteenth-century Cantonese merchants who had prospered and grown rich through commerce and trade with the West lived in considerable luxury and had a taste for rare and exotic delicacies. Cantonese cooks were encouraged to create increasingly elaborate dishes, using the most costly ingredients; and to this day, good Cantonese cooking tends to be the most expensive. The two most extravagant dishes of Chinese cooking, Shark's Fin Soup and Bird's Nest Soup are most delectable when made by Cantonese hands. Cantonese cuisine became the favorite of the Imperial Palace, two thousand miles away, and the Manchu court always scheduled a stay in Guangdong during its travels through China in order to taste this cooking at its best, fresh from Cantonese kitchens.

Continuous contact with foreigners meant that Cantonese cooks became masters in adapting to the tastes of the "red-haired foreign devils" as Westerners were known. Purists maintain that the tradition of sweet and sour flavoring is the result of this adaptation, although as early as 1700 a cook book gave a recipe for pork in which vinegar was the predominant flavor. Be this as it may, however, such a strong, pronounced ingredient should not be used indiscriminately, or it could swamp the more delicate flavors so typical of subtle Cantonese cuisine, in which the ideal is to cook foods, altering their color and consistency as little as possible, and to use accompanying ingredients as complements, not as disguises. Oil is used very sparingly in Cantonese kitchens. A great many dishes are steamed; the most famous of these steamed foods form a category of their own: *dim sum* or *tien hsin*, an infinite variety of bite-size delicacies, including every imaginable ingredient, which provide the equivalent of fast food for millions of Chinese, especially those living in Hong Kong.

THE COOKING OF EASTERN CHINA: The song of the carp in the Yangtze River

The coastal or eastern regions of China are so closely interlinked socially, economically, and in matters of custom that they are not clearly distinguishable or separately identifiable. The climate is predominantly subtropical, but so great is the divergence between one season and another that any number of different crops can be grown. All kinds of meat are available and there is a plentiful supply of seafood and freshwater fish to be caught in the numerous rivers and lakes (an outstanding example being the hairy crab of Shanghai).

External influences have played their role in developing the rich and varied spectrum of dishes which are typical of these regions: in the fourteenth century Hangzhou was chosen as the capital of the exiled Song court. Nanjing (Nanking) was also the capital for many years, and this era left its mark on the city, not least on its cooking.

Nanjing is the birthplace of pressed duck; Yanzhou saw the creation of such rice, noodle, and vegetable dishes as the famous Cantonese rice. Shao Shing still produces the most highly prized rice wine, while soy sauce from Amoy is considered without equal. The beautiful maidens of Suzhou enjoy legendary fame, as does its *dim sum* (*tien hsin*), while Hangzhou boasts the best fish in its lakes. Two of these eastern provinces are justly famous for products they have sent all over the world: vinegar from Zhejiang and kaolin, which is used in the manufacture of the world's finest porcelain, from Jiangxi.

Shanghai winters are always so bitterly cold that oil is used in abundance and a great many starchy foods are consumed: dumplings, spring rolls stuffed with meat and vegetables, noodles in broth. For the same reason local methods of preserving food by salting, pickling, drying, or curing have been perfected. Thousand-year-old eggs are a noteworthy example of this high level of expertise and ingenuity in preserving foodstuffs. Fujian, which was one of the last regions to come under the sway of imperial power, has not only retained its one hundred dialects, some of which hardly resemble one other, but also has one hundred distinct cooking traditions; these have one aim in common: the preparation of ingredients in such a way that they retain their original flavors.

WESTERN CHINESE COOKING: The way of Buddha

Western China was politically independent for many centuries, and only in 1252 did Kublai Khan manage to bring it under the sway of centralized imperial rule. Subsequently, outside influence never made itself felt consistently, even during the Sino–Japanese war when Chongqing (Chungking) in the province Sichuan was temporarily the capital of the country.

The food of western China is unique among the various schools of Chinese cooking, in that a tremendous quantity and variety of spices are used in the preparation of regional dishes. The reason for this and for the similarity between the cuisine of Sichuan and those of Thailand, Burma, and India probably lies in the influence of Buddhism, which was introduced from India across the province of Yunnan following the path of Buddha, and molded local habits and customs. The Buddhist monks and the merchants who followed in their footsteps brought with them spices and herbs and the art of using them for both culinary and therapeutic purposes. The fertile soil helped propagate and popularize these ingredients. Chili pepper, the strongest condiment in China, is used liberally and is a characteristic ingredient of the cuisine of western China. The most typical method of cooking, used in particular for chicken and duck, is smoking over tea leaves and camphor wood.

The provinces of Henan and Hubei are very like Sichuan, at least in their cooking. Yunnan, on the other hand, is a mountainous and forbidding region where the inhabitants wrest a living from the harsh terrain, and its cuisine has been influenced by the Moslems sent there by Kublai Khan to colonize the area and by the surrounding countries: Vietnam, Laos, Burma, and, indirectly, India.

Lo Mei Hing

Typical Chinese Utensils

The range of utensils needed to cook Chinese food is relatively small. A single pan, the wok, can be used for stir-frying, sautéing, and deep-frying; it is a thoroughly versatile piece of equipment and easy to use. A sound piece of advice is to buy just a few basic utensils to begin with, making sure that they are of good quality.

Chopsticks Fingers came first . . . and then came chopsticks. The Chinese first started eating with chopsticks under the Shang dynasty (1766–1123 B.C.). These chopsticks were made of various materials, including agate, jade, and even silver, valued for its imputed property of revealing the presence of poisoned food by turning black. Ivory chopsticks, however, have always been considered the best.

The ideograms for chopsticks are pronounced in almost exactly the same way as two other ideograms which are a wish for happiness and healthy children to a newly married couple, and, in fact, chopsticks are often given as a wedding present.

Chopsticks come in two sizes. The shorter ones are about 10 inches long and are used to transfer food from the plate or bowl to the mouth. They can be made of bamboo, plastic, or ivory and are often lacquered and decorated with various designs. The longer chopsticks, about 14 inches in length, are ideally made of bamboo and are used for such kitchen tasks as beating eggs, mixing sauces, and transferring ingredients to and from the wok or "keeping food on the move," as the Chinese say.

Wok This is the classic Chinese cooking pan, made of iron (preferable to the cheaper metal versions) from a centuries-old design. The wok is actually called *kuo* in Chinese. Its rounded shape is ideal for even distribution of heat – although it should be noted that the wok does not function as well on an electric hob as it does over gas. Woks come in various sizes, with either two metal handles or one wooden handle.

Wash the wok well with detergent before its first use and rinse it thoroughly; then dry it with paper towels. Season it by sprinkling the inside with unsalted oil (sunflower or sesame oil) and placing it over a high heat for five or six minutes. Remove the wok from the heat and, being careful not to burn yourself, rinse it immediately in plenty of hot water. Dry it with paper towels. Oil the pan again, place it over a high heat for a minute, rinse it and dry it. Repeat this operation until no more black discoloration comes off on the towels.

Once the wok is in use, it is better not to use detergents to wash it; always rinse it well under running hot water, and place it over a high heat for a few seconds to dry. The wok should always be dried very thoroughly to avoid rusting.

Wok rings can be bought separately in specialty shops if they are not sold with the wok itself, but they are not indispensable; their main purpose is to hold the wok steady on modern cookers, but stir-frying is best done over a flame without a ring.

For home use a wok of approximately 13–15 inches in diameter is ideal; any smaller size

Strainers or skimmers

Wok

Metal ladle

Huo Kuo (Mongolian hot pot)

Chinese fish server

14

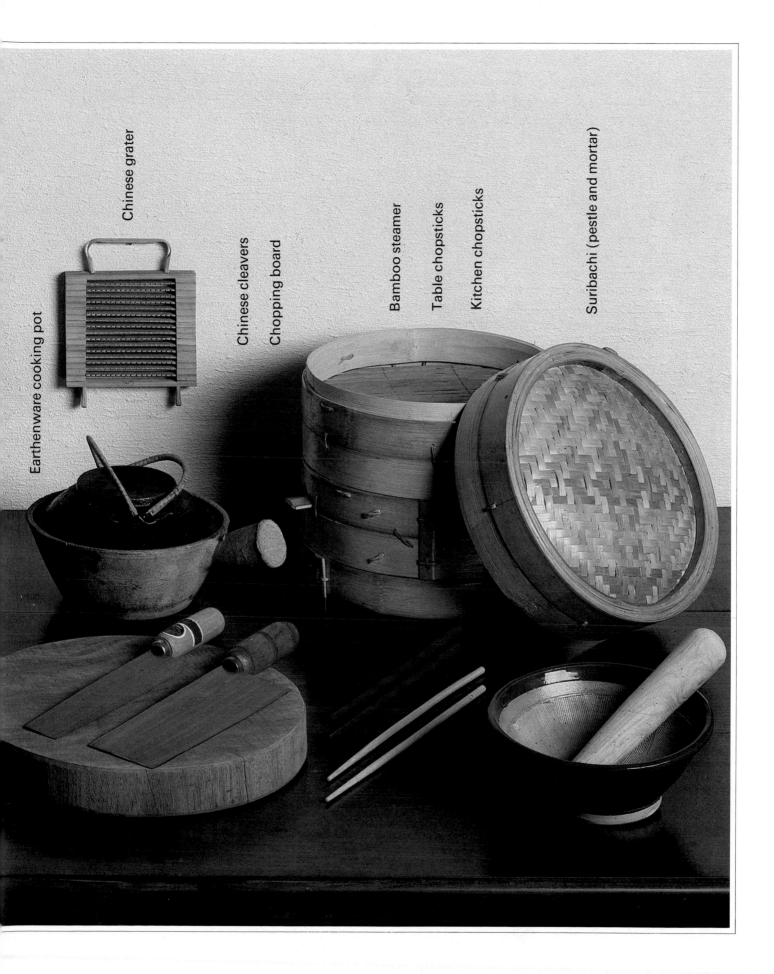

Earthenware cooking pot

Chinese grater

Chinese cleavers

Chopping board

Bamboo steamer

Table chopsticks

Kitchen chopsticks

Suribachi (pestle and mortar)

would make stir-frying vegetables or cooking Cantonese rice difficult, even for a small number of people. If too large a wok is used, the heat from a modern burner will not be evenly distributed.

Bamboo Steamer This is the ideal piece of equipment for steaming food. It is placed on a wok containing boiling water (use a ring for stability). The steamer is made of woven bamboo, and since this is porous, excess moisture from the steam does not condense on the inside of the lid and drip down, spoiling the food. Bamboo steamers come in various sizes and the smaller ones are usually used for steaming *dim sum*.

How to use steamer: fill the wok ⅔ full of water, place the bamboo steamer on top, and bring the water to a boil to produce plenty of steam, which will circulate throughout the various layers of the steamer. Place the prepared food in the steamer and top up the boiling water from time to time (never add cold water as this will take time to heat, and the flow of steam will be interrupted). Because the steamer has several layers, several dishes can be cooked at the same time. Food such as spring rolls can be placed directly on the bamboo bottom of each compartment; but foods which release fat or juice during cooking are better placed on a heat-resistant dish or a folded cloth, or cabbage or lotus leaves. Leave enough space around the sides for the steam to circulate freely. Before using a new bamboo steamer for the first time, simmer it in gently boiling water for at least ten minutes.

Chinese Cleaver This Chinese knife brings its full weight to bear on the materials to be cut. To the uninitiated or unpracticed this may seem dangerous, but a Chinese cook can chop up fowls with lightning speed and efficiency; and when leek or ginger has to be crushed with the flat of the knife blade, the practicality of this tool is really revealed. Furthermore, the ingredients can be scooped up on the broad blade. Chinese cleavers come with very broad blades or with narrower blades. The latter are lighter and sharper and are used for slicing or shredding meat, vegetables, and fruit. The broad-bladed cleaver is used for chopping through bone. The sharpened blade of a Chinese cleaver is the ideal tool for cutting up poultry or meat, bones and all, with sharp, decisive blows, while it can also be used for chopping ingredients very finely.

Huo Kuo (Mongolian hot pot) This is a brass cooking pot, about 10 inches in diameter with a small chimney in the center containing charcoal. As the charcoal burns, the liquid in the circular basin surrounding it is heated to a boil. This method of cooking is widely used in northern China. The hot pot is conveniently placed in the center of the table. Meat, fish, vegetables, etc., are sliced wafer thin, and each guest picks up the raw ingredients of his choice with chopsticks and dips them in the boiling broth to cook for a minute or two.

Chopping Board A Chinese chopping board is a round, horizontally cut piece of solid wood and is usually extremely heavy. An ordinary, less cumbersome Western-style chopping board can be substituted.

Metal Ladle and Chinese Fish Server The Chinese ladle is made of iron or steel and is shallower than its Western counterpart, adapting well to the curvature of the wok. It is used to mix and turn foods which are being stir-fried; it is also used for adding oil when frying and for countless other purposes. The Chinese fish server is used for mixing foods which are being stir-fried with little or no liquid and is ideal for turning whole fish.

Earthenware Casserole or Cooking Pot This implement is needed for slow cooking meat, giblets, and soup. In China an earthenware cooking pot with one handle, the *sha kwo*, is used.

Strainers or Skimmers These come in various sizes with long bamboo handles and wire mesh ladles. They are excellent for lifting deep-fried foods, and the fine wire mesh ladles are very efficient skimmers. It is a good idea to select a mesh ladle only a little smaller than the wok so all the fried food can be removed and drained at once as soon as it is ready. A small mesh ladle for skimming or draining individual ingredients should also be purchased.

Chinese Grater A small bamboo or ceramic grater with particularly sharp teeth, usually used for grating ginger.

Suribachi (Pestle and Mortar) A ceramic bowl with a ridged or striated inner surface, which originated in Japan is used as a mortar in which a wide variety of materials are pounded with a wooden pestle.

RECIPES

One of the problems confronting the Westerner who wants to try his hand at Chinese cooking can be the difficulty of obtaining ingredients. Climatic conditions and other factors prevent many products from being grown in the West, making it impossible to get hold of a great many of the foodstuffs which the Chinese use in the preparation of their dishes.

These obstacles should not deter the new-comer, since as we have already stressed, Chinese cooking is very versatile, and rarely does the success of a dish hinge solely upon one ingredient; another, similar ingredient can usually be substituted. Obviously a chicken cannot be used as the main ingredient in Peking Duck, and Shark's Fin Soup cannot be made with any other type of seafood, since the taste is too distinctive. The scope for improvisation in Chinese cuisine is, however, considerable, and the resulting dishes can be as appetizing as the originals. Sweet-and-sour dishes, in which the main ingredient can equally well be pork, duck, shrimp, or fish, demonstrate this flexibility. So there is no justification for giving up all thought of preparing chicken with cashew nuts because one or the other of these ingredients is unavailable: chicken with almonds will do just as well, or pork with cashew nuts; and both are equally genuine Chinese dishes. Imagination and a certain sense of what goes with what are all that are needed in order to achieve the proverbial harmony of Chinese cooking.

The essence of Chinese cooking is its everyday adaptability. Below are some Chinese ingredients and their common Western substitutes:

Rice wine (Shao Shing) can be replaced by sake, dry sherry, dry vermouth, or dry white wine.

Scallions can be replaced by leeks, shallots, or large, mild onions.

The Chinese use the same oil several times for frying, maintaining that it acquires more flavor each time it is used. Soybean oil, however, gives off a certain amount of smoke and fumes, so peanut oil is preferable.

WEIGHTS AND MEASURES

Some of the measurements may appear overprecise ($\frac{1}{3}$ teaspoon, etc.), but this serves to emphasize that where spices and flavorings are concerned, the cook should err on the side of too little rather than too much. Most of the seasonings can be adjusted to taste if desired.

As with the ingredients in Chinese food, quantities do not need to be adhered to with exact precision. If you are a little short of one ingredient, simply increase the quantity of another. Obviously this does not apply to seasonings, but here again, within certain parameters, measurements need not be too slavishly observed.

Appetizers and Snacks

Appetizers in China serve much the same purpose as in the West; they must stimulate the appetite and fill one with pleasant anticipation of the more substantial courses which are to follow but Chinese appetizers differ in one very important respect: they can all, without exception, be served with rice as a main course at any stage during the meal.

In addition to these appetizers, there is an endless variety of little snacks which form a separate category; these are the famous Cantonese dim sum *(literally "to dot the heart") or, as they are known in Mandarin,* tien hsin *("the heart-touchers"). Dim sum* include *various types of dumplings: spring rolls, steamed rolls filled with meat or vegetables, and little dishes of duck's feet, hearts, and countless other ingredients cooked in every conceivable way.*

In the tea parlors of Hong Kong and southern China these fragrant and flavorful delicacies are wheeled between the tables of the restaurant or carried on trays slung around the necks of elderly waiters or waitresses so that the clientele may pick and choose exactly what appeals to them and feel free to order as much as they wish.

Seven-color appetizer

1. CHICKEN SALAD WITH SWEET AND SOUR DRESSING

2 spring chicken leg quarters
2 cucumbers

For the sauce:
4 tablespoons light soy sauce
1½ tablespoons sugar
2 teaspoons vinegar
½ teaspoon soybean paste
5 tablespoons ground sesame seeds or sesame paste
1 tablespoon finely minced ginger root
½ teaspoon finely minced garlic
1 tablespoon sesame oil
½ teaspoon chili paste or oil
a pinch of monosodium glutamate (optional)
Preparation time: 40 minutes
220 calories; 10.5 g protein; 17.3 g fat; 7.5 g sugar

1. Place the chicken in a pan with enough cold water to cover, bring to a boil, then lower the heat slightly, and simmer for 10 to 15 minutes or until the juices run clear when a skewer is inserted. Remove the chicken, rinse under cold running water, pat dry with paper towels, and place on a plate in the refrigerator.

2. Wash the cucumber; slice it diagonally into pieces about ¾ inch long. (See notes on page 304 for details of Chinese cutting techniques.)

3. Mix all the sauce ingredients together.

4. Bone the chicken and cut the meat obliquely into ¼–½-inch slices. Arrange on top of the cucumber on a serving dish and sprinkle with the sauce.

2. CUTTLEFISH FLOWERS WITH GINGER SAUCE

½–¾ pound cuttlefish
¼ pound celery
salt
sesame oil
For the sauce:
1 ounce ginger root
2½ tablespoons light soy sauce
4 tablespoons vinegar
1 tablespoon sesame oil
a pinch of monosodium glutamate (optional)
Preparation time: 40 minutes
91 calories; 12 g protein; 4 g fat; 1.1 g sugar

1. Hold the cuttlefish under cold running water, rub the outer skin with the fingers, and pull the membrane away. Discard it. Cut off the tentacles and pull away and discard the cuttlebone, ink sac, hard mouth parts, and eyes, leaving only the body of white firm meat.

2. Rinse thoroughly. Cut into strips about 2 inches wide, following the grain of the flesh. Place the pieces on a flat surface.

3. Using a sharp knife score the pieces at an angle, in a criss-cross pattern, at ¼-inch intervals, making sure that the skin is not cut through.

4. Cut the celery into matchsticks 2–2¼ inches long, place in cold water for 10 minutes, then drain. Chop the ginger very finely and mix with the other sauce ingredients.

5. Rinse the cuttlefish in cold water, place in a saucepan of boiling water and blanch for 30 seconds; the pieces of cuttlefish will curl.

6. Drain and dry the cuttlefish and sprinkle with a pinch of salt and a little sesame oil.

7. Arrange the celery on a plate, place the strips of cuttlefish on top, and cover with the sauce.

3. MARINATED ANCHOVIES

peanut oil
1½ pounds anchovies or other very small fish, such as smelts or sprats (fresh or frozen)
1 piece of ginger root
1 large leek
1 small piece of cinnamon stick
generous 3 cups stock or water
a pinch of monosodium glutamate (optional)
1 tablespoon sesame oil
For the sauce:
4 tablespoons soy sauce
4 tablespoons rice wine
3 tablespoons sugar
2 tablespoons vinegar
pepper
Preparation time: 50 minutes
328 calories; 26.1 g protein; 17.6 g fat; 10.5 g sugar

1. Heat the peanut oil to 350°F (180°C.); add the anchovies and fry for 2 to 3 minutes, remove from the oil and drain. With the oil at 325°F. (170°C) fry for 4 to 5 minutes, or until crisp.

2. Place the ginger (cut into wafer-thin slices) with the leek (cut into small pieces) and the cinnamon in a wok or skillet and arrange the anchovies neatly on top.

3. Pour the stock or water into the wok. Mix the sauce ingredients and add 2 tablespoons peanut oil. Skim,

and simmer, covered, for 10 minutes.

4. Remove the lid, turn up the heat, and cook briskly, spooning the juices over the fish. Add 2 more tablespoons peanut oil, pouring it in so that it trickles down the pan. Finally, add a pinch of monosodium glutamate.

5. Continue cooking until the liquid has almost completely evaporated; add a little sesame oil.

6. Arrange the fish on a serving plate, pour over the remaining juices, and allow to cool.

4. SICHUAN CUCUMBER SALAD

1 pound cucumbers
salt
a small piece (1 ounce) of ginger root
2 chili peppers
2 tablespoons peanut oil
2 tablespoons sesame oil
For the sweet and sour sauce:
4 tablespoons sugar
3 tablespoons vinegar
Preparation time: 20 minutes
170 calories; 1.3 g protein; 13.3 g fat; 12.2 g sugar

1. Wash the cucumbers. Trim off the ends, cut in half vertically, and scoop out seeds. Make oblique incisions in the flesh at intervals of approximately $\frac{1}{8}$ inch. Cut the cucumber into 1-inch pieces.

2. Sprinkle the cucumber pieces with 1$\frac{1}{2}$ tablespoons salt and a little water. Place in a colander with a plate and a weight on top and leave for about 30 minutes.

3. Cut the ginger into very thin slices and slice the chili peppers into fine rings. Rinse the cucumber pieces under cold water and drain well. Place in a bowl.

4. Scatter the ginger and chili pepper over the cucumber, pour on the sugar and vinegar and mix well.

5. Pour the peanut oil and the sesame oil into a wok and heat until the oil just starts to smoke slightly. Pour the hot oil over the cucumber mixture immediately; cover and leave to stand for about 30 minutes.

For the sesame sauce:
3 tablespoons soy sauce
2 tablespoons vinegar
1 tablespoon ground sesame seeds
1 tablespoon sesame oil
1 teaspoon pepper
1 teaspoon chili oil
a pinch of monosodium glutamate (optional)
Preparation time: 45 minutes
191 calories; 7.3 g protein; 16.8 g fat; 5.2 g sugar

1. Wash the bean sprouts well; shred the ham and sweet peppers.

2. Heat 3 tablespoons peanut oil in a wok with $\frac{1}{2}$ teaspoon salt; add the bean sprouts, the ham, and peppers, and stir-fry.

3. Add 1 teaspoon each soy sauce and rice wine and a pinch of pepper. When the bean sprouts are tender drain off excess liquid and transfer to a plate.

4. Cut the dried bean curd skins in thirds. Soak in plenty of water. Spread out flat, blot away excess moisture, and place $\frac{1}{6}$ of the bean sprout mixture on the lower half of each sheet. Roll up securely.

5. Pour 1 teaspoon sesame oil into the wok to cover the surface with a thin film. Arrange the bean curd rolls in the wok and fry over a high heat until evenly browned. Allow to cool.

6. When cool, cut each roll into 6 to 8 portions.

7. Mix together the sesame sauce ingredients and pour over the rolls.

5. ABALONE IN OYSTER SAUCE

1$\frac{1}{4}$ pounds canned abalone
peanut oil
$\frac{1}{4}$ leek
a small piece of ginger root
1 tablespoon oyster sauce
2 cups stock or boiling water
sesame oil
For the sauce:
1 tablespoon soy sauce
1 tablespoon sugar
1 tablespoon rice wine
a pinch of pepper
a pinch of monosodium glutamate (optional)
Preparation time: 30 minutes
196 calories; 17.9 g protein; 10.9 g fat; 3.6 g sugar

1. Drain the abalone and cut the larger ones in half.

2. Pour 2 tablespoons of peanut oil into a wok. Stir-fry the leek, sliced into 1-inch lengths together with the pounded ginger.

3. Add the oyster sauce and then the abalone. Fry lightly, then pour in the hot stock or boiling water, and stir in the sauce ingredients.

4. Cook over a moderate heat, removing any scum from the surface. When the liquid has almost completely evaporated, add 1 tablespoon sesame oil.

5. Remove and discard the pieces of leek and the ginger. Turn off the heat, allow to cool, and serve.

6. VEGETARIAN "FISH" WITH SESAME SAUCE

$\frac{3}{4}$–1 pound bean sprouts
2 slices cooked ham
2 sweet peppers
peanut oil
salt
soy sauce
rice wine
pepper
2 sheets dried bean curd skin, approximately 8 × 18 inches

7. CHICKEN GIBLETS WITH SEAWEED

1$\frac{1}{2}$ pounds chicken giblets
1 presoaked dried green seaweed leaf, approximately 12 inches long
1 leek
a small piece of ginger root
1 small cinnamon stick
a small piece of dried mandarin peel
a little star anise
peanut oil
generous 3 cups stock or water
sesame oil
a pinch of monosodium glutamate (optional)
For the sauce:
3 tablespoons soy sauce
$\frac{1}{2}$ cup rice wine
$\frac{1}{4}$ cup sugar
Preparation time: 1 hour 15 minutes
73 calories; 28.4 g protein; 20 g fat; 14.6 g sugar

1. Wash the chicken giblets and boil them in plenty of water for 5 minutes, rinse in cold water and trim off any fat.

2. Divide the giblets into hearts, gizzards, and livers. Clean and trim the livers, removing any discolored parts; pare away the tough outer parts of the gizzards.

3. Wash the seaweed and cut into strips about $\frac{1}{2}$ inch wide. Cut the leek into 1$\frac{1}{4}$-inch lengths; pound the ginger. Wrap the cinnamon stick, the dried mandarin peel, and the star anise in a piece of cheesecloth and tie securely.

4. Pour 3 tablespoons of peanut oil into the wok and stir-fry the pieces of leek until they start to brown; turn off heat.

5. Add the ginger, seaweed, and chicken giblets to the wok; pour in the hot stock or water; then add the sauce ingredients and the little bag of spices. Turn on the heat.

6. As soon as the stock boils, lower the heat, remove any scum from the surface, and cover. Cook for 30 minutes. As soon as the chicken giblets are tender, add a pinch of monosodium glutamate (optional); increase the heat so that most of the liquid evaporates.

7. Pour in 2 tablespoons peanut oil; mix and allow the liquid to reduce until 90 percent has evaporated. Last, add 2 tablespoons of sesame oil.

Pig's tripe with pickled vegetables

An appetizer or a side-dish with boiled rice, this dish can be prepared several days in advance.

sea salt (preferably coarse)
$1\frac{1}{4}$ –$1\frac{1}{2}$ pounds pig's tripe
a small piece of leek
a small piece of ginger root
approximately $\frac{1}{2}$ pound Chinese salted white radish or mustard top (if dried salted mustard top is used, soak for 1 hour before use)
a large piece of ginger root
3 tablespoons peanut oil
1 tablespoon rice wine
a few drops of soy sauce
a few drops sesame oil
310 calories; 32.2 g protein; 17 g fat; 5.6 g sugar

1. Rub the coarse salt well into both sides of the tripe; wash very well under cold running water to get rid of the mucus, paying particular attention to the inner side. Turn the tripe over several times and make sure it is absolutely clean.

2. Boil the tripe in plenty of water with a small piece of leek and ginger. Thirty minutes' cooking will take away any trace of unpleasant smell.

3. Trim off any fat and gristle and cut the tripe into bite-size pieces.

4. Rinse the salted vegetables and cut them into pieces about the same size as the tripe; cut the large piece of ginger into very small, thin strips.

5. Heat the peanut oil in a wok and sauté the ginger until the aroma is released; add the tripe and then the salted vegetables and stir-fry.

6. Add the rice wine, trickling it down the side of the wok. Pour in enough water to barely cover the contents of the wok and cook for 20 to 30 minutes.

7. If the dish needs slightly more flavor, add a few drops of soy sauce, but remember that the salted vegetables will have added a good deal of saltiness already. Last, add a few drops of sesame oil.

Spring rolls

6–12 servings (12 rolls):
$\frac{1}{4}$ pound lean pork or chicken cut into thin strips measuring $\frac{1}{8} \times \frac{3}{4}$
   inches
2 level tablespoons cornstarch
2 tablespoons peanut oil
$\frac{1}{3}$ cup bamboo shoots cut to the same size and shape as the meat
2 large black dried Chinese mushrooms, presoaked and thinly
   sliced
1 small leek or large scallion including the green stem (finely
   chopped)
all-purpose flour
12 Chinese pancakes (see recipe on page 296)
oil for frying
For the sauce:
1 tablespoon sugar
a pinch of salt
$\frac{1}{2}$ teaspoon monosodium glutamate (optional)
$\frac{1}{2}$ tablespoon dark or "black" soy sauce
2 teaspoons light soy sauce
2 tablespoons chicken stock (see recipe on page 296)
1 tablespoon peanut oil
a few drops of sesame oil
1 tablespoon all-purpose flour
320 calories; 12 g protein; 25 g fat; 20 g sugar

1. Sprinkle the meat with the cornstarch and mix; leave to stand for a few minutes.

2. Heat the peanut oil in the wok and stir-fry the meat, the bamboo shoots, and the mushrooms for 1 minute.

3. Add the sauce ingredients and stir-fry until the liquid has evaporated; add the finely chopped leek. Transfer to a plate and leave to cool.

4. Prepare a paste for sealing the pancake rolls by dissolving 1 tablespoon of flour in 1 tablespoon of cold water. Add 2–3 tablespoons boiling water and stir.

5. Place some of the filling along the lower half of each pancake; lift up the lower edge, fold it over the filling, tuck in the edges at both ends, and roll up neatly, sealing the final flap with the flour and water paste.

6. Fry the rolls in plenty of hot oil (350°F/180°C) and serve while still piping hot and crisp.

Fried surprise rolls

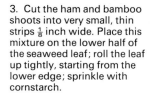

2 leaves dried purple (nori) seaweed
cornstarch as required
$\frac{1}{4}$ pound finely sliced pork belly
salt
pepper
a pinch of monosodium glutamate (optional)
1 slice cooked ham, cut just less than $\frac{1}{4}$ inch thick
6 bamboo shoots (boiled fresh or canned)
2 eggs
a pinch of salt
1 tablespoon cornstarch
1 tablespoon water
$\frac{1}{4}$ cup chopped shrimp
20 cashew nuts
oil for frying
batter (see recipe on pages 156–157)
389 calories; 13.9 g protein; 30.8 g fat; 14.8 g sugar

1. Spread one of the leaves of seaweed out flat and dredge the surface with cornstarch.

2. Cut the pork belly slices in half and then into rectangles; place them on the seaweed leaf; sprinkle evenly with salt, pepper, and a pinch of monosodium glutamate (optional).

3. Cut the ham and bamboo shoots into very small, thin strips $\frac{1}{8}$ inch wide. Place this mixture on the lower half of the seaweed leaf; roll the leaf up tightly, starting from the lower edge; sprinkle with cornstarch.

4. Beat the eggs well with salt and the cornstarch dissolved in the water; beat or mix in a blender and then use this mixture to make a very thin omelet, rather like a crepe, but rectangular, measuring about 6 × 8 inches.

5. Place the omelet on a board or working surface; dredge lightly with cornstarch, covering the entire surface.

6. Spread the chopped shrimp evenly and very delicately all over the surface of the omelet, leaving a border of $\frac{1}{2}$ inch along the lower edge. Spread the filling less thickly for a width of $2\frac{1}{4}$ inches along the upper edge of the rectangular omelet.

7. Remove the salt from the cashew nuts by rubbing with a damp cloth; arrange the nuts in a line along the lower edge of the omelet. Roll the omelet up neatly, bringing the lower edge over the cashew nuts to start with. Dredge the rolled omelet with cornstarch.

8. Dip the rolls in the batter and fry in very hot oil until they are crisp and golden brown. Cut into portions as desired and serve.

Pumpkin and pork rolls

These rolls are similar to spring rolls but have a golden pumpkin filling. They are slightly sweet and floury and make a very appetizing snack.

1½–1¾ pounds pumpkin
1 leek
3–4 dried black Chinese mushrooms
3 tablespoons peanut oil
4 ounces lean ground or very finely chopped pork
scant ½ teaspoon salt
a pinch of pepper
all-purpose flour
8–10 pancakes (see recipe on page 296)
oil for frying
339 calories; 10.5 g protein; 26.7 g fat; 18 g sugar

1

2

3

4

1. Remove seeds from pumpkin, cut off skin, and slice the flesh into small pieces. Place in a bowl in the bamboo steamer. Steam the pumpkin over a moderate heat until it is tender.

2. Turn off the heat and work the pumpkin flesh through a strainer or food mill while it is still very hot.

3. Cut the leek lengthwise and then crossways so that it is chopped into very fine pieces; place the dried mushrooms in a bowl and cover with boiling water. Allow to stand for 15 to 20 minutes. Squeeze to extract most of the moisture and cut off and discard the stems. Chop the mushrooms.

4. Heat the peanut oil in the wok, stir-fry the leek for a few seconds and then add the mushrooms, followed by the ground or finely chopped meat. When the meat has browned, season with salt and pepper.

5. Mix the puréed pumpkin with the meat, spread the mixture out in a very shallow baking pan or plate, and divide into 8 to 10 portions.

6. Prepare the sealing mixture for the rolls: dissolve 1 tablespoon flour in $\frac{1}{2}$–1 tablespoon water; then add 2–3 tablespoons boiling water and stir.

7. Taking the pancakes one by one, spread them flat on the board or working surface; place a portion of the filling on the lower half, pick up the lower edge and fold over the filling; fold in the sides; then roll up the pancake.

8. Moisten the top edge with the flour and water paste and press gently to secure. Fry the rolls in oil heated to a temperature of 325°F (160°C) until they are crisp and golden.

5

6

7

8

Crispy fried shrimp snacks

1 h

A crunchy snack made with minced shrimp, these little balls also make a delicious and unusual canapé to go with an aperitif or Chinese wine.

$\frac{1}{4}$ cup fresh pork fat
$\frac{1}{4}$ pound sliced white filleted fish (sea bass, flounder, cod, haddock, etc)
$\frac{1}{4}$ pound peeled shrimp
1 small piece of leek
1 small piece of ginger root
1 egg white
1 tablespoon rice wine
$\frac{1}{4}$ teaspoon salt
a pinch of pepper
a pinch of monosodium glutamate (optional)
2 tablespoons cornstarch
8 slices of bread
$\frac{1}{2}$ cup white sesame seeds
4 hard-boiled quail eggs
1 small slice cooked ham, thinly sliced
parsley
$\frac{1}{2}$ cup sliced almonds
oil for frying
506 calories; 24 g protein; 30 g fat; 35.4 g sugar

1. Slice the pork fat and the fish very thinly with a very sharp knife, then chop finely.

2. Wash the shrimp and remove the black intestinal vein. Chop finely and combine with the fish and pork fat. Simmer the leek and ginger together for a few minutes to obtain a lightly flavored stock.

3. Place the chopped mixture in a bowl; stir in a little of the water in which the leek and ginger have simmered, add the egg white, and then stir in the rice wine. Mix well, stirring in the salt, pepper, and monosodium glutamate (optional).

4. Beat vigorously, always working in the same direction to obtain a firm, smooth paste. Finally, work in the cornstarch.

5. Take 4 slices of bread, remove the crusts, and arrange the slices on top of one another in two pairs, aligning the slices neatly. Cut into fours and trim the corners to make circles.

6. Work about ⅓ of the fish-and-pork-fat mixture into small balls, approximately 1 inch in diameter, place one ball between two circles of bread and press down. Smooth the sides of the sandwich with a knife. Roll the sides in the sesame seeds, pressing the seeds against the filling so they adhere firmly.

7. Proceed as directed above with the remaining 4 slices of bread but shape the squares into ovals instead of circles. Place a mound of filling on half the bread slices, press a hard-boiled quail egg into the filling, and cover with chopped ham and finely chopped parsley. Mound the remaining filling on the remaining small ovals of bread and then stick the sliced almonds firmly into the filling so that the resulting canapés resemble pine cones.

8. Heat the oil to 250°F (120°C), i.e., not very hot, and place the prepared canapés very carefully in the oil. Increase the temperature of the oil gradually until it reaches 350°F (180°C) — moderately hot. The canapés should become crisp and golden.

Steamed stuffed bean curd skins

Pork and bean thread (transparent noodles) or vermicelli wrapped in dried bean curd skins – another variation of the stuffed roll, but in this recipe the rolls are steamed.

Scant ½ pound finely chopped or ground pork
1 cup bean thread (transparent noodles)
3 large dried Chinese mushrooms
1½ teaspoons sugar
3 tablespoons dark soy sauce
1 tablespoon rice wine
1 tablespoon cornstarch
4 dried bean curd skins
a few drops of dark soy sauce
208 calories; 9.5 g protein; 12 g fat; 14.4 g sugar

1. Spread the chopped or ground pork on the chopping block or working surface and pound with the blunt edge of the cleaver – this breaks up the fibers in the meat and makes it smoother and more tender.

2. Cook the noodles in boiling water for only a few minutes, drain them, and cut them into pieces approximately 1 inch long.

3. Cover the mushrooms with boiling water and leave to stand for 15 minutes; when they have softened, squeeze free of excess water, trim off and discard the stems, and slice the mushrooms in thin strips about $\frac{1}{8}$ inch wide.

4. Place the ground pork in a bowl with the mushrooms and noodles. Add the sugar, soy sauce, rice wine, and the cornstarch; work together by hand until a homogeneous paste is formed.

5. Soak the dried bean curd skins for about 30 minutes in plenty of water, spread out very carefully on the board, and dab off excess water gently with a cloth.

6. Divide the stuffing into four portions; place the first on the lower half of one of the bean curd skins. Fold the bottom edge over the filling and roll up.

7. Repeat this process with the other bean curd skins and the remaining stuffing. Arrange the rolls carefully in a shallow dish taking care that they do not overlap. Coat them sparingly with dark soy sauce.

8. Place the dish in the bamboo steamer; cover and steam over a high heat for 20 minutes. When the rolls are ready, cut as desired and serve.

Roast pork appetizer

This is a spicy dish which takes very little time to prepare.

approximately ¾ pound soybean sprouts
½ cup bean thread (transparent noodles)
½ pound thinly sliced roast pork
For the sauce:
2 tablespoons sugar
3 tablespoons vinegar
1 tablespoon soy sauce
1 tablespoon prepared mustard
1 tablespoon sesame oil
245 calories; 25.9 g protein; 6.8 g fat; 19.3 g sugar

1

1. Wash the soybean sprouts well; remove the black seed cover from one end and the threadlike root from the other. Drain well.

2. Bring plenty of water to a boil in a large pan, add the bean sprouts, and boil until tender but still slightly crisp.

3. Drain the bean sprouts very well.

4. Place the noodles in a bowl, cover with boiling water, and leave to stand for 5 minutes.

5. Drain the noodles, cut into pieces 4 inches long, and drain once more.

6. Place the slices of pork on top of one another and cut into thin strips about 3 inches long (this gives more volume to the dish, and spreads the flavor evenly).

7. Make the sauce in a bowl by mixing together the sugar, vinegar, soy sauce, mustard, and sesame oil. Take care to mix the mustard thoroughly with the other ingredients.

8. Place the noodles on a serving plate, cover with the bean sprouts, and put the slivers of pork on top. Just before serving, pour on the sauce and mix well.

5

2

6

3

7

4

8

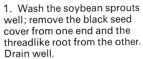

Pork kidney salad with mustard dressing

This recipe is a good example of the many imaginative and easy Chinese methods of using variety meats; it is an economical dish which takes little time to prepare.

5–6 servings:
1 large pork kidney
2 cucumbers
approximately ½ cup red seaweed
For the sauce:
2 tablespoons sugar
3 tablespoons vinegar
1 tablespoon soy sauce
1 tablespoon prepared mustard
a few drops of sesame oil
a pinch of monosodium glutamate (optional)
101 calories; 7.4 g protein; 5.5 g fat; 8.2 g sugar

1. Cut the kidney in half horizontally; this is best done by lightly pressing down on the kidney with the flat of the left hand while slicing carefully along the center of the kidney.

2. Remove the central core inside the kidney as neatly as possible – a small pair of very sharp, pointed scissors will be best for this.

3. Place the kidney in cold water for a few minutes. Bring plenty of water to a boil and place the kidney in it to cook (be careful not to overcook).

4. When the kidney is just done, drop it into a bowl of fresh cold water. This rids the kidney of any excessively strong taste and firms up the flesh.

5. Drain the kidney and cut it into small strips. Slice the cucumbers diagonally first, then cut the thin, slanting rounds into strips.

6. Shake out the seaweed and rinse in cold water; soak in cold water for 20 minutes, drain, and squeeze gently.

7. Cut the seaweed into strips of the same size as the kidney pieces. Press a very sharp Chinese fruit knife or cleaver down through the seaweed onto the board; do not use a sawing motion.

8. Blend all the sauce ingredients. Place the kidney, the seaweed, and the cucumber in a bowl, add the sauce, and mix well.

Crispy chicken and beef appetizers

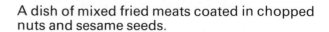

A dish of mixed fried meats coated in chopped nuts and sesame seeds.

1 cup shelled walnuts
1 tablespoon bread crumbs
scant $\frac{1}{2}$ pound young chicken breasts
salt
pepper
generous $\frac{1}{4}$ pound very thinly sliced beef
1 cup white sesame seeds
oil for frying
For the batter:
2 egg yolks
1 tablespoon water
$\frac{1}{4}$ teaspoon salt
1 teaspoon sugar
2 tablespoons cornstarch
2 tablespoons all-purpose flour
521 calories; 25.8 g protein; 37.8 g fat; 21.6 g sugar

1

2

3

4

5

6

7

8

1. Blanch the walnuts in boiling water and peel off the thin inner skins. Chop the nuts fairly coarsely before they have dried out completely and mix them with the bread crumbs.

2. Trim any gristle or sinew from the chicken breasts. Slit them open along one side and open them out. Make shallow vertical and horizontal incisions in the flesh and season lightly with salt and pepper.

3. Mix the egg yolks with the other batter ingredients: water, salt, sugar, cornstarch, and all-purpose flour. Beat very well until smooth and creamy. Pour half the batter into a separate bowl.

4. Dip the chicken breasts in the batter; if the batter does not cling to the surface of the meat satisfactorily, mix in a little more water.

5. Spread the chopped nuts and the bread crumbs in a shallow plate; place the chicken breast on the mixture and coat well on both sides.

6. Cut the beef into small slices; season lightly with salt and pepper; dip into the batter in the second bowl; and then coat with the sesame seeds in the same way you coated the chicken breasts with the nut-and-bread-crumb mixture.

7. Heat the oil until it reaches a temperature of 325°F (160°C) and fry the chicken breasts and then the small pieces of beef until they are crisp on the outside; to get a crisp crust, gradually increase the temperature of the oil while the pieces of chicken and meat are cooking, but be careful not to burn them.

8. Both the chicken breasts and the beef will take only a short time to cook; when they are done, drain briefly on paper towels and cut into small bite-size pieces.

Steamed chicken with mild garlic dressing

 30'

A light dish with a delicate garlic sauce. It is very quick to prepare.

1 piece of leek about 4 inches long
a small piece of ginger root
2 chicken leg quarters
1 teaspoon salt
1 tablespoon rice wine
1 cucumber (for the garnish)
For the sauce:
3 tablespoons soy sauce
2 tablespoons vinegar
a few drops of sesame oil
1 clove garlic (crushed or minced)
1 tablespoon finely chopped leek
1 teaspoon finely chopped ginger root
a pinch of monosodium glutamate (optional)
80 calories; 11.1 g protein; 2.6 g fat; 2 g sugar

1

2
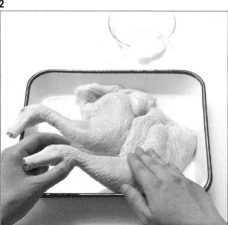

3
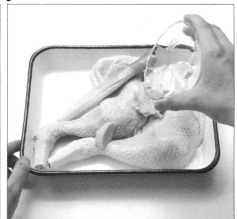

4

5

6

1. Pound the leek and the piece of ginger root with the flat of a Chinese cleaver to release their flavor.

2. Wash the chicken; dry thoroughly, place in a dish or shallow bowl, and rub with salt. Leave to stand to give the salt time to penetrate the flesh.

3. Place the leek and the ginger on the chicken legs, sprinkle with the rice wine, and place in the bamboo steamer; steam for 20 minutes over a high heat.

4. Meanwhile, mix all the sauce ingredients together.

5. When the chicken is done, remove from the steamer, allow to cool, and then remove the flesh from the bones, tearing it into small strips about 2½ inches wide.

6. Slice the cucumber lengthwise into thin strips and arrange on a serving plate. Place the small pieces of chicken in the center of the plate, pour on the garlic sauce, and serve.

Steamed chicken salad with noodles

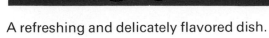

A refreshing and delicately flavored dish.

2 chicken leg quarters
salt
1 tablespoon rice wine
½ leek
1 small piece of ginger root
1 package rice noodles
2 eggs
For the sauce:
½ cup chicken stock
1 teaspoon soy sauce
2 tablespoons vinegar
½ teaspoon salt
2 tablespoons sugar
161 calories; 14.4 g protein; 5.4 g fat; 11.7 g sugar

1. Put the bamboo steamer in a wok $\frac{2}{3}$ full of boiling water. Sprinkle each chicken leg quarter with $\frac{1}{2}$ teaspoon salt and rub in well; place in a dish and sprinkle with rice wine; add the leek and ginger and place the dish in the bamboo steamer.

2. Steam the chicken legs for about 18 to 20 minutes (longer if the chicken was cold when placed in the steamer).

3. Let the chicken quarters cool a little, bend them at the joint so they come apart, and remove the flesh from the bones. Chop the flesh very finely.

4. Bring plenty of water to a boil in a large pan, and add the rice noodles attempting to separate them.

5. Stir the noodles with chopsticks, keeping them as untangled as possible.

6. After 1 to 2 minutes, test the noodles and if they are tender drain.

7. Mix together all the sauce ingredients. The salt and sugar should be added last and must dissolve completely.

8. Beat the eggs and make several very thin omelets; cut them into thin strips. Arrange the noodles on a serving dish, then cover with the chicken pieces and the strips of omelet. Sprinkle on the sauce just before serving.

Chicken gizzard salad in spicy sesame sauce

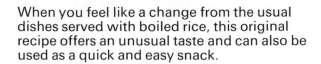

When you feel like a change from the usual dishes served with boiled rice, this original recipe offers an unusual taste and can also be used as a quick and easy snack.

5–6 servings:
15 chicken gizzards
½ leek
a small piece of ginger root
For the sauce:
3 tablespoons soy sauce
1 tablespoon vinegar
½ teaspoon sugar
1 tablespoon sesame seed oil
a pinch of monosodium glutamate (optional)
109 calories; 13.8 g protein; 5.1 g fat; 1.1 g sugar

1

2

3

1. Wash the chicken gizzards very well; bring plenty of water to a boil in a large pan; add the leek and ginger and then the gizzards.

2. Boil over a moderate heat for about 20 minutes; remove the gizzards and place them in a bowl.

3. Cover the gizzards with cold water and rinse well, changing the water several times. Drain well.

4. Carefully slice off and discard the tough, muscle-like coating that covers the meaty part of the gizzards. Cut the meaty part into thin slices which should be as even in thickness as possible, even if this means the shape of the slices varies.

5. Cut three fairly large slices of ginger root into fine strips and trim to an even size for good presentation.

6. Mix all the sauce ingredients together, using a Chinese bamboo whisk or a metal whisk to dissolve the sugar and blend in the sesame oil.

7. Add the strips of ginger to the sauce and stir, then add the sliced gizzards.

8. Mix the gizzards and sauce together very thoroughly, stirring and turning so that the gizzards will absorb the flavor and aroma of the ginger and sauce. This dish may also be served cold.

5

6

7

8

Green bean salad

A straightforward recipe for a light and appetizing first course or a side dish to serve as an effective foil for highly flavored dishes. Best served cold.

½–¾ pound green beans
salt
a small piece of ginger root
For the sauce:
1 tablespoon sugar
2 tablespoons soy sauce
½ teaspoon salt
1 tablespoon sesame seed oil
a pinch of monosodium glutamate (optional)
67 calories; 1.6 g proteins; 3.4 g fat; 7.9 g sugar

1. String the beans if necessary; wash them and then boil them in plenty of salted water; when they are tender, rinse them immediately in cold water.

2. Peel the ginger and slice into thin strips.

3. Drain the beans thoroughly; cut them obliquely into 1½–2 inch lengths.

4. Mix all the sauce ingredients together very thoroughly.

5. Add the ginger and beans to the sauce, stir, and leave to stand. Serve the salad when the beans have absorbed a good deal of the sauce and are well-flavored.

Piquant cucumber salad

A chilled salad which stimulates the appetite and is particularly tempting in hot weather.

4 cucumbers
1 teaspoon salt
1 small piece of carrot
1 small chili pepper
For the sauce:
4 tablespoons vinegar
4 tablespoons sugar
$\frac{1}{4}$ teaspoon salt
a pinch of monosodium glutamate (optional)
a few drops of sesame oil
53 calories; 0.9 g protein; 0.2 g fat; 12.9 g sugar

1. Wash and drain the cucumbers. Cut in half lengthwise and then slice diagonally. Sprinkle with 1 teaspoon salt and leave to stand for a few minutes.

2. When the cucumbers have softened slightly, rinse and drain them well.

3. Cut the carrot into thin strips; remove the seeds from the chili pepper and cut into strips. Mix the sauce ingredients together thoroughly in a bowl; add the cucumbers, carrot, and chili pepper and leave to marinate for 30 to 40 minutes, turning from time to time so that the vegetables absorb the flavor of the dressing.

Bean sprout and noodle salad

The subtle, almost bland taste of this side dish provides a good foil for other, more strongly seasoned or richer dishes.

1 leek
½ package bean thread (transparent noodles)
scant 1 pound bean sprouts
For the sauce:
½ cup vinegar
1 tablespoon salt
1 teaspoon sugar
1 tablespoon of sesame oil
a pinch of monosodium glutamate (optional)
89 calories; 3.2 g protein; 2.7 g fat; 14.2 g sugar

1

2

3

4

1. Mix the sauce ingredients together in a bowl; add the leek cut into thin diagonal slices and mix gently.

2. Soak the noodles in plenty of hot water until they turn completely transparent.

3. Drain the noodles and cut into 4-inch lengths; drain again.

4. Wash the bean sprouts meticulously and remove the little dark seed cover at one end and the threadlike root at the other. This process takes some time, but the bean sprouts will taste better and the presentation of the dish will be more elegant.

5. Bring plenty of water to a boil in a large pan, add the bean sprouts, and boil until tender but still crisp.

6. Drain quickly and allow to cool a little.

7. Add the noodles and the warm bean sprouts to the sauce and mix.

8. Chill the salad and serve very cold for it to be at its best.

5

6

7

8

Multicolored vegetable salad

A cold appetizer with a delicate flavor; the medley of colors of the ingredients gives it great visual appeal.

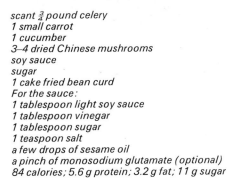

scant ¾ pound celery
1 small carrot
1 cucumber
3–4 dried Chinese mushrooms
soy sauce
sugar
1 cake fried bean curd
For the sauce:
1 tablespoon light soy sauce
1 tablespoon vinegar
1 tablespoon sugar
1 teaspoon salt
a few drops of sesame oil
a pinch of monosodium glutamate (optional)
84 calories; 5.6 g protein; 3.2 g fat; 11 g sugar

1. Wash the celery well, pull off any strings, and cut the stalk into small matchstick pieces about 2½ inches long. Place these in a bowl, cover with cold water, and when they are crisp, drain.

2. Peel the carrot and cut into matchstick pieces the same length as the celery strips; slice the cucumber diagonally across and then cut each piece into strips.

3. Place the mushrooms in a small bowl, cover with boiling water, and leave to stand for 15 to 30 minutes. Drain the mushrooms and reserve the liquid. Cut off and discard the tough stalks. Place the mushrooms in a saucepan and cover with the water in which they were soaked. Season with a little soy sauce and sugar and cook; drain well and cut into thin strips.

4. Remove excess oil from the bean curd cube by pouring boiling water over it. Cut into slices ⅛ inch thick and then into very small matchstick pieces.

5. Make the sauce, mixing all the ingredients listed above together; add the sesame oil last and mix thoroughly.

6. Add the celery, carrot, mushrooms, cucumber, and bean curd to the bowl containing the sauce; mix well. Leave to stand for about 20 minutes and then serve.

Fried stuffed lotus root and eggplant

½ large lotus root
cornstarch as required
rice flour as required
1 large eggplant
approximately ⅔ cup minced or finely chopped shrimp
oil for frying
coating batter mixture (see recipe on pages 156–157)
For the filling:
¼ pound ground or finely chopped lean pork
2 teaspoons of water taken from flavored water in which a small piece of leek and a piece of ginger have been simmered
1 tablespoon beaten egg
1 teaspoon rice wine
a pinch of salt
a few drops of soy sauce
a pinch of pepper
a pinch of monosodium glutamate (optional)
312 calories; 10.8 g protein; 18.9 g fat; 23.7 g sugar

1. Peel the lotus root and cut it into thin rounds. Soak in cold water for 15 minutes.

2. Prepare the meat stuffing as directed on page 80.

3. Drain the lotus root, pat dry, and dredge with cornstarch, take half the lotus root slices, place a small quantity of the meat filling on top of each one, and place the remainder of the lotus root slices on top to make "sandwiches." Press down gently so the filling penetrates the interior holes of the root. Press lightly on one side so that the sandwich gapes open somewhat on the other side, making it look a little like a half-open shell.

4. Dredge thoroughly with rice flour.

5. Cut the eggplant crosswise, i.e., into circles, ¼ inch thick; cut these slices in half horizontally, stopping ⅛ inch short of the edge so that the two halves are still attached. Soak in water to get rid of the bitter taste.

6. Dry the eggplant slices; dredge lightly inside and out with cornstarch. Using a small, flexible knife, fill with the chopped shrimp mixture until the open edges of the eggplant are pushed ½ inch apart by the filling.

7. Heat the oil to 340°F. (170°C.) and lower the lotus root sandwiches into the oil; reduce the heat to low; when the filled lotus root is almost cooked, turn up the heat and finish frying at 350°F. (180°C.).

8. Pick up the stuffed slices of eggplant carefully, holding them by the uncut sides and dip the open edges into the batter; deep-fry for a few minutes at 325°F. (160°C.).

Piquant turnip salad

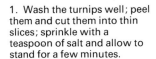

This basically simple dish owes much of its zest to the sweet and sour sauce with which it is served; the turnips should not be allowed to stand for too long in the sauce, however, or their delicate flavor will be drowned.

5–6 small turnips
1 teaspoon salt
½ carrot
1 chili pepper
For the sauce:
½ cup sugar
a few drops of sesame oil
a pinch of monosodium glutamate (optional)
82 calories; 1.3 g protein; 0.1 g fat; 19.3 g sugar

1. Wash the turnips well; peel them and cut them into thin slices; sprinkle with a teaspoon of salt and allow to stand for a few minutes.

2. When the turnips have softened a little, rinse under cold running water and drain well.

3. Cut the carrot into thin strips; remove the seeds from the chili pepper and cut into thin strips.

4. Mix all the sauce ingredients together in a bowl; add the turnips, the carrot, and the chili pepper; leave to stand for a little while, mixing and turning a few times before serving.

Cucumber and crisp cabbage salad in spicy dressing

This dish owes its distinctive taste to the use of spicy fermented soybean paste.

2 cucumbers
2 teaspoons salt
3–4 cabbage leaves
For the sauce:
1 teaspoon soy sauce
1 tablespoon hot fermented soybean paste
a pinch of monosodium glutamate (optional)
a few drops of sesame oil
25 calories; 1.8 g protein; 0.3 g fat; 3.9 g sugar

1. Trim the ends off the cucumbers diagonally and slice the cucumbers diagonally into small chunks, using the rolling knife or oblique cutting method described on page 304. Sprinkle the pieces with 1 teaspoon salt and leave to stand for a few minutes.

2. Cut out the hard ribs of the cabbage, wash well and then cut into small pieces 1½–2 inches square. Sprinkle with 1 teaspoon salt and leave to stand.

3. When the cucumber and cabbage slices have softened a little, rinse off the salt and drain.

4. Mix all the sauce ingredients together thoroughly in a bowl, add the cucumber and cabbage pieces, and stir well to let the vegetables absorb the dressing before serving.

Bean curd and shrimp salad

A very refreshing dish, with the subtle aroma and delicate flavor of sesame oil.

1 cake bean curd
1 tablespoon dried shrimp
a few chives
1 small piece of salted Chinese mustard top
For the sauce:
1 teaspoon sugar
1 teaspoon salt
a pinch of monosodium glutamate (optional)
a few drops of sesame oil
83 calories; 5.8 g protein; 3 g fat; 3.4 g sugar

1. Place the bean curd in boiling water for 2 minutes; remove, cut into pieces, and drain.

2. Soak the shrimp in water until they are plumped up and tender; chop them finely; chop the chives coarsely.

3. Rinse the mustard greens thoroughly (if dried mustard greens are used, soak them in water for a while). Chop them finely.

4. Mix the sauce ingredients together in a bowl. Place the bean curd in another bowl and work into a paste by hand or with a wooden spoon; add the chopped shrimps, the mustard greens, and the sauce. Blend all the ingredients thoroughly.

5. Arrange the mixture on a serving dish and garnish with the chopped chives.

53

Bean curd and turnip tops with thousand-year-old eggs

A recipe with a taste of spring that is quick and easy to prepare.

2 small cakes bean curd
1 bunch turnip tops or broccoli
salt
2 thousand-year-old eggs (preserved duck eggs)
4–5 slices cooked ham
For the sauce:
2 tablespoons soy sauce
1 teaspoon sesame oil
a few drops of vinegar
a few drops of chili oil
a little sugar to taste
2 teaspoons ginger juice (this is obtained by crushing ginger
   root in a garlic press)
173 calories; 13.4 g protein; 12.5 g fat; 2.8 g sugar

1. Cut the bean curd in half horizontally, place in a saucepan of gently boiling water, and simmer; remove carefully from the water so that they do not break up. Drain and chill in the refrigerator.

2. Wash the turnip tops or broccoli meticulously and place, stem downward, in lightly salted boiling water. Cook until the color turns a brighter green; drain and plunge into cold water for a couple of minutes.

1

2

3

4

5

6

3. Place the thousand-year-old eggs in water so that the ashes and dirt clinging to their shells soften and come away easily when scraped with a knife; wash the eggs, shell them, and slice them lengthwise into quarters.

4. Cut the bean curd into pieces ½ inch wide and arrange on the serving plate leaving spaces in between for the turnip tops or broccoli.

5. Squeeze the turnip tops or broccoli to rid them of excess moisture, cut into pieces about ¾ inch long, and arrange so that the flower heads are well displayed.

6. Decorate the dish with the ham, sliced in half, and the quartered thousand-year-old eggs; mix the sauce (which is served separately), adding the ginger juice last.

Chinese chicken and ham salad with noodles

A first course made with Chinese wheat-flour noodles; it also makes a very good light meal or snack on hot days.

4 bundles of fresh noodles
1 tablespoon sesame oil
3 slices cooked ham
1 tomato
3 cucumbers
¾ pound boned chicken breasts
a pinch of salt
a pinch of pepper
½ tablespoon rice wine
2 large eggs
¼ teaspoon salt
2 tablespoons peanut oil
½ tablespoon ginger juice (this is obtained by crushing small slivers of ginger root in a garlic press)
a little prepared mustard
For the sauce:
4 tablespoons sugar
6 tablespoons soy sauce
6–8 tablespoons vinegar
701 calories; 20.2 g protein; 23.1 g fat; 102.3 g sugar

1. Bring a large pan of water to a boil, throw in the noodles, and stir to keep the strands separate; cook until tender, drain and rinse in cold water. Add a few drops of sesame oil and stir so that the noodles do not stick together.

2. Shred the ham. Blanch the tomato in boiling water, then plunge into cold water, and skin. Cut into wedges ½ inch thick. Slice the cucumbers diagonally and then cut into small strips.

3. Place the chicken breasts in a small heatproof dish, sprinkle with salt and pepper, and moisten with rice wine; place in a bamboo steamer that is already hot and full of steam and cook for 8 minutes or until completely done.

4. When the chicken is cooked, remove from the steamer and cut into very small strips; strain the chicken juices produced during cooking.

5. Beat the eggs, add the salt, and mix well. Heat the peanut oil in a wok, pour in the beaten egg, and beat briskly with a fork over a high heat.

6. Add water or, preferably, stock to the juices from the chicken to make up 1½ cups of liquid; add the sauce ingredients and boil gently.

7. Add the ginger juice to the stock and juices and then pour the mixture into a bowl and allow to cool.

8. Arrange the noodles in a serving dish and place the cucumbers, tomato, ham, chicken, and eggs on top. Pour over plenty of the cold sauce. Serve with a little mustard.

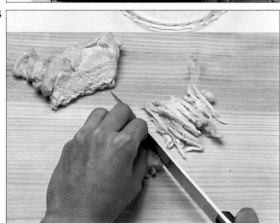

57

Steamed rice-coated pork balls

Pork rissoles covered in glutinous rice. This dish must be served piping hot or the rice will start to harden.

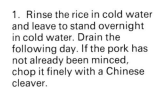

⅔ cup glutinous rice (see notes on Chinese ingredients on page 303)
1 pound lean pork, ground or very finely chopped
1 egg white
3 tablespoons soy sauce
2 teaspoons sugar
1 tablespoon rice wine
peanut oil
406 calories; 23.1 g protein; 26.1 g fat; 17.7 g sugar

1. Rinse the rice in cold water and leave to stand overnight in cold water. Drain the following day. If the pork has not already been minced, chop it finely with a Chinese cleaver.

2. Place the meat in a bowl and add the egg white, soy sauce, sugar, and rice wine. Work together lightly but thoroughly with your hands until well blended; do not pack the meat together too tightly or the balls will be heavy.

1

2

3

4

5

6

3. Oil your hands lightly and, taking a small handful of the mixture, force it out from the closed hand so that it comes out of the opening made by the forefinger and thumb.

4. Spread out the drained rice in a large flat plate and roll the meat balls in the rice so they are covered all over; press gently to make sure the rice sticks.

5. Brush a thin film of peanut oil over the bottom of a bamboo steamer or cover the bottom with a dampened but well wrung-out cloth.

6. Place the rice-covered meat balls in the steamer, leaving a little space between each one; place over a wok ⅔ full of boiling water, cover, and cook over a moderate heat for about 30 minutes.

Chiao tzu (stuffed dumplings)

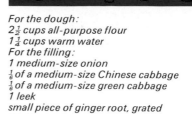

For the dough:
2½ cups all-purpose flour
1¼ cups warm water
For the filling:
1 medium-size onion
⅙ of a medium-size Chinese cabbage
⅙ of a medium-size green cabbage
1 leek
small piece of ginger root, grated
3 tablespoons sesame oil
1 tablespoon light soy sauce
a pinch of salt
2 tablespoons cornstarch
¾ cup ground pork
½ pound ground lean beef
457 calories; 19.9 g protein; 29.7 g fat; 26.4 g sugar

1. Sift the flour, gradually add the warm water, and work into a firm dough.

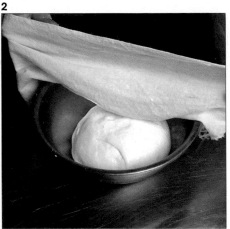

2. Place the pastry dough in a bowl, cover with a damp cloth, and leave to rest for 2 hours, then knead well, place in the bowl, cover, and leave to rest for a further 2 hours. Knead once more and then leave to stand in the bowl covered with the cloth overnight. Knead again the following day.

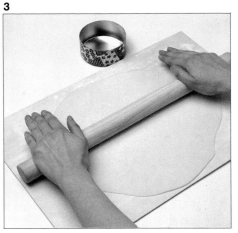

3. Dredge a large pastry board or working surface lightly with flour and roll out the pastry into as thin a sheet as possible, dredging very lightly with a little flour.

4. Cut the pastry into rounds about 4 inches in diameter with a pastry cutter.

5. The most important feature of *chiao tzu* is the excellence of the pastry, which should be smooth and very thin; this thin, silklike texture can only be achieved if the dough is kneaded and rested as directed above.

6. Prepare the filling by chopping the onion, the Chinese cabbage, the green cabbage, and the leek very finely; then pound the mixture lightly with the blunt side of a knife or cleaver.

(Continued overleaf.)

7

8

9

10

7. Wrap the chopped vegetables in a cloth; twist and squeeze tightly so that the vegetable juices are extracted.

8. Place the vegetables in a bowl and, mixing with the hands, add the grated ginger, sesame oil, soy sauce, salt, and 2 tablespoons cornstarch, then add the chopped meat. Work together until all the ingredients are blended into a smooth, homogeneous mixture.

9. To prepare the *chiao tzu* for steaming or frying moisten the edges of the circles of pastry, place a little stuffing slightly off-center on each circle and fold the pastry in half so that one side is longer than the other; pinch the ends together, make two more pleats, and close the edges firmly together.

10. To prepare the *chiao tzu* for boiling, moisten the edges of the circles of dough, place some of the filling in the center, fold the circles in half, pinch the center of the arc between thumb and fore-finger so that the dough sticks together, fold the two corners inward and upward to meet this center point, and press all the edges together to seal them.

11. To cook the dumplings in a frying pan, pour a layer of oil into a pan; when it is hot, place the dumplings in the oil as illustrated. Fry for about 2 minutes or until golden brown on the bottom. Pour water all around the dumplings and cover the frying pan as tightly as possible. Cook over a high heat until the water boils away – about 5 to 10 minutes.

12. To steam the dumplings, spread a damp cloth over the bottom of a perforated steamer; when the steamer is full of steam, arrange the dumplings neatly on the cloth and steam over a moderate heat until the pastry has become almost transparent.

13. To boil the dumplings, bring a large pan of water to a boil and add the dumplings; remove as they rise to the surface.

11

12

13

Crab and cauliflower salad

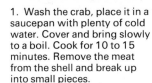

The attractive colors of this salad are matched by its flavor.

crab weighing 1½ pounds
1 medium-size cauliflower
salt
vinegar
½ onion
1 bunch of radishes
2 cucumbers
For the sauce:
4 tablespoons vinegar
2 tablespoons sugar
3 tablespoons peanut oil
1 teapoon salt.
208 calories; 16.3 g protein; 10.8 g fat
12.5 g sugar

1. Wash the crab, place it in a saucepan with plenty of cold water. Cover and bring slowly to a boil. Cook for 10 to 15 minutes. Remove the meat from the shell and break up into small pieces.

2. Cut the cauliflower into small florets, soak in salted water, and then rinse. Boil briskly in water acidulated with a few drops of vinegar until just tender. Rinse in cold water and drain.

3. Cut the onion into thin slices, rub a little salt into the slices, and wrap in a dish towel. Rinse in cold water and then squeeze tightly, twisting the cloth, to get rid of all excess moisture.

4. Trim the radishes and cut into quarters.

5. Place the cucumbers on a chopping board or working surface, sprinkle with salt, and roll against the board, pressing them so that the salt penetrates; rinse in cold water and cut vertically in half and then diagonally in pieces about ⅛ inch thick.

6. Mix the sauce in a large dish; add the rest of the ingredients; mix and serve.

Five-color hsao mai (steamed dumplings)

In the tea parlors of Guangdong (Canton) these tasty dumplings are among the *dim sum* you can sample. Filled with pork, they are topped with brightly-colored ingredients. They should be served piping hot straight from the bamboo steamer.

For the filling:
¾ pound onions
½ cup cornstarch
1¾ cups ground lean pork
20 hsao mai dough sheets (see recipe on page 296)
Seasonings:
2 tablespoons rice wine
½ teaspoon salt
½ teaspoon sugar
1 tablespoon soy sauce
a small pinch of monosodium glutamate (optional)
1 tablespoon sesame oil
a pinch of pepper
½ teaspoon chopped ginger root
For the toppings:
2–3 egg yolks
peanut oil
seaweed as required
3 slices cooked ham
1 small can crab meat
3 Chinese aromatic mushrooms (tung ku variety)
539 calories; 26.5 g protein; 29 g fat; 41 g sugar

1. To prepare the scrambled eggs for the topping, heat a little peanut oil in the wok, pour in the beaten egg yolks, and cook over a gentle heat, breaking up the egg yolks into small pieces as they set.

2. Prepare the filling: chop the onions finely, add the cornstarch and mix well by hand so that the flour is evenly distributed over the chopped onion.

3. Mix all the seasonings together. Place the ground pork in a bowl, add the seasoning mixture, and mix well until smooth.

4. Add the floured onion to the meat mixture; mix well by hand.

5. Make a loose fist, thumb upward, with one hand, stretch a dumpling sheet over the hole formed by thumb and forefinger. Place some filling in the center of the dough sheet and push down into the hole, supporting the bottom of the little bag with the little finger of the same hand.

6. When all the dough sheets are filled in this way, decorate the tops with a selection of chopped seaweed, chopped ham, scrambled egg, chopped crab meat, and the dried Chinese mushrooms (previously soaked in warm water for 30 minutes and chopped).

7. Brush the bottom of a bamboo steamer with a thin film of oil, arrange the *hsao mai* carefully in the steamer and place over boiling water. Cover and steam for 9 to 12 minutes.

65

Hsiao lung pao (steamed dumplings with meat stuffing)

24 dumplings:
For the dough:
$\frac{1}{4}$ cup sugar
scant 2 cups hot water
1 tablespoon fresh yeast
1$\frac{1}{4}$ pounds all-purpose flour
2 tablespoons shortening or lard
For the filling:
1$\frac{1}{4}$ cups ground lean pork
$\frac{1}{2}$ tablespoon soy sauce
1 teaspoon salt
1 teaspoon monosodium glutamate (optional)
1 tablespoon sesame oil
1 tablespoon finely chopped leek
$\frac{1}{2}$ tablespoon grated or finely chopped ginger root
$\frac{1}{2}$ cup water
lettuce leaves as required
380 calories; 17.5 g protein; 23 g fat; 25 g sugar

1. To make the dough: dissolve the sugar in the hot water, add the yeast, and allow to stand for 10 minutes.

2. Sift the flour; work in the fat; then add the yeast mixture. Knead, adding more flour if necessary; cover with a damp cloth and leave to rise for 3 to 4 hours in a warm place away from drafts.

3. To prepare the filling: mix the ground pork well with the other filling ingredients until they are thoroughly amalgamated.

4. Roll the raised dough into a long cylindrical sausage. Cut into 24 pieces and roll each piece into a circle with a rolling pin; each disk should measure about 4 inches in diameter.

5. Place some filling in the center of each circle of dough and enclose, forming a small ball as shown in the illustration.

6. Arrange the *hsiao lung pao* on lettuce leaves in the bamboo steamer and steam for 8 minutes over a moderate heat. Serve very hot.

Cha shao (roast pork)

This Cantonese dish can be served as a first course or as a main dish, or it can be chopped up and used as a filling for hot dumplings (*cha shao pao*).

12 servings:
3½ pounds loin of pork
6 tablespoons honey
For the sauce:
5 tablespoons sugar
1 tablespoon salt
1 cup soy sauce
1 tablespoon rice wine or dry sherry
1 tablespoon ginger juice
a pinch of red food coloring or 1 teaspoon liquid food coloring
510 calories; 26.3 g protein; 38.5 g fat; 12.3 g sugar

1. Bone the loin of pork and prick the meat all over with the point of a sharp knife. Cut into slices about 1½ inches thick.

2. Mix all the sauce ingredients together with the red food coloring and sprinkle over the meat. Leave to marinate for 1½ hours.

3. Thread one end of each strip of meat onto a metal skewer. Suspend the pieces of meat from the top rack of the oven (the pieces of meat will hang down through the rack while the skewer rests across the rungs). Leave the meat to hang and dry for 45 minutes.

4. Roast in the oven at 350°F. (180°C.) for 20 to 25 minutes, basting from time to time with some of the honey.

5. When the pork is almost done brush with the remaining honey and let it dry.

6. Serve hot or cold.

Cha shao pao (dumplings stuffed with roast pork)

24 dumplings:
For the dumplings:
1½ pounds flour
¼ cup sugar
1 tablespoon powdered yeast
2 tablespoons melted shortening or lard
For the filling:
1 tablespoon peanut oil
½ pound cha shao (see recipe on page 67), diced small
1 small leek (cleaned and trimmed)
1 slice ginger root
For the sauce:
2 teaspoons sugar
a pinch of salt
¼ teaspoon monosodium glutamate (optional)
1 tablespoon dark soy sauce
2 teaspoons light soy sauce
1 tablespoon oyster sauce
½ cup chicken stock
1 teaspoon sesame oil
a pinch of red food coloring
1 tablespoon cornstarch dissolved in 1 tablespoon water
490 calories; 24.3 g protein; 36.3 g fat; 25 g sugar

1. Sift the flour into a large mixing bowl.

2. Dissolve the sugar in the hot water, add the yeast, and mix well; leave to stand for 10 minutes.

3. Add the yeast to the flour and mix in the melted shortening or lard. Mix well, remove from the bowl, and knead for about 3 minutes; shape into a long sausage and cover with a cloth.

4. Blend the sauce ingredients together and set aside.

5. Heat the oil in the wok and fry the diced cha shao, the leek, and the ginger over a high heat for a minute. Remove the leek and ginger and discard; pour in the sauce and then add the cornstarch and water to thicken. Stir and cook until the mixture is smooth and homogeneous. Leave to cool.

6. Cut the roll of dough into 24 pieces, flattening each piece with the fingers and shaping into a disk.

7. Place a tablespoon of filling in the center of each round of dough and enclose, pinching the dough closed with the fingers. Place a piece of waxed paper or foil under each dumpling, and leave it to rise for 10 minutes.

8. Cook in a bamboo steamer for about 10 minutes, taking care to leave each dumpling enough space to expand. Do not open the steamer while the dumplings are cooking.

Pork Dishes

Because of the widely varying climate of China there are few basic foodstuffs which are not cultivated or raised there. The very wide range of dishes seems to include every taste imaginable, but everything is a matter of balance, and no one taste is allowed to overshadow another.

Pork is tender meat and can be cooked in a hundred different ways. It also goes well with almost any side dish. So it is not surprising that seven out of ten Chinese meat dishes include pork. Pork is so important in Chinese cuisine that, whereas other meats are each called by their separate names, pork is referred to simply by the generic term, "meat."

An intriguing note: the Chinese ideogram for house is made up of the basic sign for roof positioned over the ideogram for pig.

Pork and green peppers Sichuan style

A famous Sichuan dish in which the pork is stir-fried twice in the wok and flavored with soybean paste.

a piece of ginger root
1 leek approximately 4 inches long
1½ pounds leg of pork
1 tablespoon rice wine
5 green peppers
1 clove garlic, finely chopped
2 small chili peppers
1 tablespoon rice wine
2 teaspoons cornstarch
oil for frying
For the sauce:
2 tablespoons stock
2 tablespoons sugar
2 tablespoons soybean paste
¼ teaspoon salt
520 calories; 26.7 g protein; 39.8 g fat; 10.2 g sugar

1. Peel the ginger and crush it slightly with the flat of the cleaver blade; flatten the leek with the flat of the blade to release its flavor.

2. Bring a large pan of water to a boil and place the whole piece of pork in it, followed by the ginger and the leek; cook for 20 minutes.

3. Cool the pork; then cut it into approximately 1½-inch squares and then into very thin slices; place the slices of meat in a bowl and sprinkle with 1 tablespoon rice wine.

4. Cut the green peppers in half lengthwise, remove the seeds and pith, wash, and chop into pieces slightly smaller than the meat. Remove the seeds from the chili peppers and cut into rings about ¼ inch thick.

5. Mix the sauce ingredients together in a bowl, using a whisk to amalgamate the stock, sugar, soybean paste and salt.

6. Heat the wok over a high heat, pour in 2–3 tablespoons oil, and when it is very hot, add the chopped garlic, the green peppers and the chili peppers.

7. When the green peppers are tender (but still quite crisp), add the pieces of pork and sprinkle with 1 tablespoon rice wine and then add the sauce.

8. Fry over a high heat, mixing and turning; add 2 teaspoons of cornstarch dissolved in 4 teaspoons water and stir; this will give the dish body and gloss.

Sweet and sour pork

 25'

A Cantonese dish which has become a favorite worldwide. Very good with boiled rice.

¾ pound leg of pork (boned)
1 red chili pepper
2 leeks
1 teaspoon finely chopped garlic
½ small can pineapple
4 green peppers
2 teaspoons cornstarch
1 egg
cornstarch as required
oil for frying
1 tablespoon rice wine
For the sauce:
scant ⅓ cup vinegar
1 tablespoon soy sauce
4½ tablespoons sugar
1 tablespoon tomato ketchup
2 tablespoons Worcestershire sauce
½ teaspoon salt
536 calories; 17.2 g protein; 37 g fat; 33.9 g sugar

1

1. Cut the pork into slices about ½ inch thick and pound each piece lightly on both sides with the blunt edge of the cleaver to tenderize; then cut into bite-size portions.

2. Remove the seeds from the chili pepper and cut it into rings about ¼ inch thick. Slice the leeks into ½-inch lengths, and chop the garlic very finely.

3. Drain the canned pineapple and cut into small pieces; slice the green peppers lengthwise; remove the seeds, pith, and stem; and cut into portions the same size as the pieces of pork.

4. Mix the sauce ingredients together. In a separate small bowl or cup dissolve 2 teaspoons cornstarch in 4 teaspoons cold water.

5. Dip the pork pieces into the beaten egg and then coat with cornstarch. Heat the oil over a medium heat in the wok and fry the pork until it is cooked through. Set aside.

6. Heat 2 tablespoons oil in the wok and stir-fry the chopped garlic; as soon as this releases its aroma, add the leeks followed by the green peppers.

7. When the green peppers are tender, add the chili pepper, the pineapple, and the pork and stir-fry, mixing and turning all the ingredients briskly: moisten with the rice wine to add flavor.

8. Finally, add the sweet and sour sauce, followed by the cornstarch dissolved in water; mix thoroughly. Turn off the heat and serve.

2

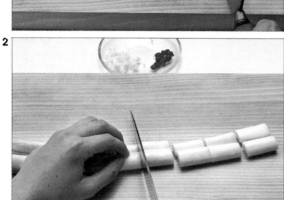

3

4

5

6

7

8

Stir-fried pork belly in sweet and sour sauce

A fuller-flavored version of the classic sweet and sour pork because of the cut of meat used.

4–5 servings:
1¼ pounds pork belly
1 tablespoon soy sauce
1 egg
cornstarch as required
oil for frying
For the sauce:
¼ cup stock
4½ tablespoons sugar
2 tablespoons vinegar
1 tablespoon soy sauce
1 teaspoon salt
1 tablespoon rice wine
To thicken:
1 teaspoon cornstarch dissolved in 2 teaspoons water
421 calories; 22.5 g protein; 40.1 g fat; 21.8 g sugar

1

2

3

4

5

6

1. Cut the pork belly into slices approximately ⅛ inch thick; place in a dish and sprinkle with the soy sauce, coating the strips of meat evenly.

2. Beat the egg and pour over the meat; dip each piece of meat in cornstarch and shake off the excess; then fry in very hot oil. When done, drain and set aside.

3. Mix the sauce ingredients together until thoroughly blended.

4. Place a wok on the burner, pour in the sauce, and cook over a fairly high heat. While the sauce is heating, dissolve 1 teaspoon cornstarch in 2 teaspoons cold water.

5. When the sauce comes to a boil, add the fried pork and cook over a high heat, mixing and turning so that the pork slices absorb the sauce.

6. Use a Chinese fish server for easy turning and mixing of the pork slices so that they will be evenly flavored; reduce the heat and stir in the cornstarch solution for a thick and glossy coating sauce.

Fried pork fillet

A sweet-salty dish eaten with boiled rice or with Chinese noodles in broth.

1½ pounds sliced fillet of pork
oil for frying
1 egg, beaten
cornstarch as required
1 teaspoon finely chopped garlic
1 tablespoon rice wine
For the sauce:
½ cup stock
scant ¼ cup sugar
2½ tablespoons soy sauce
737 calories; 22.8g protein; 65.2g fat; 12.8g sugar

1. Pound the meat lightly on both sides with the blunt edge of a cleaver and cut into small pieces.

2. Heat the oil in a wok; dip the pork into the beaten egg, coat with the cornstarch and fry until the coating is crisp and golden brown.

3. Mix the sauce ingredients together, combining the stock, sugar, and soy sauce.

4. Heat 2 tablespoons of oil in the wok, stir-fry the chopped garlic, and, as it begins to release its flavor, add the fried pieces of pork and stir-fry.

5. Sprinkle with rice wine and the sauce and cook over a high heat; if the sauce is too thin, stir in an extra teaspoon of cornstarch dissolved in 2 teaspoons water.

Pork belly with bamboo shoots

A very good example of the Chinese flair for combining complementary ingredients; the bamboo shoots balance and highlight the stronger taste of the pork.

1½ pounds pork belly in one piece
¾ pound tender winter bamboo shoots, unsalted, canned or fresh parboiled
2 tablespoons oil
a small piece of peeled ginger root, finely sliced
To flavor:
4 tablespoons soy sauce
2 tablespoons sugar
1 tablespoon rice wine
630 calories; 26 g protein; 52.6 g fat; 12.3 g sugar

1. Cut the pork belly into 1-inch squares.

2. Cut the bamboo shoots crosswise into pieces the same size as the pork.

3. Heat 2 tablespoons of oil in the wok, stir-fry the slices of ginger, add the diced pork belly, and fry over a high heat, mixing and turning so that the pork browns evenly all over.

4. Place the pork in a heavy cooking pot or an earthenware casserole; stir in the bamboo shoots and the flavoring of soy sauce, sugar, and rice wine; add enough water to just cover the meat; mix; and place over the heat.

5. Cook over a high heat until the water comes to a boil; turn the heat down to very low, cover, and cook for about 1 hour. When nearly all the liquid has reduced or been absorbed, the dish is ready to serve.

Stir-fried pork with soybean paste

A highly-flavored dish, best served with a light broth.

4–5 servings:
a $\frac{3}{4}$-pound piece of boned leg of pork
1 egg white
cornstarch as required
oil for frying
$\frac{3}{4}$ pound fresh spinach, well washed and trimmed
1 teaspoon salt
1 cup water
a few drops of sesame oil
a pinch of monosodium glutamate (optional)
For the sauce:
1$\frac{1}{2}$ tablespoons soybean paste
1 tablespoon sugar
1 tablespoon soy sauce
391 calories; 16.4g protein; 32.7g fat; 7.6g sugar

1. Slice the pork thinly and then cut into matchstick pieces about $\frac{1}{4}$ inch wide; mix the egg white with the pork strips, coating them thoroughly; then dredge with cornstarch.

2. Heat the frying oil to about 200°F. (90°C.) or until it sizzles; add the meat and fry briskly, taking care that the pork strips do not stick together as they fry; as soon as the meat turns from pink to white on the outside, remove it from the wok and drain.

3. Heat 2 tablespoons of oil in the wok, add the spinach (dried with paper towels) and stir-fry over a high heat.

4. As soon as the spinach has softened add 1 teaspoon salt and the water; cover and cook until tender; drain and keep warm.

5. Tip the cooking water from wok and dry; heat 1 tablespoon oil and pour in the sauce ingredients, adding a few drops of sesame oil and a pinch of monosodium glutamate (optional).

6. As soon as the sauce comes to a boil, add the meat and cook briefly over a high heat, mixing and turning so that the pork is evenly flavored with the sauce. Serve the meat on the bed of warm spinach as illustrated.

Fried pork balls

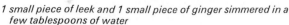

Little meat balls which can be dipped in a variety of sauces, according to taste.

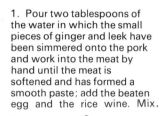

1 small piece of leek and 1 small piece of ginger simmered in a few tablespoons of water
1¼ cups ground lean pork
1 beaten egg
1 tablespoon rice wine
¼ teaspoon salt
¼ teaspoon soy sauce
a pinch of pepper
a pinch of monosodium glutamate (optional)
1½ tablespoons cornstarch
½ teaspoons sesame oil (optional)
oil for frying
For sweet and sour sauce (optional): see step 6
337 calories; 14.3g protein; 28.6g fat; 3.4g sugar

1. Pour two tablespoons of the water in which the small pieces of ginger and leek have been simmered onto the pork and work into the meat by hand until the meat is softened and has formed a smooth paste; add the beaten egg and the rice wine. Mix.

2. Add the salt, soy sauce, pepper, and monosodium glutamate and stir until the mixture is well blended.

3. Add the cornstarch and stir well; at this point ½ teaspoon sesame oil can be combined with the mixture to give it more flavor.

1

2

3

4

5

6

4. Shape the pork balls by taking a small quantity of the meat mixture in the left hand, form a fist, enclosing the meat, and then squeeze the meat out through the hole formed by thumb and forefinger, producing a small ball.

5. Fry half the pork balls, drain and set aside; fry the other half and drain. Heat the oil in the wok or skillet to 350°F. (180°C.) or until it is hot and almost smoking; fry the first batch of pork balls again until they are crisp and crunchy on the outside. Repeat with second batch.

6. Sweet and sour sauce is optional: Make about ⅓ the quantity given in the recipe on pages 132–133, add 2 tablespoons of chopped leek and ½ teaspoon of finely chopped fresh ginger, and cook as directed.

Thrice-cooked pork

4-5 h

A dish which is cooked in three stages: first
boiled, then fried, and finally steamed.

2 pounds pork belly in one piece
1 leek
a piece of ginger root
oil for frying
1 star anise
½ tablespoon cornstarch
For the sauce:
4–6 tablespoons soy sauce
1 tablespoon sugar
1 tablespoon rice wine
½ cup of the liquid in which the pork has been cooked
662 calories; 33.5g protein; 55.8g fat; 4.3g sugar

1. Bring plenty of water to a boil in a large pan; place the pork belly in the boiling water for a few minutes; remove the pork and place in a fresh pan of boiling water together with a whole leek and the ginger, sliced wafer thin. Cover and cook for approximately 30 to 40 minutes.

2. Mix the sauce ingredients together.

3. When the pork is done, allow it to cool slightly, drain, and dry with paper towels. Heat plenty of oil to 350°F. (180°C.) (hot and almost smoking) and fry the pork until it is well colored all over.

4. Remove the pork from the wok or skillet and immediately rinse in very cold warer; when it is cold enough to handle, slice it at right angles to the grain of the meat into rectangular pieces about $\frac{1}{4}$ inch thick.

5. Place the sliced pork, fat side down in a heatproof dish; add the star anise and the sauce, sprinkling it evenly over the meat.

6. Place the dish in a bamboo steamer, over boiling water producing plenty of steam; cook over a moderate meat for about 2 hours, topping up the boiling water with hot water whenever needed to avoid burning the steamer.

7. Remove the dish from the steamer and allow it to cool; place in the refrigerator and remove the layer of fat which will form on the surface. Return the dish to the steamer and cook for a further 1 to 2 hours or until the pork is very tender. Transfer to a hot serving dish.

8. Pour the juices which have been produced during cooking into a saucepan, bring to a boil, and then stir in the cornstarch dissolved in 1 tablespoon cold water. Cook briefly and then pour over the pork.

83

Shizitou casserole (braised pork balls)

Large pork rissoles which are first fried and then braised with Chinese cabbage. A hearty dish for cold days.

2 h

$1\frac{3}{4}$ cups ground lean pork
1 tablespoon finely chopped leek
scant $\frac{1}{2}$ teaspoon ginger juice
$\frac{1}{3}$ teaspoon salt
1 tablespoon rice wine
a pinch of pepper
1 egg
$\frac{1}{2}$ tablespoon sesame oil
2 tablespoons cornstarch
oil for frying
5–6 leaves of Chinese cabbage
1 tablespoon rice wine
$\frac{1}{3}$ cup soy sauce
381 calories; 19 g protein; 28.7 g fat; 9.2 g sugar

1. Spread the ground pork out on the chopping board and chop it even more finely with the cleaver, chopping in both directions to make sure that the consistency is very soft and that no lumps of meat remain.

2. Place the pork in a bowl, add the finely chopped leek, ginger juice, salt, rice wine, and pepper; work together well by hand.

3. Add the egg to the mixture and stir in the sesame oil and cornstarch; continue kneading until smooth and homogeneous. If the mixture is too firm, add a little water.

4. Divide the mixture in four; oil the palms of the hands lightly and make four large rissoles. Slap the rissoles sharply from one hand to the other to help firm them up.

5. Heat the oil in a wok, lower the pork rissoles into the hot oil, and fry over a high heat until the outside of the pork balls is crisp and sealed; lower the heat and continue cooking until the rissoles are golden brown. Drain and set aside.

6. Wash and drain the Chinese cabbage leaves; cut into pieces 2–2½ inches long; fry in oil until they are tender. Drain.

7. Line the bottom of an earthenware casserole or cooking pot with some of the cabbage leaves, place the rissoles on the bed of leaves, and top with the rest of the cabbage. Sprinkle with rice wine and soy sauce.

8. Add approximately 1 quart water, just enough to cover the contents of the casserole; bring to boil over a high heat, reduce the heat, cover, and cook slowly for about 1 hour.

Boiled pork with garlic sauce

A very simple dish, made extremely original and appetizing by the subtle garlic sauce.

1½ pounds boned shoulder of pork
a small piece of ginger root
½ leek
1 tablespoon rice wine
For garlic sauce:
1 large clove garlic
1 teaspoon sugar
1 tablespoon soy sauce
a few drops of sesame oil
a pinch of monosodium glutamate (optional)
281 calories; 30.6g protein; 15g fat; 2.7g sugar

1

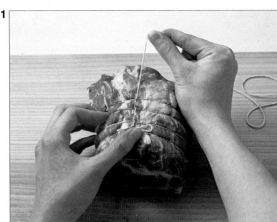

2

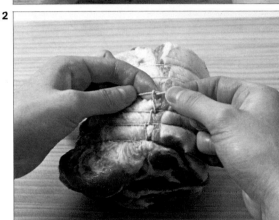

3

4

1. Tie up the boned shoulder of pork very securely as shown in the illustration, leaving intervals of about ¾ inch between the loops of string.

2. Turn the piece of pork over and secure the loops as shown, making a very compactly tied roast, knot the ends of the string tightly.

3. Peel the ginger and crush with a sharp blow from the flat of the cleaver blade; do the same with the leek.

4. Bring plenty of water to a boil in a cooking pot large enough to take the pork. Place the ginger, leek, and pork in the boiling water; sprinkle with the rice wine and cook for about 45 minutes over a moderate heat. Do not add salt.

5. To test whether the meat is cooked through, pierce it deeply with a skewer; if the juices run clear, the meat is done; if the juice is still pink, continue cooking and test again later.

6. When the pork is cooked, remove it from the pan, leave it to cool to room temperature, untie it, and carve it into thin even slices.

7. Peel the garlic and crush in a garlic press; place in a bowl.

8. Stir in the sauce ingredients. Arrange the sliced meat on a serving plate and sprinkle with the garlic sauce.

5

6

7

8

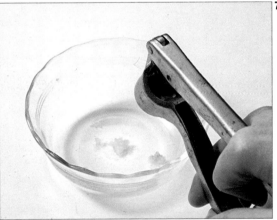

Fried pork Shanghai style

40'

The rich flavor and color of this dish are typical of Shanghai cuisine.

4 slices shoulder of pork, cut $\frac{1}{2}$–$\frac{3}{4}$ inch thick
$\frac{1}{2}$ leek
a small piece of ginger root
1 tablespoon rice wine
4 tablespoons soy sauce
2 tablespoons sugar
3–4 tablespoons oil
cornstarch as required
431 calories; 306g protein; 26.8g fat; 14.3g sugar

1

5

2

6

3

7

4

8

1. Pound first one side of the pork slices and then the other with the blunt edge of a cleaver – this is the ideal tool to use since it tenderizes the meat and also breaks up the fibers so that the flavorings can penetrate easily.

2. Bring the flat of the cleaver down on the leek in one sharp blow; repeat this with the peeled ginger; this will help to release the flavor.

3. Lay the pork slices out flat in a dish, place the leek and ginger on top. Mix the rice wine with the soy sauce and the sugar and sprinkle all over the meat. Leave to stand for 20 to 30 minutes to allow the meat to absorb all the flavors.

4. Heat 3–4 tablespoons oil in the wok; stir-fry the leek and ginger. Coat the pork slices lightly with cornstarch.

5. Shake off any excess cornstarch and fry the pork, stretched out as flat as possible, in the flavored oil. It is advisable to fry the pork slices two at a time.

6. Fry over a high heat until browned on one side, turn, and when both sides have browned, lower the heat and cover the wok.

7. Cook until the pork is tender and well browned all over. Cook the remaining slices in the same manner.

8. When all the pork is cooked, cut it into strips about $\frac{1}{2}-\frac{3}{4}$ inch wide and arrange on the serving dish. The slices are best cut with a very sharp cleaver; cut straight down through the meat, pressing firmly down on the cleaver; do not use a sawing motion which would break up the meat.

Stir-fried pork and potatoes

$\frac{1}{2}$ pound sliced leg of pork
$\frac{1}{4}$ pound carrots
$\frac{3}{4}$ pound potatoes
4 tablespoons oil
For the marinade:
1 teaspoon soy sauce
$\frac{1}{2}$ teaspoon sugar
1 tablespoon peanut oil
1 teaspoon cornstarch
For the sauce:
1 tablespoon soy sauce
1 teaspoon sugar
1 tablespoon rice wine or dry sherry
$\frac{1}{2}$ teaspoon salt
a pinch of monosodium glutamate (optional)
250 calories; 12.6g protein; 14.5g fat; 16.3g sugar

1. Cut the pork slices into thin strips, place in a bowl, and add the marinade of soy sauce, sugar, oil, and cornstarch. Mix very well by hand and leave to stand for a little while for the flavoring to penetrate the meat.

2. Cut the carrots into thin strips the same size as the pork.

3. Peel the potatoes and cut to the same size as the carrot strips. Bring a large pan of water to a boil; parboil the potato strips and drain.

4. Heat 2 tablespoons oil in a wok; fry the pork lightly, keeping the strips as separate as possible. When just done, remove from the wok and set aside.

5. Wipe the wok clean, heat 2 tablespoons of fresh oil, and stir-fry the carrots and the potatoes; when they are just tender, add the pork and stir-fry all the ingredients together briefly.

6. Mix the sauce ingredients and pour into the wok; mix quickly but thoroughly and serve.

Stir-fried pork and celery

The crisp, crunchy consistency of the celery contrasts agreeably with the tender pork.

¾ pound celery
a small piece of leek
a small piece of ginger root
oil for frying
¼ pound finely chopped or ground pork
For the sauce;
1 teaspoon soy sauce
1 tablespoon rice wine
2 teaspoons sugar
1 tablespoon soybean paste
a pinch of monosodium glutamate (optional)
If required:
cornstarch dissolved in double the quantity of water to thicken the sauce
77 calories; 5.8g protein; 11.5g fat; 4.2g sugar

1. Wash the celery thoroughly, remove the strings, and cut into ½-inch pieces.

2. Bring a large saucepan of water to a boil and parboil the diced celery. Drain and set aside.

3. Finely chop enough leek to yield 1 tablespoonful; peel the ginger and chop very finely, to yield 1 teaspoonful.

4. Prepare the sauce by mixing all the ingredients together, making sure the soybean paste is smoothly blended.

5. Heat 2 tablespoons of oil in the wok and lightly stir-fry the chopped leek and ginger; once they have started to release their aroma, add the pork and stir-fry, stirring constantly to keep it from sticking or forming lumps; mix in the celery and keep turning to ensure an even cooking.

6. Pour in the sauce and cook briskly; be sure that the sauce is absorbed evenly.

7. If the liquid seems too thin, dissolve a small quantity of cornstarch in double that quantity of water and stir into the wok.

Green chili peppers stuffed with pork

A full-flavored dish. The brilliant green of the peppers makes for attractive presentation.

generous $\frac{1}{4}$ pound finely chopped or ground pork
20 green chili peppers
oil for frying
To flavor:
$\frac{1}{4}$ teaspoon salt
2 teaspoons soy sauce
1 teaspoon sugar
2 tablespoons rice wine
a few drops of sesame oil
a pinch of monosodium glutamate (optional)
256 calories; 10.4g protein; 17.8g fat; 6.9g sugar

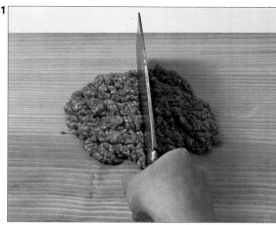

1. Spread the ground meat out on the chopping board and, using the sharp edge of the cleaver, go over the meat chopping downward first horizontally and then vertically to help soften the pork further and avoid the formation of lumps in the stuffing mixture.

2. Place the meat in a bowl, add the flavoring ingredients, and work in well with the hands until a smooth paste is obtained.

3. Wash the peppers; slit them carefully down one side, stopping short of both ends so that they do not open into two halves.

4. Remove the seeds delicately, using a chopstick or small spoon handle.

5. To avoid splattering when the peppers are fried in oil, dry very thoroughly with paper towels or a dry cloth.

6. Open the slits in the peppers carefully and fill with the stuffing, adding a little at a time, until the firmly packed meat is bulging out of the openings.

7. Heat 2 tablespoons of oil in a wok, place the stuffed peppers, meat side downward in the oil, and fry over a medium heat until the meat is browned.

8. Turn the peppers with a spatula, cover, turn down the heat, and cook through. Check every so often to make sure they do not stick and burn.

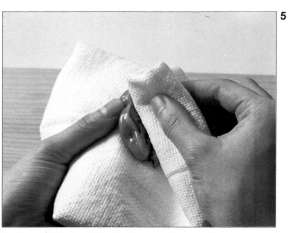

93

Sichuan ground pork and bean thread noodles

A robust, peppery dish, typical of Sichuan.

2 ounces bean thread (transparent noodles)
3 tablespoons peanut oil
2 tablespoons of leek, ginger, and garlic, finely chopped
 together
1 teaspoon hot soybean paste
½ pound ground pork
1 tablespoon rice wine
3 cups stock
a pinch of salt
2–3 tablespoons soy sauce
cornstarch mixed with water
a few drops of sesame oil
2–3 very small eggplants
oil for frying
364 calories; 9.1 g protein; 29.1 g fat; 15.7 g sugar

1. Wash the noodles, boil until they are tender, drain, and cut into 1½–2-inch lengths (this is most easily done with scissors).

2. Heat 3 tablespoons of oil in a wok; add the chopped mixture of leek, ginger, and garlic; and stir-fry. Do not allow the condiments to brown. When they have started to give off their aroma add the hot soybean paste.

3. Stir-fry for a little longer and then add the ground pork; stir-fry, mixing well to avoid lumps forming. Add the rice wine pouring it in down the side of the wok and cook until the meat has browned.

4. Add the stock, season with salt and soy sauce, and cook slowly.

5. Add the noodles, and then the cornstarch dissolved in water (about 1 tablespoon dissolved in 2 tablespoons water should suffice to thicken the liquid and give it more body); add a few drops of sesame oil for extra flavor.

6. Wash the eggplants well and slice crossways into rounds.

7. Heat some oil in the wok and fry the eggplant slices briskly; when they are tender, remove with slotted spatula allowing them to drain.

8. Serve the pork and noodles in a deep serving dish with the fried eggplant slices arranged in the center.

Beef Dishes

The Chinese have never been great eaters of beef, since cattle are raised and kept for other purposes. Since time immemorial, oxen and water buffalo have been the faithful servants and friends of the Chinese, useful as beasts of burden and working animals. The time finally comes, however, when these animals can no longer work; few of their owners can afford to be sentimental and allow them to pass an idle retirement, and so they usually end up in the cooking pot.

The relative scarcity of recipes for beef in Chinese cooking may be explained by the fact that the beef is usually from old animals and is therefore tough or it may be because of the dislike many Chinese have for red meat (more marked in previous centuries). What beef dishes there are can usually be found in the north and west of China, where Islam has made a greater impact, reducing the consumption of pork.

Beef is usually cut into very thin slices, across the grain, or ground, flavored with ginger and scallions and used as a stuffing for dumplings. Thin slices of beef are also treated with spices, dried, and eaten as snacks.

Sichuan beef with ginger and green peppers

This dish has the strong flavors characteristic of Sichuan cooking and should be accompanied by rice.

½ pound lean beef
¼ teaspoon salt
½ egg white
1 teaspoon cornstarch
5 green peppers
¼ pound bamboo shoots (canned, unsalted or fresh, parboiled)
oil for frying
1 teaspoon finely chopped garlic
1 tablespoon finely chopped leek
1 teaspoon finely chopped ginger root
1 tablespoon rice wine
sesame oil
For the sauce:
1 teaspoon sugar
2½ tablespoons soy sauce
1 teaspoon vinegar
If required:
1 teaspoon cornstarch dissolved in 2 teaspoons water to thicken the sauce
209 calories; 11.9 g protein; 15.7 g fat; 4 g sugar

1. Cut the beef into thin slices and then into thin strips $\frac{1}{4}$ inch wide. Season with salt, dip in the egg white, and then sprinkle with the cornstarch mixing well by hand.

2. Cut the green peppers in half lengthwise, remove the seeds and pith, and shred into very thin strips less than $\frac{1}{8}$ inch wide; cut the bamboo shoots into similar-sized strips.

3. Stir-fry the strips of beef in fairly hot oil, taking care that they do not stick to one another; remove as soon as they have turned whitish.

4. Heat the wok and pour in 2 tablespoons oil; when this is hot stir-fry the chopped garlic, leek, and ginger briskly over a high heat.

5. Once the ginger has turned golden brown and has started to release its aroma, add the shredded green peppers and the bamboo shoots. Stir-fry briefly over a high heat.

6. When the peppers and bamboo shoots are nearly tender, add the beef and sprinkle with 1 tablespoon rice wine; stir-fry all the ingredients together.

7. Pour the sauce over the contents of the wok and stir-fry the ingredients rapidly to allow them to absorb the flavor evenly.

8. Finish by adding a few drops of sesame oil to give the dish extra flavor, if the sauce is too thin, stir in 1 teaspoon cornstarch dissolved in 2 teaspoons water.

Beef and Chinese white radish in soy sauce

A Sichuan specialty which involves long, slow cooking and has a spicy flavor.

$1\frac{1}{4}$ pounds shin of beef
1 tablespoon rice wine
$\frac{1}{2}$ tablespoon soy sauce
1 tablespoon cornstarch
oil for frying
a 4-inch length of leek
4–5 slivers of ginger root
1 star anise
5–7 tablespoons soy sauce
$2\frac{1}{4}$ pounds Chinese white radish.
348 calories; 29.2g protein; 17.9g fat; 14.8g sugar

1. Dice the beef into 1–1½ inch cubes, place in a bowl, sprinkle with rice wine and soy sauce, add the cornstarch and mix well by hand.

2. Heat plenty of oil in a wok; add the meat and fry quickly over a high heat until the beef is well browned. If desired, the beef can be given more color by shallow-frying. Drain.

3. Place the meat in a heavy pan together with the leek, sliced diagonally into thin rounds, and the slightly crushed ginger; cover with 6–7 cups water.

4. Add the star anise and ⅓ of the soy sauce (about 2 tablespoons). Bring to a boil over a high heat, skim, cover the pan, and turn the heat down to low. Simmer for about 2 hours.

5. The remaining soy sauce will be added to the beef later on if the flavor needs strengthening.

6. Peel and slice the Chinese radishes into pieces about 1½–2 inches long; cut these pieces vertically in half or in quarters if they are very large. Trim the edges to round them off.

7. When the beef is very tender, add the radishes and continue cooking over a low heat.

8. When the liquid in the pan has reduced by half, taste the sauce and add the reserved soy sauce if needed. Continue cooking until the radishes have reached a really tender, almost buttery consistency.

Stir-fried beef with green beans

An appetizing dish, which is easy to prepare.

5 ounces thinly sliced lean beef
1 teaspoon sugar
1 tablespoon soy sauce
1 teaspoon cornstarch
1 teaspoon peanut oil
7 ounces green beans
1 teaspoon salt
1 cup water
½ can straw mushrooms
oil for frying
1 tablespoon finely chopped leek
1 teaspoon sugar
1 tablespoon soy sauce
1 tablespoon rice wine
a pinch of monosodium glutamate (optional)
a few drops of sesame oil
170 calories; 9.4g protein; 12.5g fat; 6.1g sugar

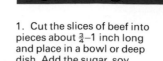

1. Cut the slices of beef into pieces about ¾–1 inch long and place in a bowl or deep dish. Add the sugar, soy sauce, cornstarch and peanut oil; mix well and leave to marinate.

2. String the beans if necessary, wash, and cut into 1¾–2-inch lengths.

3. Heat a wok, pour in 2 tablespoons oil, and stir-fry the beans lightly; add the salt and the water, cover, and simmer until the beans are tender. Remove from the wok and drain.

4. Drain the canned straw mushrooms.

5. Heat 2 tablespoons of oil in the wok, add the marinated beef, and stir-fry lightly – the meat should still be a little pink.

6. In another pan, heat 2 tablespoons of oil and stir-fry the chopped leek; when the leek starts to release its aroma, add the mushrooms and the beans.

7. Stir-fry these briefly and then add the meat, sugar, soy sauce, rice wine, and monosodium glutamate (optional). Stir-fry quickly over a high heat, and add a few drops of sesame oil to give the dish more flavor.

Stir-fried beef and onions

The well-chosen combinations of ingredients makes this a mouth-watering dish which is no trouble to prepare.

7 ounces thinly sliced lean beef
10 ounces onions
oil for frying
For flavoring and coating the meat:
1 tablespoon soy sauce
½ egg white
1 teaspoon cornstarch
For the sauce:
1 tablespoon rice wine
1 tablespoon sugar
2 tablespoons soy sauce
a pinch of monosodium glutamate (optional)
277 calories; 13.4g protein; 17.6g fat; 12.3g sugar

1. Cut the meat into very narrow strips, place in a bowl, and mix well with the soy sauce. Leave to stand.

2. Peel the onions; cut in two vertically and then slice horizontally (across the layers).

3. Heat 3 tablespoons oil in the wok and stir-fry the onions to a light golden brown. Do not allow to burn or crisp. Set aside.

4. Mix the beef by hand, first with the egg white and then with the cornstarch. Stir-fry gently in oil in a separate skillet over a fairly low heat – use chopsticks to separate the shreds of beef. As soon as the beef is done, remove the whole lot at once, using a mesh ladle. Drain.

5. Place the wok containing the onion over a fairly low heat, add the cooked beef, and stir in the sauce ingredients: rice wine, sugar, soy sauce, and monosodium glutamate (optional). Stir-fry briefly and then serve.

Sichuan braised shin of beef with Chinese cabbage

2 h 30'

A spicy dish from Sichuan which needs long, slow cooking.

1½ pounds shin of beef in one piece
5 tablespoons peanut oil
½ Chinese cabbage
2 tablespoons rice wine
5–6 cups water
1 teaspoon hot soybean paste
⅓ – ½ cup soy sauce
1 teaspoon sesame oil
1 tablespoon cornstarch
467 calories; 38.6g protein; 30.8g fat; 6g sugar

1. Cut the beef into pieces about 2 inches wide and $\frac{3}{4}$ inch thick; it is best not to cut the pieces too small or they will become dry and tasteless during the lengthy cooking process.

2. Heat the peanut oil in the wok and fry the beef over a high heat until it is well browned on all sides.

3. Wash the Chinese cabbage, place in a large saucepan of hot water, and boil until just tender. Rinse in cold water and cut lengthwise into strips $\frac{3}{4}$ inch wide. Squeeze gently to get rid of excess liquid.

4. Place the meat in a large saucepan, add 2 tablespoons rice wine, 5–6 cups water and the hot, peppery soybean paste; bring to a boil quickly over a high heat, leaving the pan uncovered.

5. As soon as the water comes to a boil, turn down the heat and remove any scum from the surface with a skimmer. Cover and simmer slowly for about $1\frac{1}{2}$ hours.

6. When the beef is quite tender, place the Chinese cabbage strips on top of it and add stir in half the soy sauce.

7. Cook for another 30 minutes, by which time the flavoring should have been absorbed by the meat and vegetable. Add some or all of the remaining soy sauce, depending on how pronounced a taste you like; add a few drops of sesame oil for extra flavor.

8. Mix the cornstarch with 2 tablespoons water, take the cabbage off the heat, and stir in the thickening mixture. once the sauce has thickened, the dish is ready to serve.

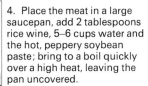

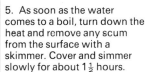

Sweet and sour beef rissoles

Made with beef, this dish is less rich and more digestible than the pork version.

$\frac{3}{4}$ pound finely chopped or ground beef
oil for frying
1 onion
4 sweet peppers
4 slices pineapple
1 chili pepper
a small piece of garlic
1 tablespoon cornstarch
To bind and flavor the beef balls:
$\frac{1}{2}$ beaten egg
$\frac{1}{2}$ teaspoon salt
1 tablespoon cornstarch
2 tablespoons water
For the sauce:
$\frac{1}{4}$ cup stock
generous $\frac{1}{2}$ cup sugar
1 tablespoon soy sauce
2 tablespoons vinegar
1 teaspoon salt
1 teaspoon rice wine
526 calories; 17.3 g protein; 31.1 g fat; 20.7 g sugar

1

1. Spread the ground beef out on a chopping board and, using the cleaver, chop it in both directions to make it smooth. Place in a bowl and add the beaten egg, salt, cornstarch, and water. Knead well.

2. When the mixture forms a smooth paste, shape into balls about 1 inch in diameter. To make well-shaped rissoles, take a small amount of the mixture in one hand and close the hand to make a fist, squeezing the meat out into a small ball through the hole formed by thumb and forefinger.

3. Heat the oil to medium hot in a wok, and fry the beef balls until they are well-browned all over. Use chopsticks to keep them from sticking to each other while cooking; drain and set aside.

4. Cut the onion in half and then slice it thinly. Cut the sweet peppers in half vertically, remove the seeds and pith; drain the juice from the pineapple slices; and cut both the peppers and the pineapple into small pieces.

5. Remove the seeds from the chili pepper and cut it into $\frac{1}{4}$ inch-thick rings; finely chop enough garlic to yield 1 teaspoonful. Mix all the sauce ingredients together.

6. Heat 2 tablespoons of oil in the wok, stir-fry the garlic and, as soon as it starts to release its aroma, add the peppers, onion, and pineapple.

7. When these are tender, add the beef balls and stir-fry; sprinkle with the chili pepper rings. Finally, pour in the sauce and mix quickly.

8. When the sauce has started to bubble, add the cornstarch dissolved in 2 tablespoons water; stir quickly to thicken the sauce evenly.

5

2

6

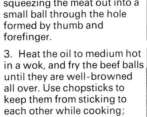

3

7

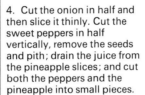

4

8

Cantonese beef with oyster sauce

A famous dish from Canton. The flavor of the oyster sauce heightens and enhances the contrasting taste of the beef.

1 pound thinly sliced lean beef
½ egg white
1 teaspoon cornstarch
1 small clove garlic
oil for frying
2 tablespoons peanut oil
1 tablespoon rice wine
1 teaspoon cornstarch
For the sauce:
⅓ cup oyster sauce
1 teaspoon sugar
2 tablespoons stock
343 calories; 26.4g protein; 21.8g fat; 8.2g sugar

1. Cut the beef into bite-size pieces, place in a bowl, and mix well with the egg white and the cornstarch.

2. Chop enough garlic to yield 1 teaspoonful. Mix the sauce ingredients and set aside.

3. Heat the oil until only moderately hot, add the beef, and fry lightly; separate the pieces with chopsticks as they cook. Drain and set aside.

4. Heat the wok and, when it is hot, pour in 2 tablespoons peanut oil and stir-fry the finely chopped garlic. When the garlic starts to give off its aroma, add the beef and sprinkle with the rice wine.

5. Add the sauce, mixing and turning well to make sure the meat is evenly covered; thicken and glaze the sauce by adding the cornstarch dissolved in 2 teaspoons of water.

Chicken and Duck

Chicken is as versatile as pork in Chinese cooking, providing another source of delicately flavored, tender meat which presents few problems, even for the inexperienced cook. The eating of its flesh is not proscribed by any religion, which is another reason for its widespread popularity. However, the fowl so beloved of the Chinese is not the watery, almost tasteless product of factory farming which all too often we in the West have to eat, but a very different bird which has grown to early maturity scratching around in farmyards and courtyards, nourished on a wide variety of foods. The Chinese also eat their chickens extremely fresh – as soon after they have been killed as possible – and for this reason the birds are usually bought at street markets and taken home alive.

Duck demands a little more skill for successful preparation. If inexpertly cooked it can be fatty and indigestible or tough and rubbery; if overdone, the flesh is dry. Duck has a distinctive taste and consistency and has a lower ratio of meat to bone than chicken. It is also less versatile and combines well with a narrower range of ingredients.

It is difficult to assign a particular role to duck in Chinese cuisine. Its pronounced flavor precludes it from being an everyday food, and its lower meat yield means it can be quite expensive, but with a little care duck can be a delectable treat, and in Chinese hands it has become a delicacy known all over the world, as anyone who has tasted Peking Duck would agree.

Stir-fried chicken and cucumbers

A light, low-calorie dish with a delicate flavor.

7 ounces chicken breasts
½ egg white
1 teaspoon cornstarch
2 cucumbers
oil for frying
1 small slice ginger root
1 tablespoon rice wine
a few drops of sesame oil
For the sauce:
1 tablespoon soy sauce
1 teaspoon sugar
½ teaspoon salt
a pinch of monosodium glutamate (optional)
a pinch of pepper
219 calories; 11.4g protein; 17.6g fat; 2.8g sugar

1. Cut the chicken breasts into thin, diagonal slices. (Hold the chicken breasts firmly with the left hand and cut carefully with the knife at a 45-degree angle to the chopping board, working from right to left.) Dip the slices in the egg white and then in the cornstarch.

2. Cut the cucumbers in half lengthwise and then slice diagonally into ¼-inch-thick pieces.

3. Heat the oil over a low heat and fry the chicken gently. Remove the chicken and drain.

4. Heat a wok and, when it is hot, pour in 2 tablespoons oil; stir-fry the ginger and, once it has started to give off its aroma, add the cucumbers.

5. Add the chicken and sprinkle with the rice wine and the sauce ingredients. Stir-fry quickly over a high heat.

6. Finally add a few drops of sesame oil.

Chicken and cashew nuts Sichuan style

7 ounces chicken breasts
½ egg white
1 teaspoon cornstarch
a pinch of salt
oil for frying
3 green peppers
3½ ounces bamboo shoots, parboiled
2 ounces cashew nuts
1 teaspoon finely chopped garlic
1 tablespoon rice wine
a pinch of monosodium glutamate (optional)
For the sauce:
1 tablespoon soybean paste
1 tablespoon soy sauce
2 teaspoons sugar
½ tablespoon vinegar
¼ teaspoon salt
317 calories; 14.8g protein; 23.7g fat; 11.5g sugar

1. Dice the chicken breasts into ½-inch pieces; dip in the egg white and then in the cornstarch mixed with a pinch of salt.

2. Heat some oil until fairly hot and fry the diced chicken. Drain.

3. Slice the peppers in half vertically; remove the seeds, stems, and pith; cut into ½-inch squares.

4. Cut the parboiled bamboo shoots to the same size as the peppers. Mix the sauce ingredients together in a bowl.

5. Fry the cashew nuts in moderately hot oil until they are lightly browned and crunchy.

6. Heat 2 tablespoons of oil in the wok and stir-fry the garlic until it starts to release its aroma; add the bamboo shoots and the peppers and stir-fry.

7. Add the chicken and cashew nuts, sprinkle with rice wine, and pour in the sauce. Stir-fry all the ingredients briefly over a high heat and add a pinch of monosodium glutamate (optional) to heighten the flavor.

Stir-fried chicken with ginger

This is a seasonal dish with a pleasant piquant taste of ginger root.

10 ounces chicken breasts
1 tablespoon rice wine or dry sherry
½ teaspoon salt
1 tablespoon rice wine
2–4 ounces ginger root
a generous pinch of salt
4 green peppers
1 teaspoon finely chopped garlic
1 egg white
1 tablespoon cornstarch
oil for frying
For the sauce:
½ teaspoon salt
2½ tablespoons vinegar
3 tablespoons sugar
1 tablespoon tomato ketchup
If required:
1 teaspoon cornstarch dissolved in 2 teaspoons water to thicken
  the sauce
303 calories; 17.2g protein; 18.9g fat; 13.6g sugar

1

1. Slice the chicken diagonally into bite-size pieces; hold the chicken breast firmly with the left hand and, with the knife at a 45-degree angle to the surface, slice across the grain of the meat; begin from the right-hand end and shear off the slices. Place the meat in a bowl and mix with ½ teaspoon salt and 1 tablespoon rice wine.

2. Remove the leaves from the ginger; wash, dry, and cut lengthwise into wafer-thin slices. Sprinkle with a pinch of salt and leave to stand.

3. Cut the peppers in half lengthwise; remove the seeds, stems, and pith; and cut into even-sized triangular pieces.

4. Place all the sauce ingredients in a small saucepan and heat, mixing well. As soon as the liquid comes to a boil, remove from heat, and set aside to cool.

5. Squeeze out the ginger which will have been softened by the salt; add to the tepid or cold sauce and leave to stand.

6. Mix the chicken with the egg white and then with the cornstarch; fry in fairly hot oil, stirring and turning to prevent crisping or browning.

7. Heat 2 tablespoons of oil in the wok; stir-fry the finely chopped garlic until it starts to give off its scent; add the peppers and the ginger (removed from the sauce and drain).

8. When the peppers are tender, add the chicken and rice wine, pour in the sauce and stir-fry over a high heat. If the sauce is too thin, stir in 1 teaspoon cornstarch dissolved in 2 teaspoons water.

2

3

4

5

6

7

8

Fried chicken Chinese style

 40'

Crisp and full of flavor, chicken fried this way is delicious dipped in tomato ketchup.

2–3 servings:
2 spring chicken leg quarters
½ beaten egg
4 tablespoons cornstarch
a few drops sesame oil (optional)
oil for frying
To flavor:
¼ teaspoon salt
2–3 drops of soy sauce
1 teaspoon rice wine
a pinch of pepper
a pinch of monosodium glutamate (optional)
255 calories; 25.7g protein; 12.4g fat; 8.3g sugar

1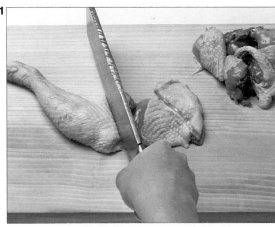

2

3

4

1. Wash and trim the chicken legs; dry with a cloth or paper towels. Using a cleaver, chop through the bone into triangular, bite-size pieces.

2. Gently mix the beaten egg and the flavoring ingredients together in a bowl and add the chicken pieces.

3. Sprinkle with the cornstarch and mix well by hand. Leave to stand for 5 minutes. If a slightly stronger flavor is preferred, add a few drops sesame oil.

4. Heat plenty of oil in a wok or a deep-fryer. The temperature indicator on an electric deep-fryer should be set at 350°F. (180°C.). If a wok is used, test the temperature of the oil by dropping in a little coarsely chopped leek; if the leek travels to the edge of the pan and browns quickly, the oil should be hot enough.

5. Lower the chicken pieces into the oil one by one, working as quickly as possible to ensure even cooking; if the skin of the chicken flaps loose, press it back into place for attractive presentation.

6. Adding the chicken to the oil will have lowered the temperature to about 300°F. (100°C.). Maintain this lower temperature by turning down the heat; when the chicken is half done, remove the pieces from the oil and prick them with a skewer to make them cook through more quickly. Lower them into the oil once more.

7. When the chicken is nearly cooked, increase the heat so that the oil is really hot; this will make it easier to drain the chicken so that it does not taste oily.

8. If desired, the flavor can be heightened by stir-frying the drained chicken pieces briefly in another skillet with a few drops of sesame oil and a tablespoon of finely chopped leek.

5

6

7

8

Chicken and pork in savory batter

The meat is encased in an extra-light batter made with oil and baking powder and seasoned with sesame seeds and seaweed.

3–4 servings:
3 chicken wings
a pinch of salt
a pinch of pepper
a pinch of monosodium glutamate (optional)
cornstarch as required
3 ounces pork tenderloin cut into chunks
batter as required (see recipe on pages 156–157)
a pinch of black sesame seeds
one leaf nori *(purple seaweed), presoaked*
oil for frying
345 calories; 12g protein; 21.3g fat; 25.6g sugar

1. Sever the main joint of the wing; cutting off the last two sections from the fleshier section required for this recipe. These tips can be used to make stock. Snip the tendons carefully to release the flesh from the bone. Hold the bone vertically, cutting and rolling the flesh downward, rather like peeling off a glove, working it away from the bone and keeping it as intact as possible. Stop just before reaching the end of the bone. The flesh should end up with the skin on the inside and still attached to the tip of the bone.

2. Season the chicken with salt, pepper, and monosodium glutamate (optional) and dredge lightly with cornstarch.

3. Season the pork with salt, pepper, and monosodium glutamate (optional) and coat with cornstarch.

4. Make the batter and pour slightly less than half into a second bowl. Stir the sesame seeds into the smaller quantity and the shredded seaweed into the larger bowl, mixing well.

5. Heat the oil to medium hot in a wok or deep-fryer; dip the chicken wings into the sesame seed batter and the pork into the seaweed batter.

6. Fry the coated portions at a medium-hot temperature until they are almost cooked; turn up the heat so that the oil reaches a temperature of 350°F. (180°C.) and finish frying.

Sweet and sour chicken legs

2 teaspoons salt
pepper
4 plump spring chicken leg quarters
a small quantity of chopped leek and ginger
1 tablespoon rice wine
oil for frying
cornstarch as required
For the sweet and sour sauce:
3 ounces leek
1½ ounces ginger root
a small bunch of parsley
4 tablespoons soy sauce
4 tablespoons sugar
4 tablespoons vinegar
3 tablespoons stock or hot water
a pinch of monosodium glutamate (optional)
1 tablespoon sesame oil
299 calories; 25.3g protein; 14.3g fat; 15.7g sugar

1. Rub ½ teaspoon salt and a pinch of pepper into each leg quarter. Pound the chopped leek and ginger briefly and mix with the chicken legs; add 1 tablespoon rice wine and leave for 30 minutes for the chicken to absorb the flavors.

2. Bring a large pan of water to a boil; add the chicken legs one at a time. Allow the water to come back to a boil, turning the legs every now and then. Remove from the heat and take out the chicken legs. Tie a piece of string around each drumstick end and hang up to dry for 1 to 2 hours.

3. Start to prepare the sweet and sour sauce by dicing the leek and chopping the ginger and the parsley, all very finely. Heat plenty of oil.

4. Untie the chicken legs and coat them with cornstarch, rubbing it well into the flesh. Lower the legs carefully into the boiling oil, reduce the heat, and fry for 5 to 6 minutes. Increase the temperature of the oil and continue cooking until the chicken is golden brown and the coating is crisp.

5. Meanwhile, mix together all the sauce ingredients including the leek, ginger, and parsley.

6. Chop each chicken leg cleanly (ideally with a cleaver) into 5 to 6 pieces and place on a warmed serving dish. Cover with the sweet and sour sauce.

Chicken with Chinese white radish

A homey, satisfying dish which nonetheless needs painstaking preparation.

2 boned chicken leg quarters
a 4-inch length of leek, cut into thin rings
a small piece of ginger, sliced wafer thin
2 tablespoons soy sauce
1 tablespoon rice wine
cornstarch as required
oil for frying
1 small Chinese white radish
1 tablespoon rice wine
a few drops of soy sauce
1 teaspoon salt
If desired:
1 star anise
a little sugar
a few drops of sesame oil
227 calories; 10.4g protein; 12.5g fat; 17g sugar

1. Cut the boned chicken into pieces 2–2$\frac{1}{2}$ inches wide and place in a bowl; marinate with sliced leek, the lightly pounded slices of ginger, the soy sauce, and the rice wine.

2. Leave the chicken to absorb the flavors for 1 to 2 hours, turning every now and then. Remove the chicken from the marinade, dry with a cloth or paper towels, and coat with cornstarch.

3. Heat the oil in a wok, shake off any excess cornstarch, and fry the chicken. Turn the pieces regularly with a Chinese scoop or spatula so that they brown well all over.

4. Cut the Chinese white radish into 1$\frac{1}{2}$–2-inch lengths, peel and pare the edges, rounding off the corners.

5. Place the pieces of chicken, radish, rice wine, a few drops of soy sauce, and salt in a saucepan, pour in enough cold water to just cover and place over the burner.

6. At this point add the star anise, a very little sugar, and a few drops of sesame oil if a stronger, more robust flavor is desired.

7. Turn on the heat and, when the water comes to a boil, carefully skim off any scum. Have a bowl of water near the cooking pot to rinse the mesh ladle or skimmer between uses.

8. Cover the saucepan and lower the heat; shake the pan gently from time to time to prevent the contents sticking and burning; simmer for 1 hour, until the radish is tender.

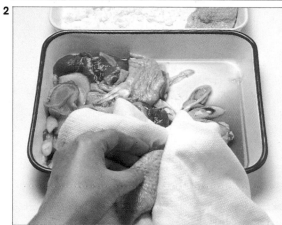

Simmered chicken giblets

A tasty and frugal dish; the chicken giblets are
cooked and then allowed to stand in their
juices to absorb all the flavor.

10 ounces chicken livers
10 ounces chicken gizzards
1 leek
a small piece of ginger, sliced wafer thin
1 tablespoon rice wine
scant 1 tablespoon sugar
$\frac{1}{3}-\frac{1}{2}$ cup soy sauce
1 star anise
344 calories; 26.8 g protein; 23.5 g fat; 3.8 g sugar

1. Wash the chicken livers well and trim away the bile ducts and any discolored portions; trim the gristle and white parts from the gizzards.

2. Place the giblets in a bowl or colander and wash under running water until completely clean.

3. Bring a saucepan of water to a boil and add the giblets; turn down heat and simmer gently; remove them from the pan as soon as they have changed color and rinse in cold water.

4. Wash well again in several changes of cold water; if this procedure is not followed thoroughly enough, the giblets will still have a rather strong taste.

5. Place the giblets in a saucepan with the leek (cut in two or more pieces) and the sliced ginger; add enough water to cover.

6. Add the rice wine, sugar, soy sauce, and star anise and bring quickly to a boil.

7. Once the liquid has boiled, lower the heat and simmer very gently. Skim off any scum, cover, and cook slowly for about 30 minutes.

8. Turn off the heat and let the giblets cool in the liquid to absorb their full flavor. Once cold, drain and slice them thinly.

Sichuan chicken with chestnuts

In this Sichuan dish the sweet taste of the chestnuts marries well with the flavor of chicken.

3 chicken leg quarters
1 leek
a small piece of ginger
2 tablespoons soy sauce
1 teaspoon rice wine
a pinch of salt
a pinch of pepper
cornstarch as required
oil for frying
2 cups stock
15 dried chestnuts (soaked overnight)
256 calories; 11.4g protein; 12.7g fat; 22.9g sugar

1. Chop the chicken legs into pieces with a cleaver.

2. Slice the leek and ginger very thin.

3. Place the chicken, leek, and ginger in a bowl; add the soy sauce, rice wine, salt, and pepper. Mix well and leave to marinate for about 30 minutes.

4. Wipe the chicken with paper towels, coat with cornstarch and deep-fry in very hot oil until crisp and golden brown on the outside.

5. Pour the stock into a pan, add the marinade in which the chicken was left to stand, and then the fried chicken. Bring to a boil over a high heat and then lower the heat. Cook over a medium heat for about 20 to 30 minutes.

6. Remove the leek and ginger from the pan and discard; add the presoaked chestnuts and cook for about 10 minutes or until they have absorbed the flavors and juices.

Empress chicken wings

4–6 servings:
12 chicken wings
½ leek
a small piece of ginger
cornstarch as required
oil for frying
For the marinade:
½ tablespoon rice wine
1 tablespoon soy sauce
For the stock:
3 cups water
1 tablespoon soy sauce
½ tablespoon rice wine
1 heaping teaspoon sugar
½ pound spinach
2 tablespoons peanut oil
a pinch of salt
1 tablespoon rice wine
1 cup water
346 calories; 21.4g protein; 22.3g fat; 13.4g sugar

1. Wash the chicken wings well, cut off the tips, and reserve; slice the leek and the ginger finely.

2. Place the chicken wings, leek, and ginger in a bowl and add the marinade made with the rice wine and the soy sauce; mix and leave to stand for 30 minutes.

3. Remove the chicken wings from the marinade and pat dry with paper towels or a cloth. Coat evenly with cornstarch and fry lightly in plenty of hot oil.

4. Pour the 3 cups water into a pan, add the soy sauce, rice wine, and sugar, along with the leek and ginger from the marinade and the wing tips.

5. Add the fried chicken wings and bring to a boil over a high heat; once the liquid has come to a boil, lower the heat and cook for about 40 minutes.

6. Wash the spinach thoroughly and stir-fry lightly in 2 tablespoons peanut oil; season with a pinch of salt and 1 tablespoon of rice wine; add 1 cup boiling water; as soon as this comes back to a boil, remove the spinach and drain.

7. Arrange the chicken wings and spinach on a serving dish; chop the spinach in half if it is too long.

Paper-wrapped Cantonese chicken

An elegant Cantonese dish in which the chicken is cooked *en papillote* to keep all its flavor. This is a good conversation piece for a dinner party. Beef, fish fillets, or shrimp can be cooked in the same way.

5 ounces boned chicken breasts
3 presoaked Chinese mushrooms
a small piece of ginger
2 ounces parboiled fresh or canned bamboo shoots
a small bunch of chives
2 tablespoons peas
12 squares parchment or greaseproof paper cut to measure 6 × 6 inches
oil for frying
For the marinade:
1 teaspoon soy sauce
½ teaspoon salt
1 tablespoon rice wine
a pinch of pepper
a few drops of sesame oil
a pinch of monosodium glutamate (optional)
1 teaspoon cornstarch
174 calories; 10.2 g protein; 13.4 g fat; 3.3 g sugar

1

2

3

4

1. Remove the strip of white gristle on the inside of each chicken breast, pulling it gently away from the flesh with one hand while cutting carefully with a very sharp knife; pull the last few inches away with a sharp tug.

2. Having trimmed all the chicken breasts in this way, slice them diagonally into small pieces.

3. Drain the mushrooms, and squeeze them gently to get rid of excess moisture; remove the stems and slice the caps into thin strips. Peel the ginger; cut into 2–3 thin slices and then into strips.

4. Shred the bamboo shoots and snip the chives into very short lengths. If fresh peas are used, boil until tender in salted water; if frozen, place in a bowl, cover with boiling water, and leave to stand for a few minutes.

5. Place the chicken breasts in a deep dish or bowl together with the ingredients you have just prepared, sprinkle with the marinade, and mix well with chopsticks to make sure it is absorbed evenly.

6. Spread the parchment or greaseproof paper squares on a working surface, brush the center of each square with a little oil, and place a portion of the chicken and vegetable mixture on the oiled patch.

7. Take the lower corner and fold over the chicken to meet the opposite top corner, forming a triangle. Fold back the apex of the triangle of the top layer of wrapping; bring first the right-hand point and then the left of the base of the triangle into the center, folding them neatly. By now the package should look rather like an open envelope; fold the apex of the triangle down toward you, over the folded-in sides and tuck the point neatly underneath the fold.

8. Heat plenty of peanut oil in the wok until it is only fairly hot; fry the rectangular packages gently, turning carefully. When the chicken has turned a whitish color, it is ready to be served. Each guest unwraps his or her own package with chopsticks.

5

6

7

8

123

Fried chicken with curry seasoning

The unmistakable flavor of curry seasons the chicken, and the turmeric in the curry gives it an appetizing color.

a 1¾-pound chicken, carved or chopped into fairly small portions (use a cleaver)
1 teaspoon salt
1 tablespoon rice wine
oil for frying
For the sauce:
1½ teaspoons curry powder
1 teaspoon sugar
½ teaspoon salt
1 tablespoon soy sauce
1 tablespoon rice wine
447 calories; 26.3 g protein; 36.2 g fat; 0.8 g sugar

1. Place the portions of chicken in a fairly deep-sided heatproof dish that will fit into a bamboo steamer; sprinkle with the salt and the rice wine and rub these into the flesh so that the flavor penetrates. See that the chicken is evenly spread out in the dish. Use two dishes and two steamers if necessary.

2. Place the dish in the steamer, which should already be hot and full of steam. Cover and steam for about 20 minutes over rapidly boiling water.

1

2

3

4

5

6

3. When the chicken is cooked through, remove from the steamer. Drain off and reserve the juices produced during cooking.

4. Place the chicken in another dish and mix well with the curry sauce. Leave to stand so that the chicken pieces are well seasoned.

5. Heat plenty of oil in a wok. Pat the chicken portions with paper towels to remove any excess moisture and fry them one by one until well browned.

6. Mix the curry sauce remaining after marinating the chicken with the reserved cooking juices; heat in a small saucepan and serve with the chicken.

Chicken with green peppers and bamboo shoots

a small piece of leek
a small piece of ginger
3–4 green peppers
5 ounces boiled fresh or canned bamboo shoots
7 ounces boned chicken breasts
½ egg white
1 teaspoon cornstarch
oil for frying
2 tablespoons peanut oil
For the sauce:
1 tablespoon rice wine
½ teaspoon salt
½ teaspoon sugar
a pinch of monosodium glutamate (optional)
194 calories; 13.7 g protein; 12.9 g fat; 3.2 g sugar

1. Finely chop enough leek to yield 1 tablespoon; peel the ginger and finely chop enough to yield 1 teaspoon.

2. Wash the green peppers and cut in half vertically; remove seeds, stems, and pith and shred, cutting along the grain of the flesh.

3. Cut the bamboo shoots into strips the same size as the peppers.

4. Shred the chicken breasts, place in a bowl, and mix well with the egg white and the cornstarch.

5. Heat the oil until fairly hot and deep-fry the shredded chicken, using chopsticks to keep the strips separate. Drain well.

6. Heat 2 tablespoons peanut oil and stir-fry the chopped leek and ginger; add the peppers and the bamboo shoots and, when these are tender, stir in the chicken. Moisten with the rice wine and then mix in the other sauce ingredients: salt, sugar, and monosodium glutamate (optional).

Simmered chicken livers

A very economical recipe made more exotic by the flavor of star anise.

5–6 servings:
½ leek
a small piece of ginger, peeled
8 chicken livers
1 star anise
1 tablespoon sugar
1 tablespoon rice wine
3 tablespoons soy sauce
1 cup water
239 calories; 37.9g protein; 6.2g fat; 4.3g sugar

1. Pound the leek once or twice with the flat of the cleaver blade and do likewise with the ginger; their flavors will then be released more readily when they are simmered with the chicken livers.

2. Wash the chicken livers under cold, running water. Snip away the bile duct and any discolored parts. If chicken hearts are also used, cut them open, wash, and trim.

3. Place the livers (and the hearts if used) in an earthenware cooking pot, add the leek, ginger, star anise, sugar, rice wine, soy sauce, and 1 cup water; stir and place over a high heat.

4. As soon as the water comes to a boil, lower the heat so that the contents of the cooking pot simmer very gently. Cook until all the liquid is absorbed, stirring and turning every now and then. Do not allow the livers to dry out; they should be very moist.

5. Slice the chicken livers in half and arrange on a serving dish.

Peking duck

5 h
30'

A very old tradition has it that the technique for preparing Peking duck was invented by a cook to one of the emperors of the Ming dynasty (1368–1644). In those days ducks raised in the Changjiang (Yangtze) River Valley were used for this recipe. In the sixteenth century the Ming emperors made Beijing (Peking) their capital, and the technique of preparing ducks spread to all the popular eating houses of the city, since many of their owners had once been cooks at the imperial palace. Many years later, in 1866, in the fourth year of the reign of the Emperor Tong Zhi of the Qing dynasty, a certain Yang Quan-ren opened an eating house outside the Qianmen gate of Beijing. The speciality of the Quanjude restaurant was duck, prepared according to the original, classic recipe of the imperial palace.

Towards the end of the Qing dynasty, breeding experiments with ducks led to a new strain, a white duck raised for its extremely tender flesh and delicate skin. As the years went by the technique of cooking duck was performed still further, and the restaurant became very famous.

10–12 servings:
1 whole duck, weighing about 6½ pounds, plucked but undrawn and with the head left on
about 2 inches of the white parts of 12 scallions or leeks
2 tablespoons molasses or treacle
24 pancakes, 4 inches in diameter (see recipe on page 296)
For the sauce:
4 tablespoons sugar
4 tablespoons sweet bean paste
2 tablespoons sesame oil
(This sauce can be replaced by hoisin sauce which is readily available from oriental stores.)
490 calories; 24.5g protein; 24g fat; 13g sugar

1

1. Wash the duck and cut off the feet. Make sharp notches all round the end of the scallions along the grain of the stem. Place in a bowl of iced water for 1 to 2 hours so that the ends curl into feathery flowers. This should be done before roasting the duck.

2. With a small, sharp knife pierce the duck's neck in the front below the head, making a cut just large enough to insert a straw between the skin and the flesh; blow air between the skin and flesh until the whole duck is expanded; this is vital to achieve really crackly yet succulent skin.

3. Make a small slit, as shown in figure 3 and draw the duck. Do not worry about air escaping, enough will remain between skin and flesh.

4. Wash the duck inside and out and sew the slit up tightly with kitchen thread or cotton.

5. Trim off the wing tips and hang the duck up over a basin.

6. Pour about 4 cups boiling water over the duck; leave it to dry a little. Combine the molasses with 1 cup boiling water and pour evenly all over the bird; baste well and repeat the process several times. Leave the bird hung up in a warm dry place or in the sun for up to 4 hours or until the skin is completely dry. Cut the head off the duck and place the duck, breast downward, in a large roasting pan and roast in a preheated oven at 400°F. (200°C.) for 20 minutes. Turn and continue cooking for a further 20 minutes. Place the roasting pan in a pan of hot water (bain marie) over a low heat for a few minutes, then return to the oven for a final 20 minutes' roasting, turning again half way through this cooking period.

7. While the duck is roasting, prepare the sauce: mix the sugar with the sweet bean paste and a generous ½ cup of water. Heat the wok and pour in the sesame oil, add the sauce mixture and cook until it thickens. As an alternative, ready-made hoisin sauce does very well.

8. Remove the duck from the oven and carve off thin horizontal slices and meat; place on a serving dish. Each person helps himself to a pancake, takes some duck, dips the end of a scallion in the sauce, and places it on the duck. The pancake is then rolled around the duck.

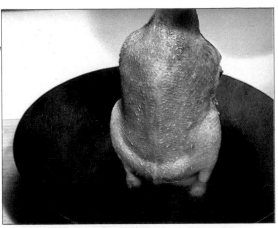

5

2

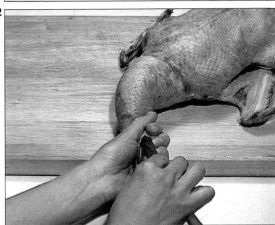

3

6

7

4

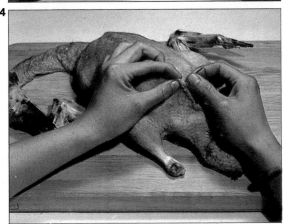

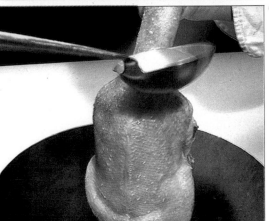

8

Hsiang su fei ya (classic spiced duck)

3 h

12 servings:
1 duck weighing about 4½ pounds
oil for frying
For the sauce and marinade:
1 tablespoon freshly ground black pepper
1 tablespoon salt
1½ teaspoons five-spice powder
½ teaspoon monosodium glutamate (optional)
1 teaspoon dry sherry
2 slices ginger root, finely chopped
1 small leek or shallot, finely chopped
2 tablespoons dark soy sauce
470 calories; 22g protein; 38.5g fat; 8g sugar

1. Clean the duck (if fresh, remove the oil sacs above the tail); wash and dry thoroughly.

2. Toast the fresh, coarsely ground pepper in a wok without any oil for 2 minutes over a moderate heat. Add the salt and remove from the heat. Mix all the other sauce ingredients together and add to the wok, followed by the ginger, leek, and dark soy sauce. Rub the duck all over, inside and out, with this mixture, working it well into the skin; then leave it to penetrate for 6 hours.

3. Place the duck on a heatproof dish in a bamboo steamer and steam it for about 2½ hours, until it is very tender. Remove from steamer and pat dry with paper towels, tipping any liquid out of its cavity. Leave to cool.

4. Heat plenty of oil in the wok over a high heat and fry the duck until the skin is brown and very crisp. Baste constantly with the oil.

5. Remove the duck from the wok and drain on paper towels.

6. Cut into fairly small, thickish pieces as shown in the illustration and arrange on a serving dish.

130

Fish and Seafood

Outside in the moonlit garden,
our servant sets about his task of cleaning a golden carp
with such vigor that the scales fly far and wide,
high enough to reach the sky; perhaps the stars up there in
the heavens are the carp's golden scales.

—*From an old Chinese poem dedicated to the carp of the Yellow River*

The ideogram which stands for fish is pronounced in the same way as the word for prosperity and plenty, an indication of the importance of fish and seafood in the Chinese diet.

Carp is the most highly prized of all the fish. Apart from being valued as a delicacy, it has a special significance for the Chinese. An old legend in Chinese literature tells of a carp which swam against the current of the river in the hope of becoming a powerful dragon; the fish therefore became a synonym for the perseverence and driving ambition required of any young student who strove to qualify for a coveted position in the mandarin hierarchy, a goal not easily attained and one which required great courage and self-sacrifice. Fish are the most popular motif used for the decoration of buildings and especially for people's homes, since it is a traditional belief that the fishes' habit of swimming in pairs symbolizes happiness in marriage.

Crispy fish in sweet and sour sauce

The crisp deep-fried fish is covered with thick sweet and sour sauce, resulting in a pleasing contrast of texture and flavor.

2 whole fish (whiting, porgy, sea bream, or the like)
oil for frying
For coating the fish:
1 egg white
½ teaspoon salt
1 tablespoon rice wine
a pinch of pepper
1 tablespoon water
3 tablespoons cornstarch
Vegetables for the sauce:
¼ carrot
2 dried Chinese mushrooms, presoaked
1 small bamboo shoot
1 green pepper
¼ leek
a small piece of ginger root
For the sweet and sour sauce:
5 tablespoons sugar
4 tablespoons vinegar
1 teaspoon soy sauce
½ teaspoon salt
3 tablespoons tomato ketchup
½ teaspoon cornstarch
376 calories; 14.4g protein; 13.5g fat; 50g sugar

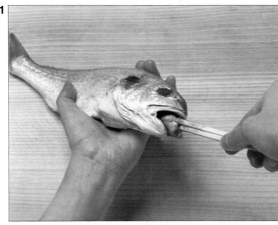

1. Clean the fish, trim the fins, and make a very small incision by the ventral fin – just big enough to draw out the intestines. Draw out the remaining innards through the fish's mouth using chopsticks.

2. Cut out the gills (the red, spongy matter in the head) and wash the fish well. Make diagonal slashes in the sides of the fish about 1 inch apart, cutting through to the bone and rotating the blade from right to left to lift the flesh partly away from the bone, but not completely severing it.

3. Mix the egg white with the salt, rice wine, pepper, water and cornstarch. Coat the fish with this mixture, rubbing it well into the fish and into the diagonal slashes.

4. Dredge the fish all over, inside and out, with cornstarch. Hold them by their tails and shake or knock them to remove the excess.

5. Heat plenty of oil to 350°F. (180°C.) in a deep-fryer. Grasp the fish firmly by its tail and hold over the hot oil; spoon the hot oil very carefully over the slashes 2 or 3 times to open them up. Deep-fry the fish.

6. Remove the fish when they are crisp and place them, belly down on a wire rack; cover with a cloth and press gently to soften (the flesh will give slightly and absorb more of the sauce).

7. Cut the vegetables for the sauce, into matchstick strips and stir-fry them in two tablespoons of oil, adding those which will take longest to cook first. When they are all lightly browned and tender, set aside.

8. Heat 3 tablespoons of oil with the sauce ingredients; add 1 tablespoon oil, trickling it down the side of the wok, and $\frac{1}{3}$ cup of water. As soon as the mixture comes to a boil, add the vegetables, stir, and pour over the fish.

133

Fried fish in egg batter

The batter used for this recipe is delicate and melts in the mouth, but care must be taken to have the oil at the correct temperature or the crust will burn.

20 small fresh fish fillets (sole, plaice, flounder, striped bass, or sea bass)
½ teaspoon salt
a pinch of pepper
1 teaspoon rice wine
1 tablespoon cornstarch
oil for frying
For the batter:
2 egg whites
2 tablespoons cornstarch
2 tablespoons all-purpose flour
a pinch of salt
a pinch of monosodium glutamate (optional)
263 calories; 26.7 g protein: 12 g fat; 10.4 g sugar

1. Use only the freshest fish fillets or buy fresh nonoily white fish such as those suggested above and carefully gut and fillet the fish.

2. Lay the fillets flat on a plate and season with salt, pepper, and rice wine; leave for a few minutes and then mix with the cornstarch.

3. Whisk the egg whites until stiff but not dry, add the cornstarch, the sifted all-purpose flour, the salt and the monosodium glutamate (optional); mix gently with a metal spoon, taking care not to stir too much or the egg whites will release too much air and the batter will not be light enough.

4. Heat plenty of oil to 275°F. (140°C.); dip the fish in the batter and deep-fry a few at a time.

5. Turn the fish while frying and gradually increase the temperature to 335°F. (170°C.); remove and drain the fish when they are only pale golden brown, or the batter will lose its delicate texture and be too crisp.

Braised fish and bean curd

A very hot and spicy dish braised in an earthenware cooking pot.

4 steaks of firm-fleshed fish (carp, bream, bass, cod, or fresh tuna)
2 cakes bean curd
1 leek
a small piece of ginger root
3–5 tablespoons peanut oil
1–2 chili peppers
For the sauce:
1 tablespoon sugar
1 tablespoon rice wine
$\frac{1}{4}$–$\frac{1}{2}$ teaspoon chili bean paste.
generous $\frac{1}{2}$ cup soy sauce
328 calories; 27.1 g protein; 21.1 g fat; 8.2 g sugar

1. Rinse and dry the fish steaks; cut the bean curd into small squares (about 8 squares per bean curd); cut the leek into thin, diagonal slices and the ginger into wafer-thin slices.

2. Heat 3–5 tablespoons oil; brown the fish steaks well on both sides over a high heat.

3. Line the bottom of an earthenware cooking pot with a layer of leek slices, place the fish steaks on top, surround with the bean curd squares, and top with the ginger slivers and chili peppers.

4. Mix together the sauce ingredients: sugar, rice wine, chili bean paste, and soy sauce and pour over the fish. Cover and cook over a moderate heat for 20 to 25 minutes. From time to time tip up the earthenware dish, collect the juices and sauce in a ladle, and moisten the top of the fish and bean curd.

Steamed fish

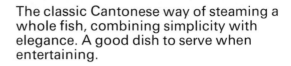

The classic Cantonese way of steaming a whole fish, combining simplicity with elegance. A good dish to serve when entertaining.

1 whole very fresh nonoily, white fleshed fish, such as bass, carp, mullet, etc, weighing approximately 1¼ pounds
2–3 dried Chinese mushrooms, presoaked
2 slices ginger root
2 slices ham
1 leek
1 tablespoon rice wine
a few drops of sesame oil
2 tablespoons soy sauce

190 calories; 28.8 g protein; 6.3 g fat; 1.6 g sugar

1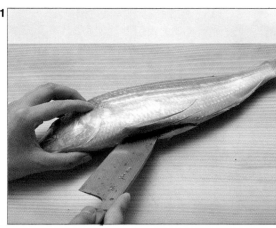

2

3

4

1. Always use the freshest fish for this recipe; slit the fish's belly and remove the guts. (Make the slit slightly to one side so you can serve the fish with the slit out of sight.)

2. With a sharp knife remove the scales from the fish; wash it well in cold running water inside and out and pat dry.

3. Soak the Chinese mushrooms in water for 20 minutes, then drain. (Ordinary mushrooms are a poor substitute.) Remove the stems and slice the caps into thin strips about $\frac{1}{8}$ inch wide.

4. Pound one slice of ginger with the blunt edge of the cleaver; cut the second slice into thin strips.

5. Shred the ham and cut the leek into two pieces, each 4 inches long.

6. Place the pounded slice of ginger in the stomach of the fish; lay the fish on its side in a heatproof dish with one piece of leek under its head and the other under its tail. Sprinkle the shredded ginger, ham, and mushrooms over the top of the fish.

7. Moisten the fish with 1 tablespoon rice wine and a few drops of sesame oil for flavor; place the dish in the bamboo steamer which should already be full of steam.

8. Steam the fish over rapidly boiling water for 15 to 20 minutes without opening the steamer; when the fish is done, remove the slice of ginger from the inside of the fish. Place the fish on a heated serving dish and sprinkle with the rice wine while still hot.

5

6

7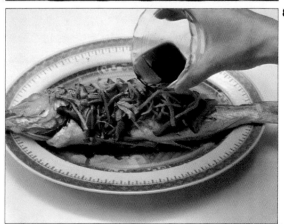

8

Mackerel in sweet and sour sauce

Boiled rice is the best accompaniment for this fish in its sweet and sour sauce, made with plenty of tomato ketchup.

4 medium-size bluefish, horse mackerel, ordinary mackerel, or scad
2 tablespoons fresh ginger juice
1 tablespoon rice wine
1 onion
2 green peppers
peanut oil for frying
1 clove garlic
cornstarch as required
For the sauce:
4 tablespoons tomato ketchup
1 tablespoon sugar
1 tablespoon soy sauce
2 teaspoons Worcestershire sauce
$\frac{1}{2}$ cup stock
To thicken:
2 teaspoons cornstarch dissolved in 4 teaspoons water
314 calories; 15.8 g protein; 15.7 g fat; 26.5 g sugar

1

2

3

4

1. Choose the freshest fish available. Using a very sharp knife, cut away the line of spines (Atlantic mackerel has far fewer than horse or Jack mackerel), working from the tail toward the head. Cut off the head and gut the fish; wash in cold running water and drain.

2. Lay the fish on a working surface and fillet by inserting a very sharp knife between the backbone and the flesh and cutting along the top of the backbone, as shown in figure 2. Turn the fish over and repeat the same process.

3. Cut the fillets into bite-size pieces, sprinkle with ginger juice and rice wine, and mix. Leave to stand for 5 to 6 minutes.

4. Peel the onion; cut it in half vertically and then into $\frac{3}{4}$-inch slices. Cut the green peppers in half lengthwise, remove the seeds and pith, and cut into $\frac{3}{4}$-inch slices.

5. Heat 3 cups peanut oil to 300°F. (150°C.); fry the onion (adding it first, as it will take longer) and the green peppers until they are lightly browned; remove with a slotted spoon and drain.

6. Dry the pieces of fish fillet with paper towels, coat with cornstarch and shake off the excess. Increase the temperature of the oil left over from step 5 to 335°F. (170°C.) and fry the fish until crisp.

7. Heat 1 tablespoon oil in the wok and stir-fry the finely chopped garlic; as soon as this starts to release its aroma, add the onion and green peppers. Stir-fry over a high heat and add the sauce ingredients.

8. When the sauce comes to a boil, add the pieces of fried fish and cook for a minute or so. Thicken the sauce by stirring in 2 teaspoons cornstarch mixed with 4 teaspoons water.

5

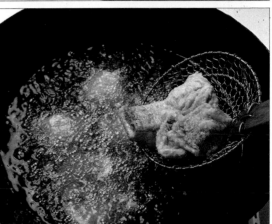

6

7

8

Cantonese pickled salmon mold

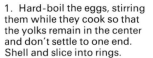

2 eggs
2 tablespoons peanut oil
2 pickled salmon steaks (or cod or halibut plus 2 teaspoons
   chopped snow pickles)
1¾ cups finely chopped or ground pork
½ egg white
½ teaspoon sugar
a pinch of salt
lard or shortening
For the sauce:
2 tablespoons stock
a pinch of salt
a pinch of monosodium glutamate (optional)
1 teaspoon cornstarch
388 calories; 28.5 g protein; 27.5 g fat; 5.1 g sugar

1. Hard-boil the eggs, stirring them while they cook so that the yolks remain in the center and don't settle to one end. Shell and slice into rings.

2. Heat 2 tablespoons oil in a wok. Fry the fish steaks until they are golden brown. Remove the skin and the bones and flake carefully. Add the snow pickles.

3. Pound the ground pork with the blunt edge of the cleaver to soften it and get rid of any remaining lumps. Place in a bowl and add the fish, egg white, sugar, and salt. Mix very thoroughly.

4. Grease the inside of a heatproof bowl with the lard, line with the sliced hard-boiled eggs and fill with the fish-and-pork mixture.

5. Place the bowl in a bamboo steamer, which should be full of steam, and cook over rapidly boiling water for 20 minutes.

6. Drain off the juice produced during steaming and mix with the stock in a small saucepan. Heat, adding the salt and monosodium glutamate (optional), followed by the cornstarch mixed with 2 teaspoons water to thicken the sauce.

7. Place a round serving plate on top of the bowl; turn upside down with a sharp jerk, releasing the mold onto the dish. Coat with the sauce.

Mackerel with five-spice seasoning

Five-spice powder is used to flavor fried mackerel. This dish is equally good hot or cold.

1 large mackerel (Atlantic mackerel)
cornstarch as required
1 quart oil for frying
For the marinade:
2½ tablespoons soy sauce
1½ tablespoons rice wine
For the sauce:
⅓ leek
a large piece of ginger root
½ teaspoon five-spice powder
4 tablespoons soy sauce
1 tablespoon sugar
½ cup water
335 calories; 16g protein; 23.2g fat; 13g sugar

1. Cut the head off the mackerel and remove the guts; wash under cold running water and dry well. Lay the mackerel out flat on a working surface or chopping board and fillet as directed on page 139, figure 2, running the knife blade along the backbone and cutting away the flesh on both sides.

2. Slice the fillets diagonally into bite-size pieces; place in a deep-sided dish or bowl and sprinkle with the soy sauce and rice wine. Leave to marinate for 15 minutes.

3. Chop the ginger and the leek very finely and mix with the five-spice powder.

4. Mix the sauce ingredients together, combining the soy sauce, sugar, and water in a saucepan and bring to a boil. When the sauce has boiled for a moment, pour into a bowl and stir in the ginger, leek, and five-spice powder.

5. Dry the marinated pieces of fish with paper towels, cover with cornstarch and shake gently to remove any excess.

6. Heat the oil to 340°–350°F. (175°–180°C.) and fry the pieces of mackerel until they are well browned and crisp; remove and drain.

7. Place the fried fish in the bowl of sauce and leave for 20 minutes to absorb the flavor before serving.

141

Fried fillets of fish mimosa

Egg yolks and whites are fried separately to make a decorative addition to the fish. This light and delicately flavored dish is perfect for entertaining.

4 eggs
½ teaspoon salt
2 tablespoons rice wine
2 tablespoons cornstarch
a small bunch of chives, chopped finely
7 ounces fillets of any white, nonoily fish
⅓ teaspoon salt
2 teaspoons ginger juice
oil for frying
4 tablespoons lard or shortening
357 calories; 17.1 g protein; 28.4 g fat; 5.1 g sugar

1. Separate the egg yolks and whites; reserve 2 tablespoons of the egg whites for later use. Add ¼ teaspoon salt to the remainder of the egg whites and mix well. Stir ¼ teaspoon salt and 2 tablespoons rice wine into the egg yolks.

2. Run the reserved 2 tablespoons of egg white through the fingers to mix the firmer, more jellied part of the white with the more liquid part. Add the cornstarch and blend. Snip the chives into small pieces.

1

2

3

4

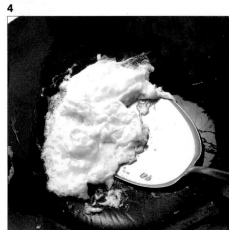

5

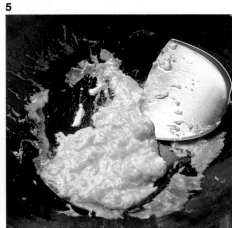

6

3. Cut the fish fillets into small, diagonal pieces; season with ⅓ teaspoon salt, 2 teaspoons ginger juice, and the egg white and cornstarch prepared in step 2. Fry briskly in oil heated to 300°F. (150°C.).

4. Heat a wok, add 2 tablespoons lard and, when the fat is hot, pour in the mixture of egg white and salt prepared in step 1. Mix and turn quickly, scraping away from the wok, until the mixture has set but is still soft.

5. Transfer the cooked egg white to a warm dish. Heat the remaining lard in the wok; pour in the egg yolk, salt, and rice wine mixture; and cook as for scrambled eggs; when the yolks are half-cooked, return the egg whites to the wok.

6. Mix and turn the scrambled egg yolks and whites briskly; add the fried fish, scooping and turning quickly, then mix in the chopped chives.

Mackerel and mixed vegetables in soybean paste sauce

A very economical and delicious method of cooking mackerel.

1 large mackerel
2 potatoes
1 carrot
1 clove garlic
2 small leeks
3–4 Chinese mushrooms, presoaked
8 snow peas
3½ cups oil for frying
cornstarch as required
2 tablespoons lard
1½ cups water
For the marinade:
4 teaspoons ginger juice
1 tablespoon soy sauce
2 tablespoons finely chopped leek
For the sauce:
3 tablespoons soybean paste
3 tablespoons soy sauce
2 tablespoons sugar
½ tablespoon sesame oil
465 calories; 19.6 g protein; 31.5 g fat; 25.3 g sugar

1

2

3

4

1. Cut the head off the mackerel and gut it; wash well. Place the mackerel on a chopping board or working surface and carefully cut along the top of the backbone; turn the fish over and repeat the operation on the other side, producing two fillets.

2. Cut the fillets into 1-inch pieces and mix well with the ginger juice, the soy sauce, and the chopped leek. Marinate the fish in this mixture for about 10 minutes.

3. Peel the potatoes and the carrot, cut them diagonally into uneven shapes, and boil until they are only just tender. Chop the garlic finely.

4. Slice the leeks into $\frac{3}{4}$-inch-wide sections. Soak the Chinese mushrooms in lukewarm water for 20 minutes (this is best done before starting to prepare the other ingredients); remove the stems and quarter the caps. Boil the snow peas in lightly salted water until they are tender but still crisp; cut each pod into two or three pieces.

5. Heat the oil to 350°F. (180°C.) and fry the potatoes until they are golden brown; drain. Keep the oil at the same temperature.

6. Coat the pieces of mackerel with cornstarch, shake off any excess, and fry the fish in the oil until well browned. Remove and drain on paper towels.

7. Heat the lard in the wok and stir-fry the garlic and leek; as soon as they have started to release their aroma, add the Chinese mushrooms and carrot and stir-fry. Pour in the sauce ingredients.

8. Pour in the water and bring to a boil; add the mackerel and the potatoes and cook for 3 to 4 minutes so they can absorb some of the sauce. Finally, stir in the snow peas quickly and serve.

5

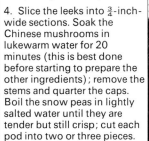

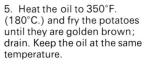

6

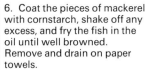

7

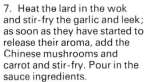

8

Steamed fish and lotus root

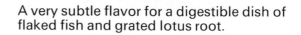

A very subtle flavor for a digestible dish of flaked fish and grated lotus root.

1 pound lotus root
vinegar
7 ounces white, nonoily fish, such as cod
2 ounces pork fat back
2 teaspoons rice wine
⅔ teaspoon salt
1 teaspoon cornstarch
lard as required
a large piece of ginger
a little parsley
249 calories; 12.3g protein; 14.4g fat; 20g sugar

1

1. Peel the lotus root and immediately transfer to a bowl of water acidulated with a few drops of vinegar. Leave for 3 minutes; then dry with paper towels. Grate finely.

2. Skin and bone the fish and chop the flesh very finely with a large kitchen knife or cleaver. Place the chopped fish in a mortar and pound well.

3. Cut the pork fat into thin slices and then chop the slices finely; add to the pounded fish in the mortar and mix and pound together until well blended.

4. Add the rice wine, the salt and the cornstarch and mix well. Incorporate the grated lotus root together with any juice produced during grating.

5. Grease a flat heatproof plate with plenty of lard. Transfer the mixture of fish and lotus root to the plate, smoothing the surface and rounding off the top and sides with a spatula.

6. Place the bamboo steamer over boiling water in the wok and allow time for it to fill with steam. Keeping the heat high, place the dish in the steamer and cook for about 8 minutes over rapidly boiling water.

7. While the fish is steaming, peel the ginger; cut into thin slices and then into thin strips. Soak in water.

8. Once the fish is cooked, remove it from steamer, sprinkle with the ginger strips (drained and dried in paper towels) and decorate with chopped parsley.

5

6

2

3

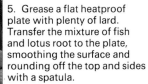

7

4

8

147

Fish fried in noodles

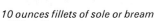 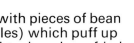

Pieces of fish are coated with pieces of bean thread (transparent noodles) which puff up and become crisp and light when deep-fried.

10 ounces fillets of sole or bream
a little salt
2 tablespoons rice wine
2 teaspoons ginger juice
a small packet bean thread (transparent noodles)
cornstarch as required
1 egg
1 quart peanut oil for frying.
For the sauce:
½ cup Chinese white radish, grated
1½ tablespoons soy sauce
1½ tablespoons vinegar
a small piece of mandarin peel or dried tangerine peel, presoaked
261 calories; 17.4g protein; 13.9g fat; 14.1g sugar

1. Remove the skin from the fish and cut into fairly large diagonal slices; place, well spaced-out, in a dish.

2. Add the salt and the rice wine and ginger juice. Leave to stand for 5 minutes; this will get rid of any fishy smell and will flavor the fish.

1

2

3

4

5

6

3. With scissors, cut the noodles into ¾-inch lengths into a plastic bag. This will prevent the noodles going in all directions when cut.

4. Coat the pieces of fish with cornstarch, dip in the beaten egg, and cover with the cut noodles, pressing them onto the fish so that they adhere.

5. Heat the oil in a wok or deep fryer to 340°F. (175°C.) and lower the coated fish pieces one by one into the hot oil; fry until crisp, but do not allow them to become darker than pale golden brown.

6. Make the sauce by mixing the grated radish with the soy sauce and a little grated mandarin peel to add more flavor. The sauce is served separately as an accompaniment to the fish.

Saury (skipper) with vegetables in sweet and sour sauce

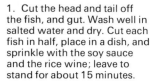

4 saury (skipper) or garfish
1 tablespoon soy sauce
1 tablespoon rice wine
3 dried Chinese mushrooms, presoaked
2½ ounces boiled fresh or canned bamboo shoots
1 chili pepper
⅓ leek
small piece of ginger root
4 tablespoons lard
2 tablespoons oil
For the sauce:
3 tablespoons soy sauce
1 generous tablespoon sugar
2 tablespoons rice wine
⅔ cup water
434 calories; 21.7 g protein; 35 g fat; 5.9 g sugar

1. Cut the head and tail off the fish, and gut. Wash well in salted water and dry. Cut each fish in half, place in a dish, and sprinkle with the soy sauce and the rice wine; leave to stand for about 15 minutes.

2. Soak the dried mushrooms for 20 minutes in lukewarm water. When they have plumped up, drain, remove the stems, and slice the mushrooms into rectangular-shaped pieces; cut the bamboo shoots into rectangles, about 1½ inches long.

3. Remove the seeds from the chili pepper and chop coarsely with the leek and peeled ginger.

4. Mix the sauce ingredients.

5. Heat the lard in a wok, dry the fish with paper towels, and fry in the hot lard over a high heat until the pieces are golden brown.

6. Remove the fish from the wok and set aside. Clean the wok and heat 2 tablespoons of oil; stir-fry the leek, ginger, and chili pepper and, as soon as they start to release their aroma, add the Chinese mushrooms and the bamboo shoots, stir-frying over a high heat.

7. Return the fish to the wok; stir in the sauce, and, as soon as it comes to a boil, lower the heat and simmer for about 15 minutes.

Cod in spicy sauce

A delicious, peppery dish which should be served with plain boiled rice.

4 fillets fresh cod or well-soaked salt cod
1 egg white
2 tablespoons cornstarch
2 cups oil for frying
1 small clove garlic
$\frac{1}{2}$ leek
7–8 chives or scallion stems (green part)
1 bean curd
2 tablespoons peanut oil
4 ounces finely chopped or ground pork
2 tablespoons soy sauce
2 cups stock (see recipe on page 296)
2 tablespoons rice wine
1 tablespoon cornstarch mixed with 2 tablespoons water
$\frac{1}{2}$ teaspoon chili powder
2 teaspoons sesame oil
313 calories; 23.6 g protein; 21.6 g fat; 5.1 g sugar

1. Cut the cod diagonally into four pieces. If salt cod is used, it must be soaked in several changes of water for 24 hours in advance or it will be too salty.

2. Agitate the egg white and press between the fingers so that the jellylike part and the liquid part blend evenly; dip the fish in the egg white and then coat with cornstarch. Fry lightly in the oil at about 300°F. (150°C.).

3. Chop the garlic and leek finely. Chop the chives into 1-inch lengths. Remove excess moisture from the bean curd by cutting the cake in half horizontally, then into eight squares and wrapping the squares gently in a clean, dry cloth.

4. Heat the wok and add the peanut oil; stir-fry the ground pork until it is well cooked and forms even, separate grains. Add 1 tablespoon soy sauce, stir, and then pour in the heated stock.

5. Add the fried cod, followed by the rice wine and the remaining soy sauce, and cook for about 5 to 6 minutes.

6. Add the bean curd and cook for a further 3 to 4 minutes; then stir in the cornstarch and water very carefully to thicken the sauce (the bean curd will break up if you mix too vigorously). Add the chili powder, chives, and a few drops of sesame oil to give the dish its finishing touch.

Fried fish with peanuts

30'

4 fillets of fish
1 tablespoon rice wine
2 teaspoons ginger juice
a small piece of ginger root
1 clove garlic
1 chili pepper
½ leek
½ cup shelled unsalted peanuts
½ leek for decoration
1 head of broccoli or Cape broccoli
salt
cornstarch as required
2 tablespoons oil
For the sauce:
4 tablespoons sweet red soybean paste
3 tablespoons rice wine or dry sherry
2 tablespoons sugar
1 teaspoon sesame oil
1 cup stock (see recipe on page 296)
450 calories; 23.5g protein; 29g fat; 21,6g sugar

1. Cut each piece of fish diagonally into three portions; place in a dish and sprinkle with the rice wine and the ginger juice; leave to marinate for 5 minutes.

2. Peel the ginger and the garlic, remove the seeds of the chili pepper, wash one piece of leek, and chop all these ingredients finely.

3. Peel off the thin brown papery skin from the peanuts and chop them coarsely, having spread them on a piece of paper on the chopping board.

4. Mix the sauce ingredients together until the soybean paste and the sugar are well blended and dissolved; add the chopped peanuts and stir.

5. Cut the remaining half leek into thin, feathery strips ready to garnish, and place in a bowl of cold water. Boil the broccoli in salted water until tender and divide into florets.

6. Coat the pieces of fish with cornstarch and fry quickly in the oil over a high heat. Add the finely chopped ginger, garlic, chili pepper, and leek mixture. Stir and turn so that they release their flavors. Pour in the sauce and cook over a moderate heat for about 10 minutes.

7. When the fish has absorbed most of the sauce, transfer to a heated serving platter. Sprinkle with the shredded leek and garnish with the broccoli florets.

Shrimp with fresh fava beans

12 large shrimp
Marinade for the shrimp:
2 tablespoons rice wine
$\frac{1}{2}$ teaspoon salt
1 teaspoon ginger juice
5 ounces fresh fava beans
salt
2 chili peppers
1 clove garlic
a small piece of ginger root
2 tablespoons lard or shortening
For the sauce:
2 tablespoons sugar
2 tablespoons rice wine
$2\frac{1}{2}$ tablespoons soy sauce
$\frac{1}{3}$ teaspoon salt
2 tablespoons tomato ketchup
$\frac{1}{2}$ cup water
390 calories; 42 g protein; 16.4 g fat; 12.9 g sugar

1. Remove the shells of the shrimp and the black vein which runs down their backs. Mix with the marinade of rice wine, salt, and ginger juice.

2. Wash the shelled beans and mix with a little salt, rubbing it into their skins. Boil until just tender and remove the thin outer skin.

3. Remove the seeds from the chili peppers and chop finely with the garlic and ginger.

4. Mix the sauce ingredients together thoroughly in a bowl, making sure that the sugar dissolves completely.

5. Heat the wok, and add 2 tablespoons lard; when the fat is hot add the drained shrimp. If the shrimp are raw, stir-fry for a few minutes until they change color; add the ginger, garlic and chili peppers. If cooked shrimp are used, add to the fat only just before the garlic and other seasonings. Stir-fry briefly over a high heat and set aside on a plate.

6. Fry the beans in the remaining fat in the wok over a high heat; when the beans are thoroughly coated and impregnated with the fat, return the shrimp to the pan, pour in the sauce, and mix quickly before serving.

Sichuan fried shrimp and peas

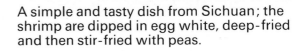

A simple and tasty dish from Sichuan; the shrimp are dipped in egg white, deep-fried and then stir-fried with peas.

1 pound shrimp
1 egg white
1 teaspoon cornstarch
peanut oil for frying
½ pound peas
1 thin slice ginger root
1 tablespoon rice wine
1 teaspoon salt
½ teaspoon sugar
a pinch of pepper
a pinch of monosodium glutamate (optional)
276 calories; 17.8g protein; 16.1g fat; 13.5g sugar

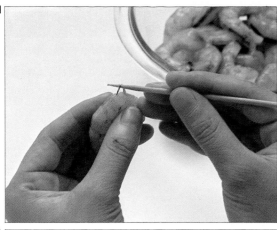

1. Peel and devein the shrimp using a toothpick or cocktail stick. Wash and drain. If cooked shrimp are used (those bought with their shells on have more flavor) there is no need to wash.

2. Dry the shrimp and mix with the egg white and cornstarch in a bowl, using your hands.

3. Fry the shrimp in oil heated to about 325°F. (160°C.), making sure they do not stick to one another; remove with a mesh ladle or perforated spoon so that they drain properly.

4. If frozen peas are used, place in a bowl and cover with boiling water; when they have completely thawed, drain.

5. Heat the wok; pour in 2 tablespoons of oil and, when very hot, add the lightly pounded ginger slice for flavor.

6. Once the ginger has started to release its aroma, add the peas and just allow to heat through; add the shrimp and stir-fry.

7. Pour in the rice wine and add the salt and sugar; season with a pinch of pepper and monosodium glutamate (optional).

8. Remove the slice of ginger and stir all the ingredients to ensure even flavoring. Do not overcook or the shrimp will begin to lose their flavor.

Cantonese fried scampi

 40'

A very digestible way of frying shellfish in a light, melting batter.

8 scampi or crayfish (with or without the heads on)
1 tablespoon cornstarch
oil for frying
For the marinade:
a pinch of salt
1 teaspoon rice wine
a pinch of pepper
a 4-inch length of leek
a small piece of ginger root
For the batter:
1 large egg, beaten
½ cup water
1 tablespoon cornstarch
1 cup all-purpose flour
1 teaspoon baking powder
1 tablespoon oil
381 calories; 29.4g protein; 16.7g fat; 26.1g sugar

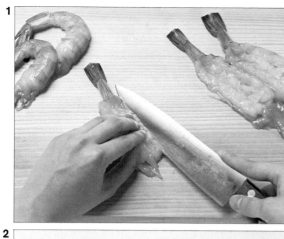

1

2

3

4

1. Shell the scampi or crayfish, remove heads and tips of tails, slit down the back without cutting all the way through, and open out flat. Make two lengthwise incisions on each side of the scampi and some shallow slashes across them.

2. Place the scampi in a shallow dish and add a marinade of salt, rice wine, pepper, chopped leek, and pounded ginger. Rub this mixture gently into the scampi so that the flavor penetrates.

3. Prepare the batter: using a whisk, beat the egg with the water and cornstarch in a bowl; sift the flour and place ready for use.

4. Add $\frac{9}{10}$ of the flour to the egg, water and cornstarch mixture and mix quickly; do not pay too much attention to the smoothness of the batter at this stage, but adjust the consistency by adding some or all of the remaining flour if needed.

5. Beat the batter until smooth; it should not be too thick; at the right consistency a ribbon of mixture will fall from the whisk when it is lifted.

6. Add the baking powder and allow to stand to 1 to 2 minutes, until the mixture bubbles and expands slightly.

7. For a really melting, crisp batter which will dissolve in the mouth add the oil and whisk in lightly and quickly.

8. Working quickly, remove the leek and ginger from the marinating scampi. Coat each scampi with cornstarch and dip in the batter, frying a few at a time until the batter is crisp, light, and golden brown.

5

6

7

8

Shrimp in tomato sauce

The varied flavors combine to make this a tempting dish.

7 ounces large shrimp
½ tablespoon rice wine
a pinch of salt
a pinch of pepper
⅓ egg white
1 rounded tablespoon cornstarch
oil for frying
1 large, ripe tomato
1–2 cloves garlic
2–3 tablespoons peanut oil
½ cup stock
⅓ tablespoon salt
1 teaspoon soy sauce
1 teaspoon rice wine
cornstarch as required for thickening the sauce
a few drops of sesame oil
243 calories; 7.3g protein; 20.5g fat; 8.8g sugar

1. Whether raw shrimp or cooked are used, shell, remove the black vein running down the shrimp's back, and place in a dish with ½ tablespoon rice wine and a pinch of salt and pepper.

2. Add the egg white to the shrimp and mix with the

fingers; then add 1 rounded tablespoon of cornstarch and mix well.

3. Pour 1–2 cups oil into the wok and heat to 260–300°F. (130–150°C.); stir-fry the shrimps until they turn pink if they are raw and for only a

minute or two if they are already cooked. Drain on paper towels.

4. Blanch the tomato in boiling water for a few seconds, rinse in cold water, and peel. Quarter, remove the seeds, and slice thinly. Chop the garlic very finely.

5. Heat 2–3 tablespoons peanut oil in the wok and stir-fry the garlic. When it starts to release its aroma, add the tomato and fry quickly; pour in the stock.

6. Season with salt, soy sauce, and rice wine. Add the cooked shrimp and then thicken the sauce by adding a little cornstarch mixed with water. Add a few drops sesame oil (approximately ½ teaspoon) for extra flavor.

Fried chili scampi

Deep-fried scampi or crayfish served with a piquant sauce made with tomato ketchup and tabasco.

15 scampi or crayfish, preferably raw
oil for frying
1 teaspoon finely chopped garlic
1 tablespoon chopped leek
1 teaspoon finely chopped ginger
1 tablespoon rice wine
1 teaspoon cornstarch
For the sauce:
$\frac{1}{2}$ cup chicken stock
$\frac{1}{2}$ cup tomato ketchup
1 teaspoon salt
$\frac{1}{2}$ tablespoon sugar
1 teaspoon tabasco sauce
258 calories; 18.6g protein; 8.8g fat; 24.3g sugar

1

1. Rinse and drain the scampi or crayfish; remove the heads by bending them over and inward, toward the tails. Remove the shells.

2. Slit the scampi down their backs with a sharp knife, stopping short of the second to last joint nearest the tail and being careful not to cut through or the scampi will separate into two halves.

3. Devein the scampi using a toothpick or cocktail stick (this black vein is actually the alimentary tract).

4. Rinse the scampi and dry with paper towels or a cloth. Snip off the tail flippers with scissors.

5. Spread the scampi on paper towels and remove excess moisture by pressing carefully with the flat of a knife blade.

6. Heat plenty of oil in a wok or deep-fryer to 340°F. (170°C.) and lower the scampi carefully into the hot oil; stir with chopsticks or tongs, remove, and drain. Chop the garlic, leek, and ginger.

7. Heat 2 tablespoons oil in the wok and stir-fry the garlic, leek, and ginger; when these start to release their aroma, add the scampi.

8. Pour in the rice wine and the sauce ingredients; stir-fry to make sure the scampi are well flavored, and then stir in the cornstarch dissolved in 2 teaspoons water to thicken the sauce so that it will coat the scampi.

5

2

6

3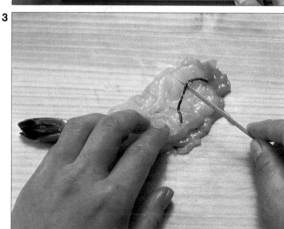

7

4

Shrimp in fluffy batter

Cornstarch is folded into beaten egg whites to make the lightest possible batter.

14 ounces shrimp in their shells
1 teaspoon rice wine
1 teaspoon ginger juice
cornstarch as required
oil for frying
For the batter:
2 egg whites
2 tablespoons cornstarch
a pinch of salt
Seasonings:
chili sauce
salt and pepper
179 calories; 10.6 g protein; 10.5 g fat; 9.6 g sugar

1. Wash the shrimp if they are raw; remove their shells and heads and the thin black vein running down their backs. Use a toothpick or cocktail stick. Leave their tails in place.

2. Place the shrimp in a dish and sprinkle with the rice wine and ginger juice, leaving them to stand for 5 to 6 minutes; this will remove any strong smell without impairing the taste.

3. Drain the shrimp and, holding them by their tails, dip them one by one into the cornstarch to coat thoroughly. Shake off excess.

4. Separate the egg yolks from the whites. Mix the whites gently to obtain an even consistency.

5. Whisk the egg whites until stiff but not too dry; the batter should be made in the proportion of 2 egg whites to 2 tablespoons cornstarch and a pinch of salt. Fold in the cornstarch gently but thoroughly.

6. Cover each shrimp with the batter; use a teaspoon to heap the light mixture onto the shrimp as it does not always cling when dipped. Holding the shrimp by their tails, lower one by one into the pre-heated oil (345°F./175°C.) and deep-fry until pale golden brown. Serve with chili sauce, freshly ground pepper and salt.

Shrimp with chili peppers Sichuan style

Chili peppers give the typical spicy Sichuan taste to large shrimp which retain all their flavor since they are fried in their shells.

12 large shrimp
1 tablespoon rice wine
1 tablespoon soy sauce
$\frac{1}{2}$ leek
a small piece of ginger
1 clove garlic
2 chili peppers
4 tablespoons oil
$\frac{1}{2}$ teaspoon cornstarch mixed with 1 teaspoon water
For the sauce:
$1\frac{1}{2}$ tablespoons soy sauce
$1\frac{1}{2}$ tablespoons sugar
2 tablespoons rice wine
2 tablespoons tomato ketchup
$\frac{1}{3}$ cup water
270 calories; 26.2g protein; 13.4g fat; 9.1g sugar

1. Rinse the shrimp, remove the black vein running down their backs by inserting a toothpick or cocktail stick between the second and third joint from the head and drawing it out between the joints of the shell. Use a pair of scissors to cut off the feelers and legs. Sprinkle the shrimp with rice wine and soy sauce and let stand.

2. Coarsely chop the leek, ginger, garlic, and chili peppers, having removed and discarded the seeds.

3. Mix all the sauce ingredients together in a bowl.

4. Heat the wok and pour in 4 tablespoons oil; when it is hot, fry the shrimp over a high heat. As soon as they change color, add the leek, garlic, ginger, and chili peppers and continue frying while stirring and turning so that the flavors blend evenly. If precooked shrimp are used, fry for 1 to 2 minutes at most before adding the condiments.

5. Pour in the sauce and continue cooking over a high heat. Mix for 1 to 2 minutes by which time the liquid should have been partly absorbed by the shrimp; thicken what remains by stirring in the cornstarch and water.

Fried crab claws

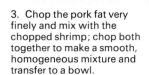

A famous Chinese delicacy, which makes a good first course for entertaining.

12 crab claws
7 ounces shrimp
1 ounce pork fat
1 egg
⅔ teaspoon salt
2 teaspoons ginger juice
1 tablespoon rice wine
all-purpose flour as required
⅔ cup fine fresh bread crumbs
4 cups oil for frying
parsley to garnish
1 lemon
freshly ground pepper or tomato ketchup
287 calories; 213g protein; 17.1g fat; 10.5g sugar

1. Remove the flesh from either side of the thin cartilage on each claw and flake very finely.

2. Rinse the shrimp if raw; devein with a toothpick or cocktail stick, peel and chop the flesh very finely.

3. Chop the pork fat very finely and mix with the chopped shrimp; chop both together to make a smooth, homogeneous mixture and transfer to a bowl.

4. Separate the egg and add the white to the shrimp-and-pork-fat mixture; add the salt, ginger juice, and rice wine and stir well. Blend in the crab meat. Divide the mixture into 12 equal portions and shape into small rissoles.

5. Press the little patties onto the base of the crab claws and coat with flour.

6. Mix 1 tablespoon water with the egg yolk; dip the bases of the claws into the egg yolk, and then coat with the bread crumbs.

7. Heat the oil to 345°F. (175°C.) and lower the crab claws into the oil; fry until well browned. Remove carefully with a slotted spoon or mesh ladle; drain.

8. Arrange the crab claws on a serving platter, sharp claws pointing inward toward the center, arrange the parsley in the middle to form a bed for the claws, and garnish with lemon wedges. Serve with freshly ground pepper or tomato ketchup.

Scallops with Chinese cabbage in creamy sauce

The Western influence present in so many recipes from southern China gives this dish a very distinctive flavor.

6 scallops
1 teaspoon ginger juice
2 teaspoons rice wine
6 large Chinese cabbage leaves
8 snow peas
$\frac{1}{3}$ carrot
$\frac{1}{4}$ leek
7 ounces honey fungus or button mushrooms
cornstarch as required
4 cups oil for frying
$1\frac{1}{2}$ cups stock (see recipe on page 296)
$\frac{2}{3}$ teaspoon salt
$\frac{1}{2}$ teaspoon sugar
1 tablespoon rice wine
$\frac{1}{2}$ cup unsweetened condensed milk
2 teaspoons cornstarch mixed with 3–4 teaspoons water
1 tablespoon melted chicken fat (taken from top of some chicken stock)
267 calories; 14.5 g protein; 16.5 g fat; 14.4 g sugar

1. Rinse and dry the scallops and snip off the thin band of tough skin surrounding them. Slice diagonally into small pieces and leave to stand in a dish with the ginger juice and the rice wine for about 5 minutes.

2. Cut the stalks of the Chinese cabbage into triangular-shaped pieces, measuring about $1\frac{1}{2}$ inches from base to apex and about $\frac{3}{4}$ inch wide at their bases. Cut the green leafy part into small pieces. Trim the snow peas and remove strings.

3. Peel the carrot and cut in half lengthwise. Notch one side of each carrot by making shallow vertical incisions down the side; in between each of these cuts make another incision, this time holding the knife obliquely so as to cut toward one of the first incisions; when the two cuts meet a small triangular section will be detached, leaving the carrot portions with a stepped appearance. Cut horizontally, producing several ladder-shaped thin slices of carrot. Boil until tender. Chop the leek; wash and slice the mushrooms.

4. Coat the scallops one at a time with cornstarch; shake off the excess. Heat the oil in the deep-fryer to 300°F. (150°C.) and deep-fry the scallops briefly.

5. Heat a little oil in the wok and stir-fry the leek; when it starts to release its aroma, add the harder, white parts of the Chinese cabbage, then the snow peas, mushrooms, green leafy parts of the cabbage, and carrots.

6. Pour in the stock and cook for 5 to 7 minutes; as soon as the vegetables are tender, add the scallops. Season with salt, sugar, and rice wine.

7. To make the sauce rich and creamy, add the condensed milk, cook for a minute or two, and then stir in the cornstarch and water to thicken.

8. If desired, the flavor can be enhanced by trickling melted chicken fat down the sides of the wok and cooking briefly before serving. This fat can be taken from the surface of chicken stock which has been made with chicken skin and other fatty parts of a chicken.

Fried sea cucumber with okra

Most Western palates will find that a taste for sea cucumbers is certainly an acquired one but this is an important dish in Chinese cookery. Long soaking is part of the protracted process which produces a gelatinous consistency.

2 ounces dried sea cucumber
straw ties or raffia
2 ounces Chinese bean thread (transparent noodles)
4 Chinese okra
salt
a small piece of ginger root
a little oil
2 tablespoons rice wine
⅔ cup stock
2 tablespoons soy sauce
3 tablespoons sweet rice wine
113 calories; 0.7 g protein; 3.8 g fat; 15.5 g sugar

1. Select black, evenly colored dried sea cucumber. Wash thoroughly in plenty of water removing any mud or dirt from between the spines.

2. Leave the sea cucumber in a bowl of cold water with the straw ties or raffia for three days to soften and plump up.

3. Squeeze the sea cucumbers to see whether soft enough to cut; when ready cut lengthwise between the spines, where the skin is relatively smooth.

4. Open up the slit and remove the innards. Wash the inside carefully.

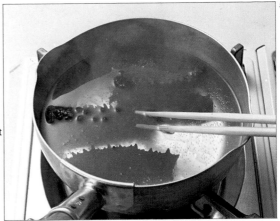

5. Continue the softening process by placing the sea cucumber in a saucepan of cold water and bringing it to a boil. Simmer the cucumber for up to $1\frac{1}{2}$ hours. While the sea cucumber is cooking pour boiling water into a bowl containing the noodles; leave to soften for a few minutes, then drain and cut into $1\frac{1}{4}$-inch lengths.

6. Rub the Chinese okra with the salt, cover with boiling water, leave to stand for a few minutes, and then drain and cut into small pieces. When the sea cucumber is tender, drain and slice thinly.

7. Peel the ginger and cut into thin strips; stir-fry in a little oil over a medium heat until it releases its aroma.

8. Add the sea cucumber to the ginger in the pan and fry; pour in the rice wine, stock, soy sauce, and sweet rice wine. Add the noodles, cook for a few minutes, and finally stir in the Chinese okra.

169

Abalone in soy sauce

Richly contrasting ingredients are blended perfectly in this dish.

5–6 dried Chinese mushrooms, presoaked
1 15-ounce can of abalone
2 tablespoons peanut oil
¼ teaspoon salt
½ teaspoon soy sauce
generous 1 tablespoon vinegar
1½ teaspoons sugar
1 teaspoon cornstarch dissolved in 2 teaspoons water
a few drops sesame oil
133 calories; 9.5g protein; 7.7g fat; 8.9g sugar

1. Soak the Chinese mushrooms in lukewarm water for 20 minutes until soft; drain, reserving the liquid, and remove the stems. Cut any large mushrooms in half.

2. Drain the canned abalone, reserving the liquid. Hold the abalone firmly with the left hand and slice them diagonally, one by one, working from right to left.

3. Make up 1 cup of liquid using liquid from the abalone and water if there is not enough.

4. Heat the peanut oil in the wok; fry the Chinese mushrooms and, once they are heated through, pour in the liquid.

5. Add the salt, soy sauce, vinegar, and sugar. As soon as the liquid boils, stir in 1 teaspoon cornstarch mixed with 2 teaspoons water to thicken.

6. Add the abalone and cook very briefly and gently, just enough to heat through. Sprinkle with a few drops sesame oil to add flavor.

Squid flowers with leek

The flavors of garlic and leek bring out the delicate taste of the squid, and the subtle color scheme of ivory and green makes a very attractive dish.

1 squid
1 small leek
3 tablespoons oil
1 teaspoon finely chopped garlic
1 tablespoon rice wine
1 teaspoon tabasco sauce
$\frac{2}{3}$ teaspoon salt
$\frac{1}{2}$ teaspoon sugar
$\frac{1}{2}$ cup stock
1 teaspoon cornstarch
120 calories; 8.8g protein; 8g fat; 3.6g sugar

1. Cut off the squid's tentacles, wash well, and cut into $\frac{1}{2}-\frac{3}{4}$-inch pieces. Rub the thin outer skin from the body of the squid under running water; pull away and discard the center bone, ink sac, head, and inner organs. Rinse thoroughly, dry, and cut down one side to open out.

2. Place the body of the squid, inner side up, on a working surface or chopping board; using a sharp knife, lightly score the squid at $\frac{1}{4}$-inch intervals; score to form a trellis pattern, making sure the skin is not cut through. Then cut the squid into rectangles about $\frac{3}{4}$ inch long.

3. Slice the leek into $\frac{3}{4}$-inch pieces.

4. Heat 1 tablespoon oil in the wok; add the squid, stir-fry lightly, and then set aside on a plate.

5. Heat 2 tablespoons oil in the wok; stir-fry the chopped garlic and leek, add the squid, and sprinkle with rice wine; stir-fry briefly.

6. Add the tabasco, salt, sugar, and stock; cook over a high heat until the squid has curled well. Thicken the sauce with 1 teaspoon cornstarch dissolved in 2 teaspoons water.

Fried squid with jellyfish

Squid:
2 dried squid
1 teaspoon bicarbonate of soda
3–4 dried Chinese mushrooms
3½ ounces carrot
1 stalk celery
3½ ounces snow peas
oil for frying
salt
1 cup water
For the sauce:
2 teaspoons sugar
1 tablespoon soy sauce
½ teaspoon salt
1 tablespoon rice wine
198 calories; 28.6g protein; 5g fat; 8.9g sugar
Jellyfish:
1¼ pounds turnips
1 teaspoon salt
3½ ounces dried jellyfish
½ cup sugar
½ cup vinegar
a few drops of sesame oil
148 calories; 3g protein; 5.2g fat; 22.6g sugar

SQUID (main dish)
1. Soak the dried squid in water overnight; boil it in water with 1 teaspoon bicarbonate of soda until tender. Drain and score in a trellis pattern (see page 171) and cut into pieces. Cut the tentacles into 1½-inch lengths.

2. Soak the Chinese mushrooms in water for 20 minutes; remove the stems and cut the caps in half. Slice the carrot ¼ inch thick; cut the celery into thin slices

3. Remove the strings from the snow peas and stir-fry in 2 tablespoons oil; add 1 teaspoon salt and 1 cup water, cover, and cook until tender but crisp.

4. Stir-fry the carrot and celery in 2 tablespoons oil;

add the mushrooms and the squid and finally the snow peas. Pour in the sauce ingredients. Stir-fry briefly before serving.

JELLYFISH (side dish)
1. Peel the turnips and cut into 1½–2-inch strips; sprinkle with 1 teaspoon salt and leave for 30 minutes.

2. Soak the dried jellyfish in hot water (about 110°F./55°C.) for about 30 seconds. The jellyfish should curl up when soaked; drain and rinse immediately in cold water.

3. Mix the sugar, vinegar, and sesame oil; stir in the jellyfish.

4. Add the rinsed and drained turnips, mix well, and serve cold.

Cantonese fried squid and vegetables

25'

2 large squid
1 teaspoon rice wine
1 teaspoon ginger juice
cornstarch as required
1 medium-size onion
4 large fresh Chinese mushrooms or dried Chinese mushrooms, presoaked
3 ounces boiled fresh or canned bamboo shoots
a 4-inch length of carrot
2 ounces snow peas
3 tablespoons lard or shortening
1 teaspoon cornstarch
For the sauce:
1 tablespoon rice wine
1 teaspoon sugar
1 teaspoon salt
$\frac{1}{2}$ cup water
249 calories; 25.2 g protein; 11.7 g fat; 9.1 g sugar

1. Place the squid in a large bowl of water; pull away the tentacles and carefully draw out ink sac and inner organs; peel off the skin and pull away the center bone. Slit the bodies of the squid and open them out flat. Score a trellis pattern (see page 171) and cut the squid into pieces 1 inch square.

2. Flavor the squid by sprinkling with the rice wine and the ginger juice. Coat lightly with cornstarch, drop into briskly boiling water to blanch, and remove after a few seconds; drain.

3. Cut the onion into eight segments, separate the layers. Remove the mushroom stems and cut the caps in four; cut the bamboo shoots, into small rectangular pieces.

4. Use a sharp knife to score grooves along the carrot and slice about $\frac{1}{4}$ inch thick. Boil for a few minutes and drain. Trim the snow peas and remove strings, cut in half obliquely and boil in salted water until they turn a vivid green.

5. Mix all the sauce ingredients together.

6. Heat the wok; add the lard and when it is hot add the vegetables in the following order; onions, mushrooms, bamboo shoots, and carrot rounds. Pour in the sauce.

7. Add the squid and stir-fry over a high heat; add the cornstarch dissolved in water and finally the snow peas.

Squid balls

Crisply fried squid balls that melt in the mouth.

3 squid
$\frac{1}{3}$ leek
a small piece of ginger root
2 tablespoons cornstarch.
4 cups oil for frying
1 tablespoon peanut oil
1 tablespoon sugar
1 tablespoon soy sauce
For the batter:
1 egg white
2 tablespoons cornstarch
1 teaspoon water
277 calories; 24.4g protein; 14.8g fat; 10.5g sugar

1

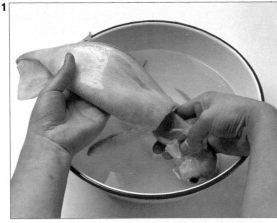

1. Place the squid in a large bowl of water. Remove the central bone or beak and the tentacles together with the innards of the squid, keeping them intact.

2. Pull the thin skin off the squid, trim off or pull away the cartilaginous tips on either side, and slit the body of the squid open.

3. Cut the thick band of flesh to which the tentacles are attached and open them out; trim off the hard, inedible parts and discard. Blanch the tentacles in boiling water, dislodging the suckers by running the back of a knife down the tentacles. Rub off the skin with a cloth or rub and peel it off with the fingers.

4. Cut the leek into strips and then cut the strips across, producing very small pieces. Peel the ginger and chop it very finely.

5. Chop each squid's body and tentacles very finely, transfer to a mortar, and pound well with the pestle. To thicken the mixture add 2 tablespoons cornstarch and mix.

6. Blend the batter ingredients together. Shape the squid mixture into small balls about ¾ inch in diameter, coat with the batter, and then deep-fry in oil heated to 340–350°F. (175°C.) for about 3 minutes. Drain and keep hot.

7. Empty the oil from the wok and wipe it clean; heat 1 tablespoon peanut oil and stir-fry the ginger and leek until they start to release their aroma. Add the sugar and soy sauce.

8. Add the squid balls and cook just long enough for the soy sauce to be partially absorbed.

5

2

6

3

7

4

8

Stir-fried squid and seaweed

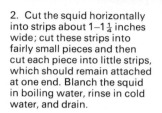

2 squid
1 ounce fresh or dried seaweed (kombu *variety*)
1 leek
1 clove garlic
3–4 snow peas
2 tablespoons lard.
For the sauce:
2½ tablespoons soy sauce
1 tablespoon vinegar
2 teaspoons cornstarch
2 tablespoons water
206 calories; 24.8g protein; 10.5g fat; 5.2g sugar

1. Place the squid in a large bowl of water; pull off the tentacles drawing out the innards of the squid without breaking them up. Slit the bodies and open them up; rub off the skin and remove the cartilaginous tips on either side.

2. Cut the squid horizontally into strips about 1–1¼ inches wide; cut these strips into fairly small pieces and then cut each piece into little strips, which should remain attached at one end. Blanch the squid in boiling water, rinse in cold water, and drain.

3. Wash the seaweed and leave it in cold water for a little while to become firm again (if dried seaweed is used, presoak). Cut it into strips. Slice the leek and garlic very thinly; trim and boil the snow peas for a short time in salted water to intensify the color; then cut them in half obliquely.

4. Mix the sauce ingredients (soy sauce, vinegar, cornstarch, and water) well until the cornstarch has thoroughly dissolved.

5. Heat the lard in the wok; stir-fry the garlic and leek and, as soon as they start to give off their distinctive aroma, add the squid and the seaweed. Stir-fry briefly over a high heat; add the sauce and mix briskly. Add the snow peas; when these have heated through the dish is ready to serve.

Stir-fried squid and asparagus

2 squid
1 teaspoon rice wine
1 teaspoon ginger juice
2 teaspoons cornstarch
8 asparagus spears (with tips)
$\frac{1}{3}$–$\frac{1}{2}$ Chinese white radish
1 bamboo shoot
2 tablespoons oil
1 cup stock (see recipe on page 296)
$\frac{1}{2}$ teaspoon salt
1 teaspoon sugar
1 tablespoon rice wine
1 tablespoon rendered chicken fat
To thicken:
2 teaspoons cornstarch dissolved in 4 teaspoons water
279 calories; 26.6 g protein; 11.6 g fat; 8.8 g sugar

1. Pull the tentacles carefully away from the bodies of the squid, removing the innards without breaking them; rub and peel off the thin skin and trim off the cartilaginous tips on either side of the opening. Slit the squid open, following the instructions on page 175; cut the squid vertically into three sections. Holding the knife at an oblique angle to the working surface, score the three sections vertically and quite deeply and then cut the scored strips horizontally into small pieces $\frac{1}{2}$–$\frac{3}{4}$ inches wide.

2. Flavor the squid with the rice wine and ginger juice, mixing well; then coat with cornstarch. Blanch in boiling water and then rinse in cold water and drain.

3. Cut any woody parts off the asparagus stems and boil the spears in salted water until the tips are just tender; rinse in cold water and cut into 1$\frac{1}{2}$-inch lengths.

4. Peel the Chinese white radish, cut into small rectangular pieces, boil until just tender, and drain; cut the bamboo shoot into rectangular pieces.

5. Heat the oil in the wok and fry the pieces of radish and bamboo shoot over a high heat. Add 1 cup stock and cook for about 5 to 7 minutes.

6. Add the sugar, salt, and rice wine; stir and then add the pieces of asparagus. As soon as the liquid returns to a boil, add the squid and cook briskly for a few minutes until the squid has curled. Stir in the cornstarch dissolved in water to thicken the sauce a little and finish by trickling the rendered chicken fat down the inside of the wok. Stir once more and serve.

Squid with fresh ginger juice and green beans

A crisp, fresh-tasting dish to which the ginger juice gives a pleasantly strong, piquant flavor.

2 squid
a pinch of salt
a few drops of sesame oil
7 ounces green beans
2 tablespoons salt
For the sauce:
2 tablespoons fresh ginger juice
2 tablespoons soy sauce
2 tablespoons vinegar
1 teaspoon sugar
1 tablespoon sesame oil
174 calories; 24.7 g protein; 6.6 g fat; 2.8 g sugar

1. Clean the squid as instructed on page 175; slit them to open out flat with the inside facing upward. Holding the knife at a 45-degree angle to the working surface, score a trellis pattern as illustrated below.

2. Cut the squid bodies into bite-size pieces, blanch in boiling water for 1 to 2 minutes, and rinse in cold water. Drain and season with salt and sesame oil.

3. String the beans if necessary; wash and drain well. Sprinkle with the 2 tablespoons salt and mix well; boil rapidly for 2 minutes; rinse in cold water and then drain and cut into $1\frac{1}{4}$–$1\frac{1}{2}$-inch pieces.

4. Mix the sauce ingredients together in a bowl (ginger juice, soy sauce, vinegar, sugar, and sesame oil).

5. Having made sure that the squid and beans are well drained, add them to the sauce and mix thoroughly, so that they are well coated and flavored.

Fried oysters

14 ounces shucked oysters
$\frac{1}{3}-\frac{1}{4}$ leek
a small piece of ginger root
cornstarch as required
1 leaf purple nori seaweed
4 cups oil for frying
For the batter:
2 small eggs
$\frac{1}{2}$ teaspoon salt
2 tablespoons water
8 tablespoons all-purpose flour
For the garnish:
1 radish
For seasoning:
lemon
mustard
soy sauce
vinegar
277 calories; 14.6g protein; 15g fat; 20.4g sugar

1. Choose oysters of roughly the same size for this recipe, place in a large strainer and immerse in a bowl full of salted water to remove grit and impurities. Drain the oysters and spread out in a strainer; pour plenty of boiling water over the oysters and allow to drain well and cool.

2. Chop the leek finely and grate the ginger.

3. Mix the oysters with the chopped leek and the grated ginger in a dish and leave them to absorb the flavors for 5 minutes. Take up the oysters and coat with cornstarch.

4. Prepare the batter by beating the eggs in a bowl; stir in the salt and water and then the sifted flour.

5. Fold the leaf of nori seaweed in half, use kitchen tongs to hold very briefly over a flame (or place for a few seconds under a preheated broiler). Wrap the seaweed in a cloth and rub gently to break the leaf into tiny pieces. Add to the batter and mix well.

6. Heat the oil in the wok to 350°F. (180°C.); dip the oysters in the batter and fry until crisp. Transfer to a serving dish and garnish with a radish cut into a flower shape. (Leave the radish to soak in cold water for 10 minutes in advance so it will open out.) Season the oysters at the table with lemon, mustard mixed with soy sauce, or soy sauce and vinegar, according to taste.

Stir-fried oysters and bean curd

A hot dish in which the bland bean curd absorbs the delectable if delicate flavor of the oysters as well as the flavor of the sesame oil.

10 ounces small shucked oysters
a small piece of leek
a small piece of ginger root
1½ cakes bean curd
2 tablespoons fermented black beans
½ leek
4 tablespoons peanut oil
a small bunch of parsley
For the sauce:
1½ tablespoons soy sauce
1 tablespoon sugar
2 tablespoons oil
2 teaspoons sesame oil
366 calories; 17.9g protein; 27.1g fat; 9.7g sugar

1. Place the oysters in a large strainer and immerse in salted water, moving the strainer from side to side to remove any grit. Add the small pieces of leek and ginger, finely sliced, to a large saucepan of boiling water; lower the oysters into the boiling water for a few seconds to blanch and then drain.

2. Cut the bean curd vertically into three pieces and then into smaller pieces about ½ inch thick. Boil in the flavored water for 1 minute and drain carefully.

3. Chop the ½ leek and the black beans finely.

4. Mix the sauce ingredients together.

5. Heat the wok, pour in the peanut oil, and when it is very hot, fry the chopped leek and beans; add the oysters and the bean curd and stir-fry over a high heat, taking care not to break up the bean curd too much; pour in the sauce all at once and cook for 2 minutes to allow it to penetrate the oysters and bean curd. Turn onto a serving dish and garnish with parsley.

Egg Dishes

Eggs play a supporting, but nonetheless vital, role in Chinese cooking, since eggs can be used to complement or blend with an endless variety of ingredients. A beaten egg added to soup not only makes it look attractive but also sets off the taste. Egg is unequalled as a binding agent: Egg whites are used for making Chinese coconut cake, and the yolks are used for sealing such foods as spring rolls.

Hard-boiled eggs are peeled, simmered in stock flavored with soy sauce, and eaten as a popular snack; or their shells are gently cracked and the hard-boiled eggs are then simmered in a mixture of tea and soy sauce; when they are peeled they reveal an attractive marbled pattern.

Thousand-year-old eggs are the product of an extremely ancient and ingenious method of preserving duck eggs which keep less well than chicken eggs. A mixture of lime, pine ash, salt, and rice husks is plastered all over the eggs, which are then buried for two to four months. During this period the coating gradually dries and the lime produces a reaction in the eggs, transforming the whites into a firm, translucent amber-colored jelly and making the yolks turn green. These duck eggs have a very distinctive taste and are usually served as a snack with slices of ginger which have been soaked and softened in vinegar. Sometimes special seasonings are mixed with the preserving substance to add extra flavor. Pickled duck eggs are another favorite; these are eaten hot with a bowl of boiled rice (or, best of all, with Congee rice – the typical Shanghai breakfast). The yolks of duck eggs are also dried in the sun and used to fill the moon cakes which are eaten as festival fare.

Although chicken and duck eggs are the most widely used, pigeon eggs and quail eggs also make frequent appearances on Chinese menus.

Chinese eggs and bacon

A full-flavored and spicy dish which is best
eaten with plain boiled rice.

14 ounces pork belly
4 dried Chinese mushrooms
1 leek
2 ounces dried shrimp
2–3 tablespoons peanut oil
4 eggs
$\frac{1}{3}$ cup soy sauce
1 tablespoon rice wine
1 teaspoon sugar
a pinch of five-spice powder.
531 calories; 18.6g protein; 49.1 g fat; 3.4g sugar

1. Dice the pork belly into $\frac{1}{2}$-
inch cubes; soak the Chinese
mushrooms in water for 20
minutes and, when they have
softened and expanded, drain.

2. Remove the stems from the
mushrooms and cut the caps
into pieces approximately $\frac{1}{2}$-
inch square. Chop the leek
finely. Soak the dried shrimp
in water and when plump,
drain reserving the liquid.

1

2

3

4

5

6

3. Heat the oil in the wok and
stir-fry the leek; when it starts
to release its aroma, add the
shrimp and stir-fry these for a
few minutes.

4. Add the mushrooms and
the pork belly and stir-fry over
a high heat; when the meat
has changed color, add the
soy sauce, rice wine, sugar,
and five-spice powder and
transfer all the ingredients to a
fairly deep saucepan.

5. Add enough stock made up
from the liquid in which the
shrimp were soaked, topping
up with water if necessary, to
just cover all the ingredients in
the saucepan.

6. Add the peeled hard-boiled
eggs, placing them on top of
the other ingredients so that
they do not touch the bottom
of the pan. Cover and cook for
about 1 hour.

Five-color omelet

Simple and quick to prepare and attractive in presentation, this delicious dish can be enjoyed at any time of year.

2 slices cooked ham
½ bunch scallions
3–4 ounces boiled fresh or canned bamboo shoots
3 fresh or canned Chinese mushrooms
6 eggs
½ teaspoon salt
½ teaspoon sugar
a pinch of monosodium glutamate (optional)
oil for frying.
230 calories; 11.2 g protein; 19.1 g fat; 3,2 g sugar

1

1. Cut the ham into thin strips; chop the scallions into pieces about $1\frac{1}{2}$–2 inches long. If scallions are not in season, use finely shredded leek.

2. If fresh bamboo shoots are used, wash them well and boil them until tender; shred into small strips the same size as the ham. Remove the stems from the mushrooms and cut the caps into strips the same size as the ham and bamboo shoots.

3. Beat the eggs in a bowl. (Always use very fresh eggs when making an omelet.)

4. Mix in the salt, sugar, and monosodium glutamate (optional) and beat the eggs briefly but energetically, lifting the mixture to incorporate as much air as possible.

5. Add the ham, scallions, bamboo shoots, and mushrooms and stir well.

6. Heat 2–3 tablespoons oil in a wok; pour the whole omelet mixture into the wok at once, cook until just set, using a spatula or a Chinese scoop or turner to make sure the ingredients are evenly spread throughout the omelet.

7. When the omelet has set on one side, turn it over, dividing it into three portions; then scoop the three portions together again.

8. When the omelet has set into a nicely rounded shape, cover and cook for a very short time and then serve. The whole of this operation will only take a few minutes.

5

2

6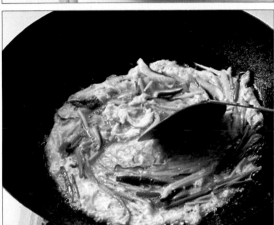

3

7

4

8

Fried eggs, tomatoes, and mushrooms

¼ ounce dried Chinese wood-ear fungus
2 eggs
a pinch of salt
2 ripe tomatoes
oil for frying
1 teaspoon sugar
1 tablespoon soy sauce
a pinch of monosodium glutamate (optional)
128 calories; 4.1 g protein; 10.5 g fat; 5.7 g sugar

1. Soak the dried fungus in warm water for 20 minutes, wash well, dry and chop the larger pieces in half.

2. Beat the eggs in a bowl together with a pinch of salt.

3. Make a shallow crisscross incision in the skin on the top of each tomato and place in a bowl; cover with boiling water and remove after 5 to 10 seconds; rinse in cold water and peel off the skin. Chop roughly.

4. Heat the wok and pour in 3–4 tablespoons oil. When the oil is hot, pour in the beaten eggs.

5. Scoop and turn the omelet mixture, using a scoop, until it is half-cooked – just set.

6. Remove the omelet mixture from the wok; pour in 2 tablespoons oil and heat. Add the chopped tomato and stir-fry lightly. When the tomato has just heated through, return the eggs to the pan, add the fungus, and cook briefly, scooping and turning.

7. Sprinkle with the sugar, soy sauce, and monosodium glutamate (optional), mixing quickly before serving.

Tea eggs

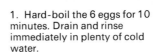

The eggs are boiled in a mixture of tea and soy sauce and then peeled to reveal an attractive marbled pattern; their taste is also enhanced.

6 servings:
6 eggs
2 teaspoons tea leaves
1 star anise
1 teaspoon sugar
¼ teaspoon salt
1 tablespoon soy sauce
2 cucumbers
1 teaspoon salt
1 teaspoon hot soybean paste
a few drops of sesame oil
152 calories; 9.9 g protein; 11.1 g fat; 2.5 g sugar

1. Hard-boil the 6 eggs for 10 minutes. Drain and rinse immediately in plenty of cold water.

2. Roll the eggs very carefully against the working surface, pressing gently so as to form tiny cracks in the shell without rupturing the thin inner skin.

3. Place the eggs in a saucepan of water with the tea, star anise, sugar, salt, and soy sauce. Boil gently for up to 1 hour, turning the eggs now and then so that they color well. Allow the eggs to cool in the liquid.

4. Remove the eggs from the pan and peel off their shells very carefully taking care not to tear the delicate skin immediately under the shell.

5. Prepare the cucumbers by slicing them in half vertically, scoring the skin obliquely in a trellis pattern, and cutting them into small pieces 1 inch long. Place in a bowl and sprinkle with 1 teaspoon salt; when the cucumbers have softened, sprinkle with a little cold water and drain. In a separate bowl mix the soybean paste, the soy sauce, and the sesame oil; add the cucumbers and mix rapidly.

6. Arrange the cucumbers in the bottom of a bowl or serving plate and top with the tea eggs.

Scrambled eggs with shrimp

The complementary flavors of the shrimp and eggs make a clever combination for this quick and easy dish.

5 ounces shrimp
½ egg white
1 teaspoon cornstarch
oil for frying
6 eggs
½ teaspoon salt
½ teaspoon sugar
a pinch of monosodium glutamate (optional)
1 tablespoon rice wine
3–4 tablespoons peanut oil.
310 calories; 15 g protein; 26.2 g fat; 1.9 g sugar

1. Shell the shrimps and remove the vein running down their backs with a toothpick or cocktail stick; rinse and drain.

2. Place the shrimps in a bowl, add the egg white and the cornstarch and mix well with the fingers.

3. Heat the oil in the wok to 250°F. (120°C.), add the shrimp and stir-fry lightly; as soon as the shrimp change color, remove from the oil and drain. (If cooked shrimp are used, merely warm them through in the oil.)

4. Beat the eggs with the salt in a bowl; add the sugar and monosodium glutamate (optional) and stir well.

5. Heat 3–4 tablespoons peanut oil in the wok, pour in the beaten eggs, stir, and turn them with a scoop or spatula until they are half-cooked.

6. Add the shrimp and mix quickly; sprinkle with the rice wine and stir briefly before transferring to a warmed serving platter. Eat while still piping hot.

Vegetables

The balance and harmony that a good Chinese cook strives to achieve means that vegetables play a far more important part in Chinese cuisine than they do in the West, where they are usually relegated to a supporting role. The word ts'ai which is used to denote all the dishes that compose a meal actually means "vegetables." There has always been a great choice and abundance of vegetables in China. This is mainly due to the favorable climate but also stems from the Chinese habit of raising fast-growing vegetables sown between the main crops of rice and cereals, thus making the most of the limited area of arable land available. Plants which do not spread out and take up too much ground space are therefore favored, and squashes or pumpkins are ripened on the roofs of houses; vegetables such as soybean sprouts can even be grown indoors.

In addition to this, the age-old Chinese flair for making the most of every food source offered by nature means that such plants as bamboo shoots, seaweed, and water chestnuts are gathered and consumed. Such beauties of nature as the lotus are also fully exploited, hence the widespread inclusion of the plant's leaves, seeds, and root in so many recipes.

The teachings of Buddhism, which advocate vegetarianism have had a considerable influence on Chinese eating habits, and while the religion has lost much of its philosophic influence in China, its influence on Chinese cuisine is still strong. Preserved vegetables are an important addition to the Chinese diet; when vegetables are plentiful, the surplus can be dried or pickled for use when the fresh article is out of season or scarce.

Stir-fried green beans with mushrooms

A simple recipe using ingredients which are available all year round; it goes well with meat dishes.

$\frac{1}{2}$ pound green beans
4 ounces button mushrooms
oil for frying
1 teaspoon salt
1 cup water
2 tablespoons soy sauce
1 teaspoon sugar
1 teaspoon rice wine
a pinch of monosodium glutamate (optional)
a few drops of sesame oil
If required:
1 teaspoon cornstarch dissolved in 2 teaspoons water
96 calories; 2.3g protein; 7.7g fat; 6.1g sugar

1. Trim, wash, and dry the beans and slice them obliquely into $1\frac{1}{2}$–2-inch lengths.

2. Trim and wash the mushrooms, cutting the larger ones in half.

3. Heat a wok over a high heat and pour in 2 tablespoons oil, swirling it round the inside of the wok to coat it thoroughly.

4. When the oil begins to smoke, add the beans and stir-fry, tossing vigorously.

5. Once the beans have absorbed most of the oil, season with salt and pour in the water; cover and cook until tender and then transfer to a plate and discard the liquid from the wok.

6. Heat the wok again over a high heat; pour in 2 tablespoons oil and, when it is very hot, return the beans to the pan and add the mushrooms; stir-fry again, tossing the ingredients.

7. Season with the soy sauce, sugar, rice wine, and monosodium glutamate (optional), mixed together in advance. Add a few drops of sesame oil for extra flavor.

8. If the sauce needs thickening, stir in 1 teaspoon of cornstarch mixed well with 2 teaspoons water.

191

Stir-fried snow peas with soybean paste

A vegetable dish with a well-defined, mildly spicy flavor.

3/4 pound snow peas
oil for frying
1 teaspoon salt
1 cup water
1 teaspoon finely chopped garlic
1 teaspoon soybean paste
1 tablespoon soy sauce
1 teaspoon sugar
a pinch of monosodium glutamate (optional)
a few drops of sesame oil
119 calories; 3.8g protein; 7.9g fat; 9.7g sugar

1. Trim and remove the strings from the snow peas, wash and dry.

2. Heat 2 tablespoons oil in a wok, add the snow peas and stir-fry lightly; season with salt and pour in 1 cup water.

3. Cover and cook until the snow peas are tender but still crisp; drain.

4. Remove any liquid left in the wok; pour in 2 tablespoons oil and, when the oil is quite hot, add the chopped garlic and stir-fry.

5. As soon as the garlic starts to release its aroma, return the snow peas to the wok and mix in the soybean paste, soy sauce, sugar, and monosodium glutamate (optional). Stir-fry just long enough for the snow peas to absorb the flavor of the dressing.

6. Sprinkle with a few drops of sesame oil for extra flavor and sheen.

Stir-fried cucumbers with dried shrimp

An extremely unusual combination of cucumbers and shrimp provides a delicious, quick, and easy dish.

2 tablespoons dried shrimp
2–3 cucumbers
oil for frying
1 slice ginger root
1 teaspoon sugar
$\frac{1}{2}$ teaspoon salt
1 tablespoon soy sauce
a pinch of monosodium glutamate (optional)
1 teaspoon cornstarch dissolved in 2 teaspoons water.
58 calories; 0.9g protein; 5.1 g fat; 2.2g sugar

1. Wash the shrimp and soak in water to soften and plump up; drain, reserving the liquid, and chop the shrimp into small pieces.

2. Slice the cucumbers vertically in half and then cut obliquely into pieces.

3. Pour 2 tablespoons oil into a wok and heat; when the oil is very hot stir-fry the ginger until it releases its aroma.

4. Add the chopped shrimp and stir-fry; add the cucumbers and stir-fry, keeping the heat high.

5. Season with sugar, salt, soy sauce, and monosodium glutamate (optional) and moisten with some of the liquid reserved from soaking the shrimp. Cover and cook over a low heat until the liquid has been partially absorbed.

6. Thicken the remaining juices a little by stirring in 1 teaspoon cornstarch mixed with 2 teaspoons water.

Cucumbers and scallops with mushrooms

A delicate combination of flavors, which makes a delicious and exotic dish. It is useful when unexpected guests arrive, since it is made with mainly canned ingredients.

4 cucumbers (2 if large)
1 can Chinese straw or egg mushrooms
1 can scallops
2 cups stock (including liquor from canned scallops)
3 tablespoons peanut oil
1–2 tablespoons rice wine
1 teaspoon salt
2 teaspoons cornstarch
a few drops of sesame oil
185 calories; 18.4g protein; 10.5g fat; 11.4g sugar

1. Peel the cucumbers and cut diagonally into slices about $\frac{1}{4}$ inch thick.

2. Drain the mushrooms and cut into thin slices.

3. Drain the scallops, reserving the liquor; chop the scallops finely and add the reserved juice to the stock, making up 2 cups.

4. Heat the wok; pour in 3 tablespoons oil and, when the oil is hot, stir-fry the scallops.

5. Add the cucumbers and the mushrooms; stir-fry briefly and then trickle 1–2 tablespoons rice wine down the inside of the wok. Pour in the stock.

6. When the liquid comes to a boil, season with salt and continue cooking over a slightly lower heat.

7. When the cucumbers are tender but still crisp, stir in 2 teaspoons cornstarch mixed with 4 teaspoons water, to thicken the sauce.

8. For extra flavor add a few drops of sesame oil just before serving.

Eggplant Sichuan style

The flavor of the fried eggplant is improved by the addition of ground pork.

6 very small eggplants
oil for frying
1 teaspoon finely chopped garlic
1 tablespoon finely chopped leek
1 teaspoon finely chopped ginger
scant $\frac{1}{2}$ cup ground pork
1 teaspoon rice wine
For the sauce:
1 tablespoon sugar
2 tablespoons soy sauce
1 teaspoon vinegar
a pinch of monosodium glutamate (optional)
241 calories; 5.4g protein; 21g fat; 7.5g sugar

1. Wash the eggplants, remove the stalks, and cut lengthwise into 4 to 6 pieces. Place in cold water for $\frac{1}{2}$ hour to remove any bitter taste.

2. Dry the eggplant slices thoroughly with a cloth and fry them in very hot oil.

3. Mix all the sauce ingredients together.

4. Heat 2 tablespoons oil in the wok and stir-fry the garlic, leek, and ginger; once these have started to release their aroma, add the ground pork.

5. Fry the pork making sure that it does not form lumps; sprinkle with rice wine, add the fried eggplants and pour in the sauce. Stir and turn quickly to distribute the flavor evenly.

Chinese white radish
with pork and shrimp

The finely chopped pork and shrimp enhance the subtle flavor of the white radish. An economical dish.

4–5 servings:
2 tablespoons dried shrimp
1 pound Chinese white radish
oil for frying
1 tablespoon finely chopped leek
1 teaspoon finely chopped ginger
¼ cup finely chopped or ground pork
1 tablespoon rice wine
1 cup stock
2 teaspoons sugar
3 tablespoons soy sauce
a pinch of monosodium glutamate (optional)
126 calories; 4.2 g protein; 8.1 g fat; 8 g sugar

1. Wash the dried shrimp and soak them in cold to lukewarm water until they have softened and swelled; chop into small pieces.

2. Peel the Chinese white radish; cut lengthwise into 4 or, if very large, into 6 pieces and then slice diagonally into small chunks.

3. Heat the wok over a fairly high heat and pour in 2–3 tablespoons oil; when the oil is very hot, stir-fry the chopped leek and ginger.

4. Once these start to release their aroma, add the shrimp.

5. When the shrimp have heated through, add the ground pork and mix well with a wooden spoon or scoop while cooking to keep the meat in very small pieces and prevent its forming lumps.

6. When the meat is cooked and well colored, add the white radish, mix and turn briefly, and then sprinkle with rice wine.

7. Stir-fry all the ingredients over a high heat; pour in 1 cup of stock and flavor with the sugar, soy sauce, and monosodium glutamate (optional).

8. Cover and cook over a low heat until the liquid has almost completely evaporated and the white radish is tender; any remaining juices should be absorbed by the white radish.

Stir-fried potatoes with pork

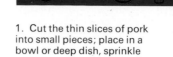

A dish which commends itself to any cook since it is both economical and digestible.

5 ounces very thinly sliced pork
1 teaspoon sugar
1 tablespoon soy sauce
1 teaspoon cornstarch
1 tablespoon peanut oil
1 pound boiling, not baking, potatoes
1 cup stock
1 teaspoon sugar
$\frac{1}{4}$ teaspoon salt
a pinch of monosodium glutamate (optional)
2 tablespoons peanut oil
276 calories; 8.7 g protein; 16.2 g fat; 23.8 g sugar

1. Cut the thin slices of pork into small pieces; place in a bowl or deep dish, sprinkle with the sugar, soy sauce, cornstarch, and peanut oil; and mix well by hand to ensure even coating.

2. Peel the potatoes and boil them whole until they are only just tender.

3. Cut the potatoes into thin slices.

4. Heat 2 tablespoons oil in a wok, add the marinated pork and stir-fry lightly over a high flame.

5. After 2 to 3 minutes, add potatoes and stir-fry. Pour in 1 cup stock and season with sugar, salt, and monosodium glutamate (optional).

6. Cover and turn down the heat; continue cooking for a short while until the meat and potatoes are tender and have absorbed the seasoning.

Bamboo shoots with spinach and mushrooms

The attractive color contrasts of the ingredients make this light vegetable dish very appetizing.

approximately 1 pound fresh spinach
3½ ounces bamboo shoots
4–5 Chinese winter (black) mushrooms
oil for frying
1 teaspoon salt
1 cup water
1 tablespoon oyster sauce
a pinch of monosodium glutamate (optional)
a few drops of sesame oil
To thicken:
1 teaspoon cornstarch dissolved in 2 teaspoons water
93 calories; 3.1 g protein; 7.9 g fat; 5.2 g sugar

1. Trim the spinach and wash it very thoroughly; pat dry and cut into 2–2½-inch pieces.

2. Boil the bamboo shoots until tender and slice thinly into small pieces.

3. Soak the mushrooms in water for 20 minutes, if they are dried; remove the stems and cut the larger caps in half.

4. Heat 2 tablespoons oil in the wok, stir-fry the spinach briefly and then add the salt and water. Cover and cook over a low heat until the spinach is tender; remove and drain the spinach.

5. Clean the wok and heat 2 tablespoons of fresh oil; when this is very hot, add the bamboo shoots and the mushrooms and stir-fry.

6. When the bamboo shoots and mushrooms are nearly done, add the spinach, stock, oyster sauce, and monosodium glutamate (optional), finishing with a few drops of sesame oil.

7. Cover and cook for 2 to 3 minutes to allow the vegetables time to absorb flavor and moisture. Before serving, thicken the sauce by stirring in 1 teaspoon cornstarch mixed with 2 teaspoons water.

Chinese white radish with crab meat

The delicate flavors of Chinese white radish and chicken are enhanced by the sprinkling of crab meat.

1 chicken wing
a small piece of leek
a small piece of ginger root
a few drops of rice wine
a pinch of salt
1 small can crab meat
$1\frac{1}{4}$–$1\frac{1}{2}$ pounds Chinese white radish
$2\frac{1}{2}$ cups stock, made up from the liquid from the steamed
  chicken and liquor from the canned crab meat
3 tablespoons peanut oil
1 teaspoon salt
1–2 tablespoons rice wine
2 rounded teaspoons cornstarch
a few drops of ginger juice
4–5 Chinese chives
313 calories; 15.7 g protein; 21.7 g fat; 11.7 g sugar

200

1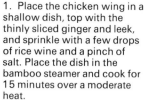

1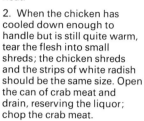

1. Place the chicken wing in a shallow dish, top with the thinly sliced ginger and leek, and sprinkle with a few drops of rice wine and a pinch of salt. Place the dish in the bamboo steamer and cook for 15 minutes over a moderate heat.

2. When the chicken has cooled down enough to handle but is still quite warm, tear the flesh into small shreds; the chicken shreds and the strips of white radish should be the same size. Open the can of crab meat and drain, reserving the liquor; chop the crab meat.

3. Cut the Chinese white radish into 1½-inch sections, then into thin slices, and finally shred these slices to the same size as the chicken. Combine the crab liquor and the juices from the steamed chicken to make up 2½ cups.

4. Heat a wok and pour in the peanut oil; when this is hot add the white radish and stir-fry until fairly tender.

5. Season with ½ teaspoon salt and flavor with 1–2 tablespoons rice wine, trickling this down the inside of the wok. Pour in the stock and cook over a moderate heat; remove any scum which forms during cooking.

6. When the Chinese white radish is tender, add the rest of the salt to taste, a little at a time. If there is too much liquid, reduce by cooking a little longer.

7. Add the shredded chicken and the crab meat, reserving a little crab for decoration. Stir and turn quickly with a spatula or scoop.

8. Stir in the cornstarch dissolved in water to thicken the sauce. Turn off the heat, add the ginger juice, and stir. Garnish with chopped chives and the remaining pieces of crab meat.

5

6

2

7

3

4

8

Stir-fried Chinese cabbage

A fresh, light, and very simple dish.

approximately 2 pounds Chinese cabbage
oil for frying
1 teaspoon salt
a pinch of monosodium glutamate (optional)
1 cup stock
52 calories; 0.8 g protein; 5.1 g fat; 1.3 g sugar

1. Wash the cabbage very thoroughly, drain in a colander or salad shaker, and cut into pieces 1–1½ inches long.

2. Heat the wok and pour in 2–3 tablespoons oil; as soon as the oil is quite hot, add the cabbage and stir-fry over a high heat.

3. Season with salt and monosodium glutamate (optional) and pour in the cup of stock. Cover and cook until tender.

4. Drain and serve.

Fried eggplant with sweet and sour sauce

The eggplants are fan-cut, fried, and served with a spicy sweet and sour sauce and garnished with plenty of sesame seeds for extra flavor.

6 small eggplants
oil for frying
For the sauce:
1 tablespoon white sesame seeds
1 chili pepper
1 clove garlic
1 tablespoon vinegar
1 tablespoon sesame oil
2 tablespoons soy sauce
1 tablespoon sugar
160 calories; 1.7g protein; 14g fat; 7.8g sugar

1. Toast the sesame seeds.

2. Remove the seeds from the chili pepper and cut into thin rings, about $\frac{1}{8}$ inch thick.

3. Crush the garlic clove.

4. Place the vinegar, sesame oil, soy sauce, sugar, sesame seeds, chili pepper, and garlic in a bowl and mix well. The sauce is now ready.

5. Remove the stalks from the eggplants and slice in half lengthwise. Score the outside of each half very deeply and obliquely, without cutting all the way through the vegetables, so that each half eggplant will fry quickly but remain in one piece.

6. Heat plenty of oil moderately hot in a wok and deep-fry the eggplants, turning them carefully every so often. Remove and drain well.

7. Arrange the eggplants, skin side upward, on a heated serving platter, pour the sauce evenly all over them, and leave to stand for a couple of minutes before serving so that the eggplants can absorb the sauce.

Ch'ao tou ya (stir-fried bean sprouts)

Not only is this vegetable very quick to prepare but it is also available all year round.

6 servings:
3 tablespoons peanut oil
2 or 3 crushed cloves of garlic
2 slices ginger root, finely chopped
1 pound fresh bean sprouts, rinsed and well-drained
½ teaspoon salt
a pinch of freshly ground pepper
1 tablespoon lard or cooking fat
1½ tablespoons light soy sauce
3 small leeks, white part only, finely shredded into thin strips about ¾ inch long
1 teaspoon sesame oil
116 calories; 3.4g protein; 4.3g fat; 3.2g sugar

1. Heat the peanut oil in the wok and stir-fry the garlic with the ginger very briefly.

2. Add the bean sprouts and salt and pepper and stir-fry quickly for a few seconds only.

3. Add the lard, soy sauce, and leek.

4. Stir-fry for 2 minutes over a high heat. When the bean sprouts are ready (they should still be crisp), sprinkle with the sesame oil.

Bean Curd Dishes

The two most important products obtained from soybeans are soy sauce and the very nutritious and versatile white bean curd, which is known as tofu. These curd cakes look similar in texture to cheese, though their taste is quite different and rather bland. Yellow soybeans are soaked and softened in water and then crushed to a powder; this is then ground once more with added water to form a purée or paste which is strained through cheesecloth. The filtered liquid is heated, combined with a little thickening agent, and then left to set in molds. The purer and fresher the water used when making bean curd, the better it will be.

Buddhist monks introduced tofu and pioneered its skilful use to replace meat which was, of course, forbidden by their religion; bean curd and its derivatives were molded and shaped to look like fish, seafoods, and other ingredients for which they were substitutes. Bean curd can be dried, fermented, or frozen, and can also be spiced to give it a stronger flavor.

Bean curd with fermented black beans Sichuan style

As with most dishes from the province of Sichuan, this is a spicy, peppery recipe.

2 cakes bean curd
1 chili pepper
1 tablespoon fermented black beans
oil for frying
1 tablespoon finely chopped leek
1 teaspoon finely chopped garlic
1 teaspoon finely chopped ginger root
5 ounces finely chopped or ground pork
For the sauce:
$\frac{1}{3}$ cup stock
2 tablespoons soy sauce
2 tablespoons sugar
1 tablespoon soybean paste
1 teaspoon hot soybean paste
$\frac{1}{4}$ teaspoon salt
1 tablespoon rice wine
a pinch of monosodium glutamate (optional)
To thicken:
1 teaspoon cornstarch
279 calories; 17.3g protein; 20g fat; 9g sugar

1. Cut the bean curd into small cubes about $\frac{1}{2}-\frac{3}{4}$ inch square. Place in one layer in a shallow pan propped up at one end so that the liquid from the bean curd will drain to the bottom.

2. Remove the seeds from the chili pepper and cut into rings $\frac{1}{4}$ inch thick; chop the black beans finely, holding the knife at both ends and pivoting on the sharper end from left to right while chopping.

3. Prepare the sauce by mixing all the ingredients thoroughly: the stock, soy sauce, sugar, soybean paste, hot soybean paste, salt, rice wine, and monosodium glutamate (optional).

4. Heat 2–3 tablespoons oil in the wok, stir-fry the finely chopped leek, garlic, and ginger briskly without allowing them to color too much.

5. When these ingredients start to release their aroma, add the ground pork, the black soybeans and the chili pepper. Stir-fry, taking care that the meat does not form lumps.

6. When the pork is cooked, add the bean curd, being very careful not to break it.

7. Pour in the sauce; stir gently, and turn all the ingredients once without breaking the bean curd, if possible. Cover and cook for about 15 minutes over a low heat, shaking the wok gently from time to time.

8. When the bean curd has absorbed most of the sauce, thicken the remainder by adding 1 teaspoon cornstarch mixed with 2 teaspoons water and distribute evenly so that the sauce is of uniform consistency.

207

Steamed bean curd and egg white

A subtle-tasting, elegant dish in which the interesting texture of the steamed bean curd and egg white provides a foil for the ham, peas, and sauce.

4–5 servings:
1 cake bean curd
2 slices cooked ham
2 tablespoons frozen peas
5 egg whites
½ cup milk
⅓ cup stock
½ teaspoon salt
1 teaspoon sugar
a pinch of monosodium glutamate (optional)
1 teaspoon cornstarch
For the sauce:
¾ cup stock
1 tablespoon rice wine or dry sherry
¼ teaspoon salt
¼ teaspoon sugar
a pinch of pepper
a pinch of monosodium glutamate (optional)
127 calories; 12.5 g protein; 6.5 g fat; 5.4 g sugar

1. Cut the bean curd into 4 pieces and push through a strainer. Allow to stand for a little while and then transfer to a piece of cheesecloth to drain away excess moisture.

2. Cut the ham into small strips about $\frac{1}{4}$ inch wide; place the frozen peas in a bowl and cover with boiling water; leave to stand for a couple of minutes and then drain.

3. Place the egg whites in a bowl, mix gently with chopsticks or a fork, making sure that no bubbles form. Add the bean curd and mix with a wooden spoon. Place the steamer over boiling water to get hot and full of steam.

4. Add the milk, stock, salt, sugar, and a pinch of monosodium glutamate (optional) to the bean curd mixture.

5. To achieve a particularly smooth, velvety consistency, push the mixture through a strainer with a slightly wider mesh than previously used; transfer the mixture to a heatproof serving bowl.

6. Place the bowl in the steamer. Steam the bean curd mixture for 20 to 25 minutes over a gentle heat until it has set. (The top should feel firm when pressed very lightly with the fingers.)

7. Meanwhile prepare the sauce by placing the strips of ham and peas together with all the sauce ingredients in a small saucepan; bring to a boil and add the cornstarch dissolved in little water. Set the thickened sauce aside.

8. When the bean curd is set, cut into it with a spoon scooping out an egg-shaped piece and let it fall back gently into the bowl upside down, repeat all the way around the bowl so that the curd looks rather like the petals of a flower. Pour in the sauce and serve.

Fried bean curd in soy sauce

2 cakes fried bean curd
a large piece of ginger root
3–4 dried Chinese mushrooms
1 tablespoon Chinese dried wood-ear fungus
approximately 30 dried lily bud stems
5 ounces leg of pork
1 teaspoon rice wine
$\frac{1}{2}$ teaspoon soy sauce
1 rounded teaspoon cornstarch
oil for frying
2–3 tablespoons peanut oil
$3\frac{1}{2}$ ounces green beans
salt
For the sauce:
3 tablespoons soy sauce
3 tablespoons water
$\frac{1}{2}$ teaspoon sugar
1 tablespoon rice wine
1 tablespoon sesame oil
To thicken:
cornstarch as required dissolved in double the quantity of water
448 calories; 24g protein; 30.7g fat; 26.3g sugar

1. Cut the fried bean curd into slices about $\frac{1}{4}$ inch thick. Shred the ginger.

2. Soak the dried mushrooms in water for 20 minutes; drain, dry and cut diagonally into thin slices. Soak the wood-ear fungus in lukewarm water for 20 minutes and snip off the hard stems.

3. Soak the lily bud stems in warm water for 30 minutes; snip if necessary to remove any woody parts and tie each stem into a knot.

4. Cut the pork into small, narrow strips, sprinkle with rice wine and soy sauce, mix and leave to marinate for 10 minutes.

5. Mix the cornstarch with the pork and stir-fry in fairly hot oil.

6. Heat 2–3 tablespoons peanut oil in the wok. Stir-fry the ginger briefly, then add the Chinese mushrooms, the fried bean curd, lily bud stems, fungus, and fried pork; stir-fry over a fairly high heat.

7. Pour in the sauce and cook over a high heat for 3 to 4 minutes, stirring and turning. Thicken the sauce by stirring in a little cornstarch mixed with water.

8. Cook the beans in boiling salted water; drain. Cut each bean obliquely into two or three pieces; stir-fry in a little peanut oil and season with salt.

9. Transfer the bean curd and other ingredients to a heated serving plate and surround with the beans.

Soups

When Tung-po was living as a hermit he used to cook a vegetable soup which, although it contained no fish, meat, or five-spice powder, was full of the savor and goodness of simple things.

—Su Shih, *In praise of Tung-po's Soup*

Soup is usually served as the last course of a Chinese meal, but, as is so often the case in Chinese cooking, this is not a hard and fast rule. Such highly prized delicacies as Shark's Fin Soup and Bird's Nest Soup are substantial and very nutritious, made with fish or meat, eggs, mushrooms, and various other vegetables. These special thick soups are served in small bowls immediately after the first course.

The soup which is most often served is, in contrast, a very light, clear vegetable broth, containing a few small pieces of meat. It is brought to the table in a large tureen and each person helps himself, ladling the soup into his own bowl and sipping it throughout the meal in place of other thirst-quenching drinks; at the end of the meal, a further, more generous helping is consumed as a very effective aid to digestion.

Yu Ch'i (shark's fin soup)

8–10 servings:
3½ ounces dried shark's fin
generous 8 cups light stock
2 scallions or thin, young leeks
3 slices ginger root
2 tablespoons peanut oil
1 cup chicken meat, shredded
½ cup shredded bamboo shoots
½ cup dried Chinese mushrooms (tung ku variety), presoaked
   and cut into small strips
1 tablespoon rice wine
2 tablespoons light soy sauce
1 tablespoon red wine vinegar
½ teaspoon sugar
½ teaspoon salt
3 tablespoons cornstarch dissolved in 3 tablespoons water
120 calories; 6.6 g protein; 4.5 g fat; 7 g sugar

1. Soak the shark's fin for 4 hours in cold water; rinse several times. Boil the shark's fin for up to 2 hours, changing the water several times and picking out any remaining foreign particles.

2. Rinse the shark's fin under cold running water for 10 minutes and then pat dry.

3. Place the shark's fin in a heatproof earthenware cooking pot, pour in 3 cups stock and add the scallions and the ginger. Bring to a boil, cover, and boil for 15 minutes. Drain the shark's fin, discarding the stock.

4. Heat the oil in a clean earthenware cooking pot, add the shredded chicken meat, and stir-fry until the flesh changes color.

5. Add the remaining stock and bring to a boil. Add the shark's fin, bamboo shoots, mushrooms, rice wine, soy sauce, vinegar, sugar, and salt and simmer over a low heat for 15 to 20 minutes.

6. Stir in the cornstarch mixed with water and simmer until the soup has thickened, stirring from time to time. Serve very hot in small bowls; a little vinegar may be added if desired.

Won ton soup

6–8 servings:
¾ pound shrimp, peeled, deveined, and chopped
1 beaten egg
2½ ounces leek, shallot, or scallion cut into thin rings
For the marinade:
1 teaspoon sugar
½ teaspoon salt
½ teaspoon monosodium glutamate (optional)
2–3 drops sesame oil
For the soup:
6 cups basic chicken stock (see recipe on page 296)
1 teaspoon salt
½ teaspoon monosodium glutamate (optional)
2 tablespoons light soy sauce
4–5 drops of sesame oil
For the won ton:
4 ounces sifted all-purpose flour
6 tablespoons mixture of beaten egg and water
cornstarch as required
430 calories; 16.5 g protein; 25.6 g fat; 23 g sugar

1. Prepare the won ton: Sift the flour on to a pastry board, make a well in the center and pour in all but 1 tablespoon of the beaten-egg-and-water mixture; mix in the flour and work the dough for about 5 minutes until smooth; add the remaining egg and water if needed. Cover with a cloth and leave to rest for 4 to 5 hours at room temperature.

2. Knead the dough briefly once more and lightly dust the pastry board and rolling pin with cornstarch. Roll the dough out into a very thin, almost transparent sheet and cut out 48 circles. These should be dusted with cornstarch, piled on top of each other, and kept in the refrigerator, covered with a cloth until needed.

3. Mix the shrimp thoroughly with the marinade and place in refrigerator for 30 minutes.

4. Place a generous teaspoon of shrimp mixture in the center of each pastry circle, brush the edges with beaten egg.

5. Gather the pastry over the filling; twist to seal.

6. Bring a saucepan of salted water to a boil and boil the won ton until they rise to the top. Drain.

7. Distribute half the chopped leek evenly in the soup bowls and place the won ton on top.

8. Bring the stock and other soup ingredients to a boil, add the remaining leek, and boil for 1 minute. Serve.

Pork and shrimp balls in broth

Pork and shrimp balls served in a delicate chicken stock. In China this soup is usually served to celebrate a male child's birthday.

4–6 servings:
7–8 cups stock (see recipe on page 296)
2 tablespoons rice wine
2 generous teaspoons salt
½–1 cucumber
a few drops of sesame oil
For the shrimp balls:
7 ounces shelled shrimp, deveined
2½ ounces fresh pork fat
1 teaspoon rice wine
½ egg white
½ teaspoon salt
1 tablespoon cornstarch
½ teaspoon ginger juice
For the pork balls:
3 small dried Chinese mushrooms (tung ku variety)
½ leek
7 ounces ground pork
½ tablespoon rice wine
a pinch of pepper
½ teaspoon salt
scant 1 teaspoon mixed peanut and sesame oils
1 small or ½ large egg
½ tablespoon cornstarch
397 calories; 22g protein; 30.9g fat; 5.9g sugar

1. Raw shrimp should really be used for this dish as they bind better and form a more homogeneous mixture for the shrimp balls. Chop the shrimp very finely and pound with the blunt edge of a cleaver to form a thick paste.

2. Dice the pork fat finely into about $\frac{1}{4}$-inch cubes – if chopped any finer it may melt during cooking.

3. Place the shrimp in a bowl, add the rice wine and mix well; stir in the pork fat, egg white, salt, and cornstarch. Mix thoroughly and add the ginger juice.

4. Shape the mixture into balls about $\frac{1}{2}-\frac{3}{4}$ inch across; a quick and easy method is to take a small portion of mixture, form a fist enclosing it, and then squeeze out a ball of mixture through the opening formed by the thumb and forefinger.

5. Prepare the pork balls next: soak the mushrooms in lukewarm water for 20 minutes, remove the stems, and chop the caps. Chop the leek finely.

6. Place the ground pork in a bowl with the rice wine and pepper, mix, and then add the leek, mushrooms, salt, mixed peanut and sesame oils, egg, and cornstarch and work together to form a smooth, homogeneous mixture. Shape into balls.

7. Pour the stock into a deep saucepan or cooking pot (preferably earthenware) and bring to a boil; add the pork balls followed by the shrimp balls.

8. When the stock returns to a boil, skim off any scum, flavor with rice wine and salt, and add the cucumber, cut into paper-thin slices. Season with pepper and a few drops sesame oil.

Mushroom soup

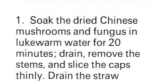

This soup is something of a luxury, since it contains several varieties of delicious mushrooms.

4–6 servings:
4–5 dried black Chinese mushrooms
$\frac{1}{2}$ cup dried wood-ear fungus soaked in water for 20 minutes
$\frac{1}{2}$–1 can straw mushrooms or egg mushrooms
2–4 leaves Chinese cabbage
3 tablespoons peanut oil
a small piece of carrot
1 teaspoon salt
5–6 cups stock
$\frac{1}{2}$ tablespoon soy sauce
1 tablespoon rice wine
$\frac{1}{2}$–$\frac{1}{3}$ teaspoon vinegar
$\frac{1}{2}$ tablespoon cornstarch
a pinch of pepper
a few drops sesame oil
105 calories; 4g protein; 10.4g fat; 9.1g sugar

1. Soak the dried Chinese mushrooms and fungus in lukewarm water for 20 minutes; drain, remove the stems, and slice the caps thinly. Drain the straw mushrooms and slice.

2. Cut the Chinese cabbage and the peeled carrots into very small, thin strips. Cut off the bottom of the wood-ear fungus (keep them separate from the mushrooms).

3. Heat 3 tablespoons peanut oil in a wok; add the black mushrooms, the straw mushrooms, the Chinese cabbage, and the carrot; stir-fry over a fairly high heat. When the vegetables are quite tender, season with salt.

4. Pour in the stock, soy sauce, rice wine, and vinegar and as soon as the liquid comes to a boil, lower the heat and continue cooking for about 5 to 6 minutes to give the vegetables time to absorb some of the liquid and flavors. Add the fungus.

5. When the vegetables are cooked, stir in the cornstarch mixed with 1 tablespoon water to thicken the soup.

6. Just before serving, add a pinch of pepper and a few drops of sesame oil.

Steamed egg soup with crab meat

An exquisitely delicate soup in which crab meat adds flavor to the steamed egg mixture.

5 eggs
a pinch of salt
a pinch of monosodium glutamate (optional)
3 cups stock
1 small can crab meat
3–4 chives
1 teaspoon cornstarch
For the sauce:
$\frac{3}{4}$ cup stock
$\frac{1}{4}$ teaspoon sugar
$\frac{1}{4}$ teaspoon salt
1 tablespoon rice wine
a pinch of monosodium glutamate (optional)
158 calories; 16.6g protein; 7.3g fat; 2.4g sugar

1. Break the eggs into a bowl and stir gently, add a pinch of salt, a pinch of monosodium glutamate (optional), and 3 cups stock; mix slowly so that the mixture does not become at all frothy.

2. Select a fairly deep, heatproof bowl which will fit in the steamer and is also decorative, since the soup will be served in this bowl. Pour the egg mixture through a fairly fine strainer into the bowl.

3. Place the bowl in the bamboo steamer, which should be full of steam; cook for 20 to 25 minutes until the surface is firm to the touch.

4. While the egg mixture is being steamed, prepare the sauce, combining all the ingredients. Chop the crab meat into small pieces; snip the chives into 1–1$\frac{1}{2}$-inch lengths.

5. Place the crab meat, chives, and sauce in a small saucepan, cook for a few minutes over a moderate heat, and then thicken by stirring in the cornstarch mixed with 2 teaspoons water.

6. Pour onto the steamed egg mixture and serve.

Crab soup

A thick soup made with crab and beaten egg; an ideal recipe for entertaining.

1 can crab meat
1 egg
3 dried Chinese mushrooms
1 cup bamboo shoots, parboiled
1 leek
a small piece of ginger root
1 tablespoon oil (or lard or cooking fat)
1 teaspoon soy sauce
1 tablespoon rice wine
6 cups stock or hot water
2 generous teaspoons salt
a pinch of pepper
a pinch of monosodium glutamate (optional)
1½ tablespoons cornstarch
parsley to garnish
107 calories; 7.7g protein; 5.5g fat; 6.9g sugar

1. Drain and chop the crab meat. Beat the egg in a bowl or cup.

2. Soak the Chinese mushrooms in warm water for 20 minutes and slice into thin

1

2

3

4

5

6

strips. Cut the bamboo shoots into strips of the same size. Cut the leek diagonally into thin slices. Chop the parsley finely and grate the ginger.

3. Heat the oil in the wok; stir-fry the mushrooms; add the leek and, when this starts

to release its aroma, add the bamboo shoots, the crab meat, and the grated ginger. Stir-fry over a high heat.

4. Sprinkle with soy sauce and the rice wine; pour in the heated stock or water; as soon

as the liquid comes to a boil, skim off any scum.

5. Season with salt, pepper, and monosodium glutamate (optional), Stir in the cornstarch mixed with a little water to thicken the soup.

6. Pour the beaten egg into the soup and mix with chopsticks so that the egg sets and is evenly distributed throughout the soup. Sprinkle with finely chopped parsley and serve.

Chicken wings and cucumbers in broth

This soup requires painstaking preparation and is usually served when entertaining special guests.

14 ounces chicken wings
3 small (or 1 large) cucumbers
1 dried Chinese mushroom
a pinch of salt
To flavor:
a pinch of salt
a pinch of pepper
1 tablespoon rice wine
a pinch of monosodium glutamate (optional)
267 calories; 19.5g protein; 18.8g fat; 3.9g sugar

1. Cut the chicken wings in half.

2. Place the wings in a bowl, cover with boiling water, stir, drain, and remove any feathers. Wash in cold water and drain.

3. Place the chicken wings in a large saucepan, add 8 cups of water, and bring to a boil quickly over a high heat reduce the heat and cook for 30 minutes until the flesh is tender; remove any scum from the surface.

4. Peel the cucumbers carefully; cut them in half vertically and then cut each strip obliquely into 4 pieces (if larger cucumbers are used, cut into quarters lengthwise and then into pieces). Soak the Chinese mushroom in warm water for 20 minutes, remove the stem, and add the mushroom to the chicken and stock.

5. Bring a saucepan of water to a boil; add a pinch of salt and the cucumbers and boil for 3 minutes; drain the cucumbers and rinse in cold water.

6. When the chicken wings are done, remove from the stock and arrange in a small heatproof dish around the mushroom, which should be placed upside down in the center; insert the pieces of cucumber between the chicken wings.

7. Strain the chicken stock, add the flavoring ingredients, and pour enough of the stock into the dish containing the chicken wings, mushroom, and cucumbers to come $\frac{4}{5}$ of the way up the dish. Reserve the remainder of the stock, keeping it hot. Place the dish in the bamboo steamer and steam the wings and cucumbers for about 15 minutes.

8. Pour the juices from the dish into the reserved stock. Place the serving bowl over the small dish from the steamer and turn the chicken wings, cucumbers, and mushroom upside down into the serving bowl. Gently pour the hot broth into the serving bowl.

Lettuce and fillets of fish in broth

3½ ounces fillets of white fish, such as halibut, cod, carp, etc.
1 teaspoon ginger juice
1 teaspoon rice wine
a pinch of salt
a pinch of monosodium glutamate (optional)
1 teaspoon cornstarch
1 lettuce
1 teaspoon peanut oil
a small piece of ginger root
1 teaspoon soy sauce
For the broth:
6 cups light stock or hot water
a pinch of salt
a pinch of pepper
a pinch of monosodium glutamate (optional)
a few drops of rice wine
a few drops of sesame oil
55 calories; 5.8g protein; 2.4g fat; 2.6g sugar

1. Slice the fish fillets obliquely into fairly thin pieces and sprinkle with ginger juice, rice wine, salt, monosodium glutamate, and cornstarch. Mix for even flavoring and coating.

2. Detach all the leaves from the lettuce, wash well. Cut the ginger into thin slices.

3. Heat the peanut oil in a wok, stir-fry the ginger, moisten with the soy sauce, and continue to cook until the full aroma is released. Pour in the stock or hot water and season to taste with salt.

4. Turn down the heat, add the pieces of fish, a few at a time, and when the liquid has come to a boil, season with salt, pepper, monosodium glutamate (optional), rice wine, and sesame oil; add the lettuce leaves and turn off the heat.

West Lake beef soup

 25'

A classic soup from Shanghai.

$3\frac{1}{2}$ ounces thinly sliced beef
3 egg whites
$\frac{1}{2}$ leek
a few golden (honey fungus) mushrooms
1 tablespoon peanut oil
1 tablespoon rice wine
6 cups light stock (or hot water)
2 heaping teaspoons salt
a pinch of monosodium glutamate (optional)
2 level tablespoons cornstarch
a pinch of pepper
To flavor:
1 teaspoon soy sauce
1 teaspoon rice wine
$\frac{1}{2}$ teaspoon sugar
$\frac{1}{2}$ teaspoon cornstarch
75 calories; 6.1g protein; 1.3g fat; 6.3g sugar

1. Cut the slices of beef obliquely into strips about $\frac{1}{4}$ inch wide. Mix all the flavoring ingredients together in a bowl.

2. Beat the egg whites with chopsticks or a fork; shred the leek. Trim the bottoms of the mushroom stems and set the mushrooms aside.

3. Heat 1 tablespoon oil in the wok; add the rice wine and then pour in the stock (or hot water) and bring to a boil.

4. Mix the flavoring mixture with the beef and leave to stand.

5. Once the stock has come to a boil, add the beef, a little at a time; season with salt and monosodium glutamate (optional). Stir in the cornstarch mixed with an equal quantity of water to thicken.

6. Pour the egg whites into the broth all at once, mixing quickly to blend evenly; add the mushrooms, shredded leek, and a pinch of pepper. Allow to boil for a few seconds and then turn off the heat.

Meatballs in broth

A full-flavored soup using a wide variety of ingredients.

$\frac{1}{2}$ pound ground pork
$\frac{1}{2}$ onion
2 teaspoons rice wine
a pinch of pepper
1 teaspoon sesame oil
3 dried Chinese winter (black) mushrooms
1 small egg
1 level tablespoon cornstarch
$\frac{1}{3}$ teaspoon salt
1 tomato
2 cabbage leaves
1–1$\frac{1}{2}$ ounces bean thread (transparent noodles)
5–6 cups stock or water
sesame oil for oiling your hands
For the final seasoning:
1 teaspoon rice wine
a pinch of pepper
1 teaspoon salt
273 calories; 13.2g protein; 18.4g fat; 13.4g sugar

1. Place the ground pork in a bowl, add the very finely chopped onion, 2 teaspoons rice wine, pepper, and 1 teaspoon sesame oil; work the mixture well by hand.

2. Soak the mushrooms in warm water; remove the stems, chop very finely, and add to the meat mixture. Mix in the beaten egg, salt, and cornstarch in that order. Blend each ingredient in thoroughly before adding the next one.

3. Blanch a ripe tomato in boiling water, rinse in cold water, and peel. Slice in half horizontally, remove the seeds, and cut each half into slices just over $\frac{1}{2}$ inch thick.

4. Cut out the ribs of the cabbage leaves and cut the leaves into small pieces. Place the bean thread (transparent noodles) in a bowl, cover with boiling water and leave to soften. Drain and snip into fairly short lengths.

5. Bring the stock to a boil in a large saucepan. Lightly oil the palms of your hands with sesame oil and shape the pork mixture into small balls, taking a small quantity of meat in one hand, forming a fist enclosing the meat, and squeezing a well-rounded ball out through the opening formed by thumb and forefinger.

6. The meat balls should be about 1 inch in diameter; lower into the boiling stock one by one.

7. Remove any scum from the stock, add the cabbage and the tomato, and boil for a few minutes longer, skimming off any scum as it forms.

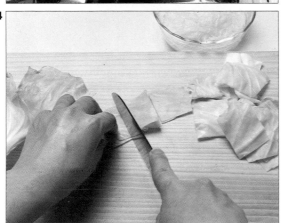

8. Add the final seasoning of rice wine, salt, and pepper and, shortly before serving, add the noodles, boil fast for a minute, and turn off the heat. Serve very hot.

Cucumber and chicken soup

A light soup with a very delicate taste. The ingredients are given the bare minimum of cooking.

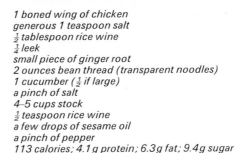

1 boned wing of chicken
generous 1 teaspoon salt
$\frac{1}{2}$ tablespoon rice wine
$\frac{1}{4}$ leek
small piece of ginger root
2 ounces bean thread (transparent noodles)
1 cucumber ($\frac{1}{2}$ if large)
a pinch of salt
4–5 cups stock
$\frac{1}{2}$ teaspoon rice wine
a few drops of sesame oil
a pinch of pepper
113 calories; 4.1 g protein; 6.3 g fat; 9.4 g sugar

1. Place the chicken wing in a heatproof dish, sprinkle with salt and rice wine, and top with the diagonally sliced leek and slivers of ginger. Place the dish in the bamboo steamer and steam for 15 to 20 minutes.

2. When the chicken is cooked, remove the skin; tear the chicken flesh by hand into long, thin strips; remove and

1

2

3

4

5

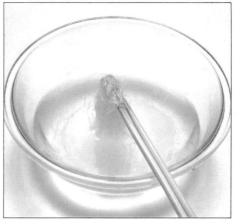

6

discard the leek and ginger and pour the cooking juices which have collected into the stock.

3. Rinse the bean thread (transparent noodles), place in a bowl, and cover with boiling water. Leave to soften for 5 minutes. Drain and cut into fairly short lengths.

4. Slice the cucumber diagonally into thin rounds, then cut each slice into thin strips.

5. Pour the stock into a deep saucepan, bring to the boil, and add salt and rice wine (the best stock, made with chicken bones and wing tips, should be used for this soup).

6. Add the bean thread (transparent noodles) to the stock followed by the strips of chicken and the cucumbers. Adjust the seasoning, adding a few drops sesame oil and a pinch of pepper. Turn off the heat.

227

Peking bean curd soup

1–2 cakes bean curd
3 slices pork belly
3 dried Chinese mushrooms
5 leaves Chinese cabbage
a few gingko nuts (use the shelled, canned variety)
$3\frac{1}{2}$ ounces ground pork
1 tablespoon rice wine
Flavoring for the pork balls:
2 teaspoons finely chopped leek
1 teaspoon grated ginger root
$\frac{1}{3}$ teaspoon soy sauce
2 tablespoons water
1 scant tablespoon cornstarch
$\frac{1}{3}$ teaspoon salt
a pinch of pepper
a pinch of monosodium glutamate (optional)
Seasoning for stock:
1 tablespoon soy sauce
1 teaspoon sugar
$1\frac{1}{2}$ teaspoons salt
a pinch of pepper
a pinch of monosodium glutamate (optional)
187 calories; 12.5g protein; 11.5g fat; 9.9g sugar

1. Cut each bean curd into 8 pieces. Cut the pork belly into pieces 2 inches long. Soak the Chinese mushrooms in warm water for 20 minutes, remove the stems, quarter the caps, and then cut obliquely into thin slices.

2. Cut the Chinese cabbage leaves in half vertically, then into 2-inch pieces, and finally shred diagonally. If unshelled gingko nuts are used, shell, boil in salted water, and peel off the thin inner skin.

3. Place the ground pork in a bowl and add the flavoring ingredients; blending well to form a firm, smooth mixture, Shape into small balls.

4. Bring 6 cups water to a boil in a large heatproof earthenware cooking pot. Lower the pork balls into the boiling water, followed by the mushrooms and the pork belly. Cook for a while before adding the seasoning and then stir in the cabbage.

5. When the Chinese cabbage is just tender, adjust the seasoning if necessary; add the bean curd, gingko nuts, and rice wine and boil for a few moments longer.

6. Serve the soup immediately, while piping hot.

Bamboo shoot soup

A fairly thick soup which is served as a foil to rich, spicy dishes.

5 ounces boiled fresh or canned bamboo shoots
2–3 cups stock
$\frac{1}{2}$ teaspoon salt
a pinch of pepper
generous 1 tablespoon rice wine
scant 1 teaspoon cornstarch
a small bunch of parsley
2–3 drops of peanut oil
2–3 drops of sesame oil
44 calories; 1.4g protein; 2.6g fat; 3.9g sugar

1. Cut the bamboo shoots in half vertically and then into thin slices as illustrated, cutting out a comb pattern down the straight side for decorative effect.

2. Bring the stock to a boil in a large saucepan, add the bamboo shoots, and, when the stock returns to a boil, season with salt, pepper, and rice wine; stir in the cornstarch mixed with 3 teaspoons water to thicken.

3. Sprinkle with coarsely chopped parsley and quickly add the peanut oil and the sesame oil and turn off the heat.

Chicken soup

An original and enjoyable soup which is made with readily available ingredients.

14 ounces Chinese white radish
10 ounces carrots
a 4-inch length of leek
a small piece of ginger
1¼ pounds chicken wings and legs
1⅓ teaspoon salt
a pinch of monosodium glutamate (optional)
a pinch of pepper
249 calories: 23.7 g protein; 12.1 g fat; 8.6 g sugar

1. Wash the white radish thoroughly and peel; cut in half vertically and then into 2-inch lengths; round off all the edges to make even, fairly regular pieces.

2. Wash the carrot well and cut into small replicas of the white radish pieces. Cut the leek in half. Pound the ginger lightly with the flat of the cleaver.

1

2

3

4

5

6
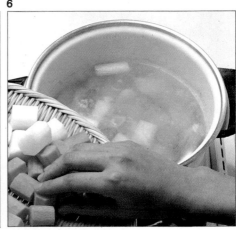

3. Chop the chicken into portions about 1½ inches square; place in a bowl and cover with boiling water. Drain.

4. Use kitchen tweezers to pluck out any remaining small feathers, quill roots, etc. Rinse in cold water.

5. Place the chicken in a large saucepan with the leek and ginger; pour in sufficient water to cover the chicken pieces. As soon as the water has come to a boil, lower the heat and simmer for 20 minutes. Skim off any scum which forms.

6. When the chicken is nearly done, remove and discard the leek and ginger. Season with salt and monosodium glutamate (optional), add the white radish and carrot, cook until these are tender, and then season with pepper and a little more salt if necessary.

Bean curd and tomato soup

The contrast in color and taste between the bean curd and tomatoes is brought out by the use of chili oil.

7 ounces pork belly, thinly sliced
2 cakes bean curd
2 tomatoes
a little parsley
2 tablespoons oil
For the marinade:
2 teaspoons soy sauce
2 teaspoons rice wine
Flavoring for the soup:
2 tablespoons soy sauce
1 teaspoon chili oil
a pinch of monosodium glutamate (optional)
a pinch of pepper
308 calories; 11.4g protein; 24.4g fat; 2.5g sugar

1. Cut the slices of pork belly into 2-inch lengths and marinate in the soy sauce and rice wine.

2. Cut each bean curd cake into 8 pieces; remove stems from the tomatoes and cut into 4–8 pieces. Chop the parsley.

3. Heat the oil in the wok, add the marinated pork belly and stir-fry until lightly browned. Add the pieces of bean curd (handling them gently so that they do not break up) and the tomatoes and stir-fry briefly. Add the soup flavoring and 4 cups hot water. As soon as the water comes to a boil, transfer carefully into an earthenware casserole dish.

4. Bring the soup back to a boil, sprinkle with parsley.

Chinese cabbage and chicken soup

The whole chicken is simmered to make this wholesome soup which is an easy and effective dish for entertaining.

5–6 servings:
a boiling fowl weighing about 3 pounds
1 small Chinese cabbage
2 teaspoons salt
a pinch of monosodium glutamate (optional)
1 tablespoon rice wine
a pinch of pepper
378 calories; 31.9 g protein; 25.8 g fat; 2.2 g sugar

1. Clean the chicken, wash well in cold water, and pour boiling water over the skin and inside the cavity to dislodge any remaining particles and loosen any quills.

2. Place the chicken in a large, heavy cooking pot or saucepan, cover with water, and bring to a boil over a high heat. As soon as the water has boiled, skim and turn down the heat. Boil gently for about 40 minutes.

3. Remove and discard the outer leaves of the Chinese cabbage, until the cabbage is about 5 inches in diameter. Cut in half and then slice each half into 4–6 pieces.

4. When the chicken is nearly done, season with salt, monosodium glutamate (optional), and rice wine; add the Chinese cabbage and cook until the chicken and cabbage are tender.

5. Transfer the chicken carefully into a heatproof serving dish, arrange the cabbage leaves around it, and pour in the chicken stock. Bring back to a boil, add a little pepper, and serve very hot.

Five-color soup

40'

5 chicken wings
10 quail eggs
2 teaspoons soy sauce
oil for frying
10 scallops
2 ounces pork belly, preferably 3 slices
3 dried Chinese mushrooms
3½ ounces boiled fresh or canned bamboo shoots
4 leaves Chinese cabbage
bean thread (transparent noodles) (approximately 1–2 ounces)
1 tablespoon peanut oil
½ leek
1 teaspoon soy sauce
1 tablespoon rice wine
5 cups hot water
1⅓ teaspoons salt
a pinch of monosodium glutamate (optional)
a pinch of pepper
434 calories; 22.3g protein; 35.4g fat; 6.7g sugar

1. Wash the chicken wings and chop in half, placing them on a heatproof dish together with the quail eggs. Cook in the bamboo steamer for 5 minutes; shell the eggs.

2. Sprinkle the wings and eggs with 2 teaspoons soy sauce, mix well, and then fry until they are golden brown.

3. Wash and trim the scallops; chop the pork into strips 2 inches long.

4. Soak the mushrooms in warm water, remove the stems, and cut the caps obliquely into thin slices. Slice the bamboo shoots thinly.

5. Cut the Chinese cabbage vertically in half, then into 2-inch pieces, and finally slice obliquely into thin strips. Cut the leek into 1¼-inch lengths.

6. Place the bean thread (transparent noodles) in a bowl, cover with boiling water and, when soft, drain and snip into 5-inch lengths.

7. Heat in the wok 1 tablespoon peanut oil and stir-fry the leek; sprinkle with 1 teaspoon soy sauce and the rice wine; add 5 cups boiling water.

8. Line an earthenware cooking pot or casserole dish with the cabbage leaves; place all the ingredients except for the scallops on the cabbage leaves, pour the prepared stock slowly into the casserole dish, and season with salt and monosodium glutamate (optional).

9. As soon as the soup has come to a boil, lower the heat, and simmer until all the ingredients are nearly done; add the scallops and cook for a few minutes only; season with pepper and serve.

Eight-treasure soup

14 ounces chicken wings
cornstarch as required
12 dried Chinese mushrooms
2 dried bean curd
10 ounces taro root
3½ ounces carrot
a small quantity of spinach
a few gingko nuts
a few dried lily buds
a little mustard
For the marinade:
1 teaspoon soy sauce
1 teaspoon rice wine
1 teaspoon sesame oil
⅓ teaspoon salt
a pinch of pepper
To flavor and season the stock:
4 tablespoons soy sauce
scant 2 tablespoons sugar
2 tablespoons rice wine or dry sherry
2 generous teaspoons salt
a pinch of monosodium glutamate (optional)
a little mustard
385 calories; 23.8g protein; 20.4g fat; 30.3g sugar

1. Chop the chicken into fairly generous pieces and sprinkle with the marinade. Mix and leave to stand and then coat each piece with cornstarch.

2. Soak the mushrooms in warm water, remove the stems, and cut the caps obliquely into thin slices.

3. Soak the dried bean curd in several changes of hot water and cut each curd into 6 pieces.

4. Peel the taro root and cut into ½-inch slices.

5. Cut evenly spaced grooves lengthwise into the outside of the carrot, slice the carrot into ¼-inch rounds to form flower shapes. Blanch the spinach for a few seconds in boiling water, drain, and cut into 1½-inch lengths.

6. Shell the gingko nuts, boil in slightly salted water, and peel off the thin inner skin, or, if possible, use the shelled canned variety. Wash and trim the lily buds and soak in water; tie each lily in a knot.

7. Bring 8 cups water to a boil in a heatproof earthenware cooking pot; add the flavoring for the stock, the Chinese mushrooms, taro root, carrots, and dried bean curd. Cook for about 10 minutes and then add the chicken wings, gingko nuts, and the lily buds.

8. Boil for a minute or two, adjust the seasoning, and add the spinach. Serve, using a little additional mustard for extra flavor.

Beef and Chinese white radish soup

A very substantial, thick soup which needs lengthy cooking and can be served as a meal in itself; its robust flavor goes well with boiled rice.

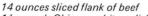

14 ounces sliced flank of beef
1¼ pounds Chinese white radish
7 ounces carrots
½–1 leek
1 clove garlic
small piece of ginger root
1 chili pepper
2 tablespoons oil
1 teaspoon salt
a pinch of pepper
a pinch of monosodium glutamate (optional)
For the sauce:
1–2 teaspoons hot soybean paste
2 tablespoons hoisin sauce
2 teaspoons sugar
3 tablespoons soy sauce
379 calories; 22.2 g protein; 23.2 g fat; 18.9 g sugar

1. The beef should be sliced thinly – about ⅛ inch thick – and cut into generous bite-size pieces.

2. Peel the Chinese white radish and slice diagonally using the rolling cut (see Cutting Techniques, pages 304–307); cut the carrot in the same fashion.

1

2

3

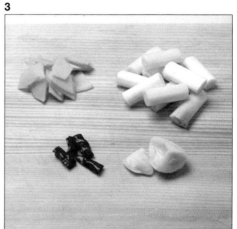

4

5

6

3. Cut the leek into 1½-inch lengths; slice the ginger finely and pound the garlic with the flat of the cleaver. Cut the chili pepper in half.

4. Heat the oil in a wok and stir-fry the garlic over a moderate heat until it releases its aroma; add the leek and the ginger and stir-fry well. Add the chili pepper and the beef.

5. Turn up the heat and stir-fry until the beef has changed color, pour in the blended sauce ingredients, and stir-fry until the ingredients are golden brown.

6. Place the carrot and Chinese white radish in an earthenware casserole dish, place the beef on top, and fill the dish with hot water almost to the rim. Season with salt, pepper, and monosodium glutamate (optional) and cook for 1 hour or more over a low heat, until the beef is very tender.

Pork belly and vegetable soup

A straightforward recipe; the soy sauce and vinegar counteract the rich, rather fat pork.

7 ounces pork belly, in one piece
10 ounces Chinese white radish
14 ounces Chinese cabbage
1 teaspoon salt
a pinch of monosodium glutamate (optional)
1 tablespoon rice wine
a pinch of pepper
soy sauce
vinegar
201 calories: 9.2g protein; 15.6g fat; 4.8g sugar

1. Place the piece of pork belly in a deep saucepan, cover with water and bring to a boil.

2. Lower the heat as soon as the water boils and cook for about 15 minutes. Drain and cool; cut into thin slices. Strain the cooking liquid and reserve.

3. Peel the Chinese white radish and slice into $2\frac{1}{2}$-inch lengths; cut these pieces into rectangles 1 inch long and $\frac{1}{8}$ inch thick.

4. Cut the Chinese cabbage in half lengthwise and then into $2\frac{1}{2}$-inch lengths.

5. Pour the reserved stock into a large saucepan and bring to a boil, season with the salt and monosodium glutamate (optional), add the Chinese white radish and cook for about 5 minutes; add the Chinese cabbage and boil for 5 minutes more.

6. When the vegetables are tender, sprinkle the pieces of pork into the soup; season with rice wine and pepper and serve at once. Serve with a mixture of soy sauce and vinegar for each person to add as desired.

Pork belly and mushroom soup

This dish can be eaten hot, but it is equally good cold and can therefore be prepared in advance.

5 dried Chinese mushrooms
1¼ pounds pork belly, in one piece
2 leaves dried seaweed (kombu variety), each about 12 inches long
7 ounces boiled fresh or canned bamboo shoots
15–20 quail eggs
¾ cup soy sauce
1 tablespoon rice wine
a pinch of monosodium glutamate (optional)

1. Soak the Chinese mushrooms in warm water for 20 minutes, remove the stems and cut the caps in half or in quarters; slice obliquely into slivers.

2. Dice the pork into ¾-inch cubes; place in a large saucepan or cooking pot. Wipe the seaweed leaves with a damp cloth and add to the pork. Pour in 5 cups water; bring to a boil.

3. Once the water has boiled, turn down the heat and cook slowly until the pork is so tender that it can be pierced easily with chopsticks. Remove the seaweed when soft.

4. Cut the bamboo shoots into quarters lengthwise, then slice obliquely into irregular pieces. Place the quail eggs on a plate in a bamboo steamer and steam for 5 minutes; shell.

Cut the seaweed into strips and knot each strip.

5. Add the soy sauce, rice wine, and monosodium glutamate (optional) to the soup, followed by the mushrooms, bamboo shoots, seaweed, and quail eggs; boil for a few seconds and then reduce the heat; simmer until all the ingredients are well colored, having absorbed the soy sauce and other flavorings. Add a little water if necessary.

6. Transfer the ingredients with a slotted spoon to an earthenware serving dish, pour in the liquid, and bring to a boil before serving.

Chinese cabbage and pork soup

Ground pork is shaped into a flat cake and cooked with Chinese cabbage in flavorful stock.

7 ounces ground pork
oil
10–14 ounces Chinese cabbage
½ leek
a small piece of ginger root
½ tablespoon soy sauce
1 tablespoon rice wine
4 cups water
1 teaspoon salt
a pinch of monosodium glutamate (optional)
freshly ground pepper
For the sauce:
½ egg
1 teaspoon ginger juice
1 teaspoon rice wine
½ teaspoon salt
a pinch of pepper
a pinch of monosodium glutamate (optional)
2 tablespoons cornstarch dissolved in 2 tablespoons water
208 calories; 11.1 g protein; 14.5 g fat; 6.7 g sugar

1. Place the pork in a bowl, pour in the sauce ingredients, and mix well until smooth and well blended. Gather the meat in one hand and slap it against the inside of the bowl several

1

2

3

4

5

6

times, then mix and knead well once more.

2. Oil a slightly concave plate very lightly, place the meat on it and press out into a large hamburger about ½ inch thick using a spatula or pot scraper rinsed in cold water.

3. Cut across the Chinese cabbage, slicing it into pieces ½ inch wide; cut the leek into rings ¼ inch thick; peel the ginger and cut into thin slivers.

4. Heat 1 tablespoon oil in a wok; stir-fry the leek and

ginger and, when they start to release their aroma, add the soy sauce and the rice wine, followed by 4 cups water.

5. Season with salt and monosodium glutamate (optional), add the Chinese cabbage, and slide the pork hamburger carefully on top.

6. Cover and cook over a gentle heat for about 10 minutes; adjust the seasoning; sprinkle with freshly ground pepper. Transfer all the ingredients very carefully to an earthenware dish, bring to the boiling point, and serve.

Fish balls in broth

A mixture of fish balls and slices of fish in a clear soup; a light and digestible dish.

7 ounces swordfish (if not available, use any very dense, firm fish)
a pinch of salt
a pinch of pepper
7 ounces raw white-fleshed fish, flaked
1 tablespoon rice wine
1 bunch Chinese spring chrysanthemum flowers (not the normal garden variety)
1 stalk celery
6 cups stock
2 teaspoons salt
a pinch of monosodium glutamate (optional)
161 calories; 24.5 g protein; 2.9 g fat; 7.8 g sugar

1. Pound the swordfish lightly with the flat of the cleaver; cut into rectangular pieces $\frac{1}{2}$ inch × $\frac{3}{4}$ inch long, and $\frac{1}{2}$ inch high. Season lightly with salt and pepper.

2. If the flaked fish is a bit too dry, soften with the rice wine and a little water. Combine with the swordfish and leave to stand in the refrigerator for about 6 hours.

3. Tear the chrysanthemum flowers into small pieces by hand. Remove the strings from the celery and slice thinly.

4. Pour the stock into a large cooking pot, season with 2 teaspoons salt and monosodium glutamate (optional), and once it has come to a boil, add the flaked fish, shaped into small balls, together with the swordfish.

5. When the fish rises to the surface, add the celery and chrysanthemum flowers; season with a little more pepper and rice wine.

242

Mongolian Hot Pot Cooking

Mongolian hot pot cooking is a legacy of the ancient northern Chinese braziers, which served the dual purpose of cooking food and providing warmth for dwellings lashed by the icy northern winds during the freezing winter evenings.

A table prepared for a Huo Kuo or "fire-pot," meal is one of the most enchanting and welcoming sights imaginable. In the center of the table is a great chafing dish of shining brass with red-hot glowing coals in its chimney and hot, flavorful broth steaming in the surrounding moat. All around are placed numerous dishes on which various raw meats, fish, and vegetables, all cut into small slivers are elegantly set out. They will cook very quickly in the simmering broth. Several different kinds of sauces are also placed around the table.

Each person cooks his or her own food by holding the delicious morsels in the broth with chopsticks – the Chinese call it "rinsing" the food – while sipping some of the strong wines or spirits of the North.

The recipes that follow are adaptations of the hot-pot method in that the food is precooked and is merely kept hot in the broth as it simmers gently in the bowl of the hot pot.

Huo Kuo

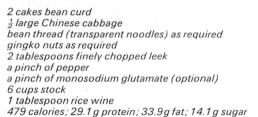

14 ounces ground pork
oil for frying
3 eggs
salt
cornstarch as required
5 dried Chinese mushrooms, presoaked
1 piece steamed white fish
7 ounces snails or oysters

2 cakes bean curd
½ large Chinese cabbage
bean thread (transparent noodles) as required
gingko nuts as required
2 tablespoons finely chopped leek
a pinch of pepper
a pinch of monosodium glutamate (optional)
6 cups stock
1 tablespoon rice wine
479 calories; 29.1 g protein; 33.9 g fat; 14.1 g sugar

1. Mix the ground pork in a bowl with 1 egg, the chopped leek, ½ teaspoon of salt, a pinch of monosodium glutamate, and a pinch of pepper. Mix by hand until smooth and homogeneous.

2. Use ¾ of this mixture to shape small balls 1-inch in diameter; lower carefully into plenty of very hot oil; turn off the heat immediately. Wait 3 minutes and then turn on the heat again. Fry briskly.

3. Beat 2 eggs well with a pinch of salt and 1 tablespoon cornstarch dissolved in water. Heat a little oil and fry the egg mixture to make a very thin rectangular omelet, rather like a crepe, measuring 6 × 8 inches; spread the remaining ground meat very carefully over it; sprinkle with a little more salt and monosodium

1

2

3

4

5

6

glutamate (optional), and then with 4 tablespoons cornstarch. Roll up and steam for 8 minutes.

4. Drain the mushrooms. Remove the stems, and slice the caps thinly. Cut the fish into several pieces. Drain the

canned snails or, if oysters are to be used, clean well. Blanch the bean curd in boiling water for 1 minute. Drain and cut into slices.

5. Boil the Chinese cabbage in salted water; chop into pieces 1½ inches wide; soften

the bean thread in boiling water, drain and cut into 4½-inch lengths. Boil the gingko nuts (canned nuts are most practical) and peel off the thin inner skin.

6. Line the bottom of the hot pot with the cabbage. Arrange

the other ingredients as shown on the facing page, pour over the cooking stock and add 2 teaspoons salt, a pinch of pepper and the rice wine. Simmer until all ingredients are tender.

Seafood hot pot

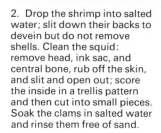

1 whole white fish or 10 ounces fish fillets
5 large shrimp
1 squid
10 clams
3½ ounces pork belly
10 ounces Chinese white radish
1 leek
a small piece of ginger root
petals of Chinese spring chrysanthemum flowers (not the
    normal garden variety) as desired
1 tablespoon peanut oil
1 tablespoon rice wine
2 teaspoons salt
a pinch of monosodium glutamate (optional)
a pinch of pepper
soy sauce
vinegar
ginger root, finely chopped
325 calories; 42.8g protein; 13.8g fat; 4.8g sugar

1. Scale and gut the fish; cut away the gills. Cut in half by running a knife down the backbone, work both sides carefully away from bones. Cut into bite-size pieces; reserve the head which will be included in the dish.

2. Drop the shrimp into salted water; slit down their backs to devein but do not remove shells. Clean the squid: remove head, ink sac, and central bone, rub off the skin, and slit and open out; score the inside in a trellis pattern and then cut into small pieces. Soak the clams in salted water and rinse them free of sand.

3. Cut the pork into 2-inch pieces.

4. Wash and peel the Chinese white radish, cut into pieces 1 inch wide, 2 inches long, and ¼ inch thick.

5. Slice the leek diagonally into 1-inch sections; slice the ginger very thinly; wash the chrysanthemum flowers and pluck off the petals.

6. Heat the peanut oil in the wok, stir-fry the leek and the ginger until they release their aroma, sprinkle with rice wine and pour in 6 cups hot water. Add the pork and Chinese white radish; season with salt and monosodium glutamate (optional). Cook until the vegetables are quite tender.

7. Transfer to the hot pot or an earthenware cooking pot, bring back to a boil, and add the fish (including the head) and clams followed by the shrimp and squid. Add the chrysanthemum petals, sprinkle with a pinch of pepper, and serve. Pass around soy sauce mixed with vinegar and finely chopped ginger as a dipping sauce.

Rice Dishes

When one Chinese person meets another the customary greeting is: "Chueh fan mei-yu?" – literally, "Eat rice? Yes? No?" It is the Chinese equivalent of the English "How are you?" The Chinese phrase reveals the fundamental importance of rice in the everyday life of millions of Chinese.

Rice has been a staple food in China for over four thousand years. There is a vast number of different varieties of rice grown in China – some say as many as seven thousand, but this is certainly an exaggeration. The polishing of rice is an ancient custom: twenty-five hundred years ago Confucius wrote that rice should be clean and white. When cooked, the rice grains should be fluffy and separate, and the knowledgeable Chinese cook will take great care to wash the rice very thoroughly before cooking (thus, incidentally, removing some of the nutritional value). Only certain varieties, such as glutinous rice, with its short, round grains, should be sticky; it is used for special dishes and puddings, desserts, and sweets.

In the recipes which follow, it should be noted that, unless otherwise stated or where the recipe obviously calls for uncooked rice, the weights given are for cooked rice. As a very approximate guide, uncooked rice yields roughly two-and-a-half times its uncooked weight, absorbing a great deal of water as it cooks.

Yangzhou fried rice

Known incorrectly as "Cantonese rice," this dish can be the last course in an elaborate meal or can be served on its own as a light and nourishing one-course meal.

3–4 dried Chinese mushrooms
sugar
soy sauce
sesame oil
3½ ounces shrimp
½ egg white
1 teaspoon cornstarch
oil for frying
5 ounces chicken breast
½ egg white
1 teaspoon cornstarch
5 ounces cold roast pork
½ cup peas
2 large eggs, beaten
2 teaspoons salt
3 cups cooked rice
a pinch of pepper
1–2 tablespoons rice wine
784 calories; 44.6 g protein; 20.2 g fat; 100.5 g sugar

1. Soak the mushrooms for 20 minutes in warm water, rinse, and remove stems; sprinkle with a mixture of a little sugar, soy sauce, and sesame oil and chop into pieces ½-inch square.

2. Wash the shrimp if raw, and shell; devein with a toothpick or cocktail stick, mix by hand with the ½ egg white and cornstarch and then stir-fry very lightly in oil at a temperature of 250°F. (120°C.). Drain.

3. Dice the chicken into ½-inch cubes, mix by hand with the other ½ egg white and cornstarch, and stir-fry in medium-hot oil taking care that the cubes do not stick to one another.

4. Dice the pork into ½-inch cubes. If frozen peas are used, cover with boiling water and then drain well. If fresh peas are used, boil briefly in lightly salted water.

5. Heat 1–2 tablespoons oil in a wok; pour in the beaten eggs, stir and, when cooked, cut into pieces about ½-inch square.

6. Clean the wok and heat 3–4 tablespoons fresh oil, add the mushrooms, pork, shrimp, and chicken. Stir-fry over a moderate heat; season with 1 teaspoon salt.

7. When these ingredients have absorbed the oil and salt, add the cooked rice (it should be tender but firm); mix and turn thoroughly to keep the ingredients from sticking.

8. Add the peas and the cooked egg, season with the remaining salt and pepper, sprinkle with the rice wine, and stir-fry over a high heat, taking care that the rice does not stick and that the grains remain separate.

Five-color fried rice

A delicious dish which can be prepared
quickly and served to special guests.

3 dried Chinese mushrooms
2 ounces cooked ham
3½ ounces pork
1 leek
2 eggs
3½ ounces shrimp
a pinch of salt
a pinch of monosodium glutamate (optional)
3 tablespoons oil
2 teaspoons soy sauce
a pinch of monosodium glutamate (optional)
a pinch of pepper
4 tablespoons lard or cooking fat
4 bowls (up to 1¾ pounds) precooked rice, (preferably boiled 24
    hours in advance)
scant ½ teaspoon salt
a pinch of monosodium glutamate (optional)
1–2 tablespoons peas, precooked
617 calories; 19.3 g protein; 30.3 g fat; 84.2 g sugar

1. Soak the mushrooms in warm water for 20 minutes, remove the stems, and cut the caps into $\frac{1}{4}$-inch squares. Dice the ham and pork to the same size; chop the leek finely. Shell the shrimp and chop into pieces $\frac{1}{4}$ inch thick.

2. Beat the eggs and season with salt and monosodium glutamate (optional). Heat 1 tablespoon oil in a wok; pour in the eggs and scramble, set aside on a plate.

3. Wipe the wok and heat 2 tablespoons fresh oil; stir-fry the mushrooms gently over a moderate heat until their full aroma is released.

4. Add the pork and stir-fry, stirring to keep the cubes from sticking to one another; when the pork has changed color, add the shrimp and the ham. Fry lightly.

5. Once the shrimp have changed color, if raw, or have heated through, if precooked, pour in 2 teaspoons soy sauce, trickling it down the inside of the wok; stir and turn, giving the soy sauce time to flavor the other ingredients, and then season with a pinch each of monosodium glutamate (optional) and pepper. Remove ingredients from the wok and set aside.

6. Clean the wok, pour in 4 tablespoons oil and heat; stir-fry the leek to flavor the oil but do not allow it to brown.

7. Add the rice and stir-fry over a moderate heat, stirring and turning continuously, taking care not to crush the rice grains. Season with $\frac{1}{2}$ teaspoon salt and a pinch of monosodium glutamate (optional).

8. When the rice is well mixed and coated with oil, add the reserved ingredients and stir-fry; add the scrambled egg and peas and mix once more before serving.

Fried rice with smoked salmon and chicken

20'

$3\frac{1}{2}$–5 ounces smoked salmon
7–8 tablespoons oil
$3\frac{1}{2}$ ounces chicken breast
2 eggs
a pinch of salt
a pinch of monosodium glutamate (optional)
a pinch of pepper
3–4 lettuce leaves
2 level tablespoons finely chopped leek
4 bowls (up to $1\frac{3}{4}$ pounds precooked rice, boiled 24 hours in
    advance)
Marinade for chicken:
1 teaspoon rice wine
$\frac{1}{4}$ teaspoon salt
a pinch of monosodium glutamate (optional)
a pinch of pepper
$\frac{1}{2}$ teaspoon cornstarch
619 calories; 23.1 g protein; 28.5 g fat; 64.7 g sugar

1. Lightly brown both sides of the salmon in 1–2 tablespoons oil; remove the bones and skin and flake finely. Shred the chicken and sprinkle with the marinade.

2. Beat the eggs, and season with salt and monosodium glutamate (optional). Cut the lettuce into $\frac{1}{4}$-inch strips.

3. Heat 1 tablespoon of oil in the wok, pour in the eggs, and mix with chopsticks or a fork so that the eggs will scramble into small pieces. Set aside on a plate. Wipe the wok and pour in 2 tablespoons of oil; stir-fry the chicken and, when cooked, remove from the wok and set aside.

4. Clean the wok and heat 3 tablespoons of fresh oil. Stir-fry the chopped leek without allowing it to color, add the rice, and stir-fry, mixing very gently but thoroughly. Add the salmon and chicken; stir-fry, stirring and turning. Season to taste with salt, pepper, and monosodium glutamate (optional).

5. Finally mix in the eggs and lettuce and stir-fry briefly before serving.

Curried fried rice with shrimp

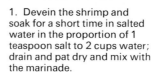 25'

7 ounces shrimp, raw or precooked, shelled
salt
4 dried Chinese mushrooms
1 small onion
1–2 tablespoons peas
5 tablespoons oil
1 tablespoon Chinese curry powder
1 tablespoon soy sauce
a pinch of monosodium glutamate (optional)
4 bowls (up to 1¾ pounds precooked rice, boiled 24 hours in
   advance)
Marinade for the shrimp:
1 teaspoon rice wine
a pinch of salt
a pinch of monosodium glutamate (optional)
½ teaspoon cornstarch
282 calories; 13.2 g protein; 18 g fat; 67.7 g sugar

1. Devein the shrimp and soak for a short time in salted water in the proportion of 1 teaspoon salt to 2 cups water; drain and pat dry and mix with the marinade.

2. Soak the mushrooms in water for 20 minutes, remove the stems, and dice the caps into ½-inch cubes. Dice the onion to the same dimensions and boil the peas in lightly salted water.

3. Heat 1 tablespoon oil in the wok; stir-fry the shrimp briskly, removing from the wok when just heated through.

4. Heat 1 tablespoon fresh oil in the wok and stir-fry the mushrooms for a few seconds, then set aside.

5. Clean the wok, heat 3 tablespoons oil, and stir-fry the onion until it is transparent and soft; lower the heat and add the curry powder; cook, stirring for a couple of minutes. Return the mushrooms to the wok and stir-fry gently. Trickle the soy sauce down the inside of the wok; once this is thoroughly warmed through, add the rice and stir-fry, stirring and turning gently but thoroughly. Season with salt and a pinch of monosodium glutamate (optional).

6. Finally, add the shrimp and peas and distribute evenly before serving.

Pai fan (boiled rice)

As in all the preceding recipes, long-grain rice should be used; its low starch content means that the grains should not stick to one another.

4–6 servings:
2⅔ cups Chinese uncooked long-grain rice
2¼ cups water
½ teaspoon peanut oil or corn oil (optional)
359 calories; 7.5 g protein; 0.8 g fat; 85.6 g sugar

1. Place the rice in a strainer and rinse under fast-running cold water.

2. Place the rice in a heavy cooking pot or saucepan and add water. Half a teaspoon oil may be added at this stage – this decreases the chances of the rice boiling over.

3. Bring the rice to a boil over a medium-high heat. When the water bubbles up, stir once with a fork to distribute the rice grains and help prevent lumping. Cover and cook for 1 minute before reducing the heat to low. Simmer for 10 minutes.

4. Turn off the heat and leave to finish cooking with the retained heat for 10 to 12 minutes longer. The rice is done when the grains are dry and separate and there are small holes or depressions in the surface of the rice.

Pork chops with boiled rice

A good snack or light, quickly prepared meal.

4 slices loin of pork, weighing about 3½ ounces each
7 ounces Chinese salted mustard top or other Chinese salted vegetable
4 eggs
a small piece of ginger root
4 tablespoons oil
4 bowls (up to 1¾ pounds precooked boiled rice)
1 cup water
For the marinade:
4 tablespoons soy sauce
2 tablespoons sugar
1 tablespoon rice wine
For the sauce:
2 teaspoons soy sauce
1 teaspoon sugar
1 teaspoon wine vinegar
695 calories; 33 g protein; 28.7 g fat; 72.2 g sugar

1. Pound the pork with the flat of the cleaver blade; snip or make small cuts where there is any fat or gristle, so that the meat does not curl when cooked.

2. Mix the marinade ingredients, sprinkle over the pork, stir and turn to distribute evenly, and leave for about 20 minutes.

3. Rinse the preserved vegetables in cold water; slice vertically into ¾-inch strips and then into small pieces.

4. Hard-boil and peel the eggs. Shred the ginger.

5. Heat 2 tablespoons oil in the wok, fry the drained pork well on both sides so that it is well browned, pour in the reserved marinade, and add the hard-boiled eggs. Cook, stirring and turning until the outsides of the eggs are lightly colored. Pour in 1 cup hot water, reduce the heat to moderate, and cook for about 10 minutes, mixing from time to time so that the ingredients color evenly.

6. Heat 2 tablespoons oil in another pan or skillet, stir-fry the ginger, and then add the preserved vegetables. Fry and add the sauce ingredients.

7. Arrange the boiled rice in the serving dish and top with the vegetables, pork, and the halved eggs. Sprinkle with the liquid left in the wok after step 5.

Boiled rice with pork and vegetables

Served piping hot, this dish can provide a meal in itself. It is best accompanied by hot green tea or a light vegetable broth.

7 ounces thinly sliced pork
7 ounces spinach or other green leafy vegetable
4 dried Chinese mushrooms
$3\frac{1}{2}$ ounces bamboo shoots
scant 1 tablespoon cornstarch
2 teaspoons sugar
a pinch of monosodium glutamate (optional)
a pinch of pepper
1 cup water
4 tablespoons oil
$\frac{1}{3}$ teaspoon salt
2 tablespoons soy sauce
1 tablespoon rice wine
4 bowls (up to $1\frac{3}{4}$ pounds) precooked boiled rice
For the marinade:
2 teaspoons soy sauce
2 teaspoons rice wine
1 teaspoon sugar
1 teaspoon cornstarch
527 calories; 17.8g protein; 17.6g fat; 73.5g sugar

1
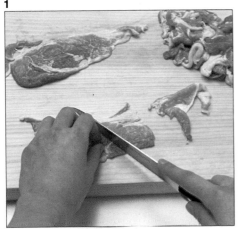

2

3

4
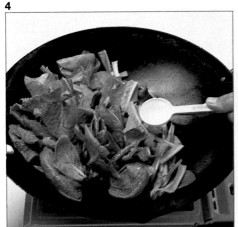

5
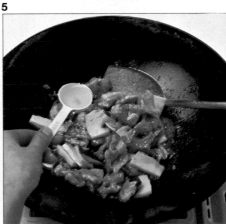

6

1. Cut the pork into bite-size pieces, mix with the marinade and leave to stand. Wash the spinach, cut into pieces about 2 inches wide, and leave in cold water to crisp until needed.

2. Soak the mushrooms in water for 20 minutes; when plump, remove the stems and slice the caps thinly and obliquely. Slice the bamboo shoots very thinly.

3. Mix the cornstarch, sugar, monosodium glutamate (optional), and pepper in a bowl with the water.

4. Heat $1\frac{1}{2}$ tablespoons oil in the wok, add the drained spinach with $\frac{1}{3}$ teaspoon salt and a very little water, and stir-fry. Drain and set aside.

5. Heat $2\frac{1}{2}$ tablespoons oil in the wok and stir-fry the mushrooms. Add the pork and, when the meat has changed color, add the bamboo shoots; sprinkle with 2 tablespoons soy sauce and 1 tablespoon rice wine.

6. Pour the mixture prepared in step 3 into the wok and, when it has come to a boil, add the spinach and cook, stirring and turning, until the sauce thickens; place on top of the hot boiled rice.

257

Rice with beef and eggs

$3\frac{1}{2}$ ounces thinly sliced prime lean beef
6 eggs
$\frac{1}{4}$ teaspoon salt
a pinch of monosodium glutamate (optional)
a pinch of pepper
1 leek
1 tablespoon soy sauce
4 tablespoons oil
2 cups oil for deep-frying
4 bowls (up to $1\frac{3}{4}$ pounds) precooked, boiled rice
For the marinade:
$\frac{1}{2}$ teaspoon ginger juice
$\frac{1}{2}$ teaspoon sugar
$\frac{1}{2}$ tablespoon rice wine
$\frac{1}{2}$ teaspoon baking powder or $\frac{1}{4}$ teaspoon dried yeast and
    $\frac{1}{4}$ teaspoon bicarbonate of soda
1 tablespoon cornstarch
2 tablespoons water
676 calories; 19.4g protein; 35.1g fat; 67.7g sugar

1. Cut the slices of beef into 1-inch pieces, mix with the marinade, and leave to stand for about 30 minutes.

2. Beat the eggs and season with the salt, monosodium glutamate (optional), and pepper.

3. Slice the leek into $\frac{1}{4}$-inch rings.

4. Mix the marinated meat with 1 tablespoon soy sauce and 1 tablespoon oil just before frying.

5. Heat the 2 cups oil for deep-frying to 325°F. (160°C.). Drain the beef and add to the oil; lower the temperature and deep-fry the beef taking care that the pieces do not stick to one another. Once the beef has changed color, remove, drain, and place together with the beaten egg.

6. Heat 3 tablespoons oil in the wok, stir-fry the leek gently, and add the beaten eggs and meat; fry over a high heat until the bottom of the egg is set and the upper portion has thickened. Turn off the heat.

7. Place the hot rice in a serving dish and arrange the beef and egg on top.

Savory rice

7 ounces thinly sliced pork
4 dried Chinese mushrooms
1 dried squid
2 cups water
1 teaspoon bicarbonate of soda
3 tablespoons Chinese dried shrimp
2 ounces Chinese sausage (or any dense, savory sausage, preferably pork)
1 leek
a small bunch of parsley
1 egg
a pinch of salt
a pinch of monosodium glutamate (optional)
5 tablespoons oil
4 tablespoons soy sauce
a pinch of monosodium glutamate (optional)
a pinch of pepper
$4\frac{1}{2}$ cups rice, uncooked long-grain rice
948 calories; 43.6 g protein; 30 g fat; 121.7 g sugar

1. Cut the pork into $\frac{1}{2}$-inch squares; soak the mushrooms in water, for 20 minutes, remove the stems, and cut the caps into pieces $\frac{1}{2}$ inch square.

2. Soften the dried squid by soaking in the water and bicarbonate of soda overnight. Cut vertically into $\frac{1}{2}$-inch strips and then into small pieces. Rinse the shrimp and drain.

3. Slice the sausage lengthwise into 6–8 strips and then into small pieces; slice the leek finely and chop the parsley.

4. Beat the egg and season lightly with salt and monosodium glutamate (optional). Cook 1 or 2 thin omelets and cut into strips.

5. Heat the oil in the wok; stir-fry the mushrooms for a few seconds, add the shrimp, and fry until they are heated through. Add the leek, pork, squid, and sausage in that order and fry, stirring and turning; sprinkle with soy sauce, monosodium glutamate (optional), and pepper.

6. Cook the rice in slightly less water than usual; when nearly done top with the contents of the wok, including the liquid; continue cooking until the rice is tender. Turn off the heat, cover, and leave to stand for a short while. Mix and transfer to a serving bowl, topping with the strips of omelet and the parsley.

Congee rice with taro root

This rice gruel is eaten for breakfast or as a snack at any time of day. Served with pickled and salted green vegetables, it becomes a full meal.

4–6 servings:
1½ cups round, short-grain rice, uncooked
¼ cup Chinese dried shrimp
1 leek
4 dried Chinese mushrooms
8–10 cups stock or water
10 ounces taro root (similar to potato in texture, but more glutinous)
5 ounces pork
3–4 tablespoons peanut oil
1–2 teaspoons salt
1 tablespoon rice wine
a pinch of pepper
½ teaspoon sesame oil
515 calories; 13.6g protein; 21.9g fat; 64.9g sugar

1. Wash the rice in a strainer under running water until the water runs clear. Drain. Wash the dried shrimps and drain well. Reserve the water used. Chop the leek finely.

2. Soak the mushrooms in water for 20 minutes, remove the stems and cut the caps into small cubes. Add the shrimp water to the stock.

3. Peel the taro root and dice; boil rapidly but briefly to remove the gelatinous quality. Dice the pork to the same size.

4. Heat the peanut oil in the wok, stir-fry the leek over a low heat, add the shrimp, and stir-fry until both release their aromas.

5. Add the mushrooms, followed by the pork. Stir-fry until the pork is well-cooked and then add the rice.

6. Stir and turn the rice well so that the grains are coated with oil. Transfer to a large, heavy cooking pot; pour in the stock, bring to a boil, skim, and then lower the heat.

7. Season with salt and rice wine; cover and cook for about 20 to 30 minutes, stirring every now and then. Add the taro root.

8. Cook, still covered, for about 1 hour longer over a low heat, stirring occasionally, bringing the rice from the bottom of the pan up to the top. If the rice tastes too bland, add a little salt. Season with a pinch of pepper and a few drops of sesame oil. The rice should look rather like porridge and be thick but soft.

261

Congee rice with chicken

Congee rice is a Chinese national standby, equally popular at breakfast, midday, or evening. Some restaurants specialize in various types of Congee rice: with chicken, as in this recipe, or more luxuriously, with abalone, porgy, shrimp, and crab.

5 cups water
a 7-ounce piece of chicken breast
1 small piece of ginger
1 leek
1 dried scallop
2 cups round, short-grain rice, uncooked
a pinch of salt
a pinch of monosodium glutamate (optional)
4 eggs
4 teaspoons soy sauce
4 teaspoons sesame oil
496 calories; 22.1 g protein; 19.7 g fat; 54.4 g sugar

1. Bring 5 cups water to a boil; boil the chicken until well done, removing any scum which forms.

2. Drain the cooked chicken and allow it to cool until it can be handled. Cut it into $\frac{1}{2}$-inch cubes and strain the stock.

3. Slice the ginger thinly and then shred. Cut the leek into 2-inch sections; slit these sections open so the layers can be opened out; cut into fine strips.

4. Soak the scallop in boiling water to allow it to soften and swell; tear into small shreds by hand; reserve the water used for soaking.

5. Wash the rice well in running water, drain, and place in a heavy cooking pot with the scallop and 10 cups of liquid made up from the chicken stock, scallop water, and, if necessary, a little more water. Bring to a boil and then reduce the heat.

6. Cook for about 30 minutes, stirring from time to time, season with salt and monosodium glutamate (optional); add the chicken and cook for a further 10 to 15 minutes. By this time the mixture should resemble a thick soup.

7. Place an egg in each individual bowl, top with a few strips each of ginger and leek, 1 teaspoon soy sauce, and 1 teaspoon sesame oil.

8. Pour the boiling rice into the bowls and serve immediately providing each person with a Chinese spoon with which to mix and eat the rice.

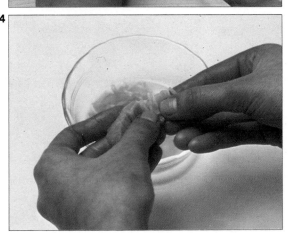

Fujian glutinous rice

This round rice is creamy white and resembles seed pearls when uncooked; it has a sticky texture when cooked and, in this recipe, forms the basis of a highly flavored dish best accompanied by hot tea or a light vegetable broth.

8–10 servings:
5 generous cups uncooked glutinous rice
1 cup fresh, unsalted, unroasted peanuts
2 ounces dried Chinese mushrooms
1 pound pork
1 leek
2 ounces Chinese dried shrimp
10 tablespoons oil
10 tablespoons soy sauce
a pinch of monosodium glutamate (optional)
a pinch of pepper
1 small bunch of parsley, finely chopped
sweet pickled ginger (optional)
538 calories; 20.5 g protein; 29.6 g fat; 95.6 g sugar

1. Wash the glutinous rice thoroughly and leave to soak in cold water overnight; drain. Boil the peanuts in water until tender, rinse in cold water and drain.

2. Soak the mushrooms in water for 20 minutes, remove the stems, and cut the caps into fairly wide strips approximately 1 inch long. Cut the meat into strips of the same size. Slice the leek into thin rings. Wash the shrimp and drain.

3. Heat 5 tablespoons oil in the wok to medium hot. Add the rice and fry, mixing and turning so that each grain is coated with oil. Add the peanuts.

4. Pour in 5 tablespoons soy sauce and continue to fry, stirring and turning so that the rice colors evenly.

5. Place the bamboo steamer over boiling water, line it with a damp piece of cheesecloth, and sprinkle the rice over the cloth, poking small holes at intervals to allow the steam to circulate freely. Cook over rapidly boiling water for about 1 hour; top up the water in the wok with boiling water when necessary.

6. Heat 5 tablespoons oil in the wok; stir-fry the mushrooms for a few seconds, push them to one side of the pan, and stir-fry the shrimp and leek in turn.

7. When the leek is very lightly browned, combine all the ingredients in the wok and stir-fry; add 5 tablespoons soy sauce and stir-fry, mixing continuously; add the pork, followed by the monosodium glutamate (optional) and the pepper.

8. Once the rice is tender, transfer it to a heated serving dish, add the other ingredients, and mix well. Serve into individual bowls and garnish with chopped parsley and little heaps of pickled ginger.

Steamed rice in lotus leaf casing

12 servings:
6 ounces coarsely chopped chicken breast
4 ounces chopped shrimp
1 teaspoon salt
½ teaspoon monosodium glutamate (optional)
1 tablespoon cornstarch
1 fresh lotus leaf or dried leaf soaked overnight in cold water
5 tablespoons peanut oil
4 ounces roast duck, coarsely chopped
*4–5 dried Chinese mushrooms (*tung ku *variety), presoaked,*
*   finely sliced with stems removed*
1 carrot, diced small
about 4½ cups precooked, steamed, long-grain rice – 1½ cups
*   uncooked rice will yield this quantity*
680 calories; 41.5g protein; 18.2g fat; 93.3g sugar

1. Mix the chicken and shrimp with the salt, the monosodium glutamate (optional) and the cornstarch and leave to stand for a few minutes.

2. Wash the lotus leaf, pat dry, and brush the inside with oil.

3. Heat 3 tablespoons oil in the wok and stir-fry the chicken, duck, and shrimp for about 1 minute. Remove and set aside.

4. In the remaining oil, stir-fry the mushrooms for 1 minute. Pour in 2 tablespoons fresh oil and fry the rice until it is lightly colored.

5. Add the chicken, duck, and shrimp, followed by the carrot and stir-fry over a moderate heat for 1½ minutes.

6. Place the rice in the lotus leaf and fold the leaf over the rice, enclosing it in a neat package. Steam in the preheated bamboo steamer for 15 minutes. Serve very hot.

Noodles

In those parts of China far from the main rice-growing areas, wheat and other cereal crops are sown to provide people with an alternative source of starch in their diet. Many different types of bread are eaten in China but there is a far greater variety of noodles, which are usually made with wheat flour but also with rice or soy flour.

Most Chinese noodles are in the form of long straight sticks. The length is due to a tradition which remains particularly strong in the northern regions of China; this legend maintains that long noodles symbolize long life; for this reason they are usually included in the main dish of a birthday feast. It is supposed to be bad luck to cut the noodles before they are presented to the guests.

Noodles can be eaten as a snack, or they may form the basis of an entire meal. At banquets, dishes are not usually accompanied by rice, but the end of the meal is often signaled by the appearance of fried rice or noodles.

Chow Mein, which consists of fried noodles with vegetables and meat, is often eaten as a meal in itself. Noodles in broth are as just as popular, making a nourishing hot dish when meat or vegetables are added.

A dish of cold noodles with sliced cucumber and chicken or other ingredients is often served as a first course but can equally well appear as one of the main dishes in a meal.

Chicken and noodle casserole

Like most Chinese noodle recipes, this can be served as a meal in itself; it is economical and simple to prepare.

4–6 servings:
½ chicken
5 ounces spinach
⅓ leek
a small piece of ginger
2 tablespoons rice wine
7–10 cups water
1–2 teaspoons salt
2 bundles (approximately ½ pound) Chinese egg noodles
464 calories; 16.6g protein; 2.8g fat; 88.9g sugar

1. Wash the chicken, place in a large pan of boiling water and blanch to remove any residue of blood, etc.

2. Wash the spinach very thoroughly; cut into 1½-inch lengths. Bring the flat of the cleaver blade sharply down on the leek and ginger for fuller release of flavor.

1

2

3

4

5

6

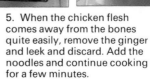

3. Place the chicken in a large cooking pot, preferably earthenware, together with the leek and ginger. Add the rice wine and salt, followed by 7–10 cups water to cover the chicken.

4. Place the cooking pot over a high heat and bring to a boil; lower the heat and skim. Cover and cook for about 1 hour, scimming whenever necessary. Boil the noodles until tender but still firm.

5. When the chicken flesh comes away from the bones quite easily, remove the ginger and leek and discard. Add the noodles and continue cooking for a few minutes.

6. Add the spinach and cook until tender but still slightly crisp; adjust the seasoning by adding a little more salt if needed.

Chinese egg noodles in broth with meat and vegetables

The delicate taste of this dish is enlivened by soy sauce. The eggs, meat, vegetables, and natural flavorings make a nourishing combination which can be varied as desired.

4 bundles fresh or dried Chinese egg noodles
8 cups stock (see recipe on page 296)
2 hard-boiled eggs
12 thin slices cold roast pork
$3\frac{1}{2}$ ounces bamboo shoots
1 pound spinach or other green leafy vegetable
$\frac{1}{2}$ leek
a little oil for frying
To flavor the stock:
$\frac{1}{3}$ leek
1 clove garlic
a small piece of ginger root
2 cups soy sauce
$\frac{1}{3}$ cup rice wine
2 tablespoons sweet rice wine
638 calories; 26.4g protein; 9.9g fat; 102.7g sugar

1

1. Heat plenty of water to the boiling point in a wok or large saucepan; shake and pull the noodles apart and boil 1–2 bundles at a time, so that they can spread out and cook more successfully.

2. Stir from time to time so that the noodles do not stick together.

3. Once the water has returned to a boil, pour in a little cold water (about 1 cup) and continue cooking.

4. Draw one of the noodles out of the boiling water with chopsticks; if it does not slide back through them it is done. Drain at once. The noodles should be cooked at the last minute just before they are served.

5. While the noodles are cooking, prepare the flavoring for the stock: stir-fry the coarsely chopped leek, garlic, and ginger and, once these are lightly browned, add the soy sauce, rice wine, and sweet rice wine.

6. Place 2–2½ tablespoons of this flavoring in each of 4 heated serving bowls; pour an equal amount of boiling hot stock into each bowl.

7. Add the well-drained, piping hot noodles to the bowls.

8. Top each bowl of noodles with a half hard-boiled egg, cut into a decorative flower shape, 3 slices of pork, and some slices boiled bamboo shoots together with the lightly boiled spinach or other green vegetable. Garnish with very finely chopped leek.

5

2

6

3

7

4

8

Noodles with pork and soybean paste

A truly robust and full-flavored recipe in which the pork is cooked with star anise and soybean paste.

4 bundles Chinese noodles (preferably fresh)
1 pound boned, rolled, and very firmly tied shoulder of pork
2 tablespoons soybean paste
2½ cups water
4 tablespoons cane sugar
3 ounces boiled fresh or canned tender (winter) bamboo shoots
⅓ leek
approximately ½ pound spinach
2 tablespoons lard or cooking fat
a pinch of salt
a pinch of pepper
7 cups stock (see recipe on page 296)
To flavor:
3½ tablespoons soy sauce
3 tablespoons rice wine
2–3 star anise
For the sauce:
4 tablespoons soy sauce
3 tablespoons rice wine
⅔ teaspoon salt
1019 calories; 39.9g protein; 48g fat; 108.5g sugar

1. Rub the pork all over with the soybean paste and leave to stand for 2 hours.

2. Place the flavoring ingredients (soy sauce, rice wine, and star anise) in the wok, bring to a boil, and add the pork in its covering of soybean paste. Cook the pork, turning very frequently, and, when it is well moistened on all sides, pour in $2\frac{1}{2}$ cups boiling water. Reduce the heat.

3. Cover the wok and cook for about 30 minutes over a low heat.

4. Add the sugar and simmer for about 1 hour, turning the pork now and then. The pork will absorb the liquid and flavoring and turn a rich brown color.

5. Boil the bamboo shoots; slice into small, diagonal pieces. Cut the leek into $1\frac{1}{2}$-inch sections. Trim the spinach, wash well, and cut in half.

6. Heat the lard or cooking fat in the wok; add the salt and stir-fry the spinach and leek briskly. Add the bamboo shoots and stir-fry all these vegetables together briefly; season with a pinch of salt and a pinch of pepper and turn off the heat.

7. Boil the noodles in plenty of water until tender; drain and place in a heated serving bowl; top with the pork, carved into thin slices, and the spinach.

8. Add the sauce ingredients to the stock, bring to a boil and pour into the serving dish.

Chinese noodles with scrambled eggs and leeks

1 leek
5 ounces shrimp
4 tablespoons lard or cooking fat
a small piece of ginger root
4 eggs
4 bundles fresh Chinese egg noodles
8 cups stock (see recipe on page 296)
1 tablespoon salt
$\frac{1}{4}$ cup rice wine
For the marinade:
$\frac{1}{4}$ teaspoon salt
$\frac{1}{2}$ tablespoon rice wine
1 teaspoon cornstarch.
645 calories; 204g protein; 19.8g fat; 92.3g sugar

1. Wash the leek and cut into 1-inch lengths.

2. Devein the shrimps and mix with the marinade of salt, rice wine, and cornstarch.

3. Heat 2 tablespoons lard or cooking fat in a wok; add the shrimp and stir-fry briskly over a high heat for a minute or two; remove from the wok and set aside.

4. Chop the ginger and stir-fry in the remaining fat in the wok; add the leek and stir-fry.

5. When the leek is soft, add the shrimp, heat through and add the beaten eggs. Mix well over a high heat, combining all the ingredients in the wok. Divide the contents into 4 portions and set aside to keep warm.

6. Boil the noodles in plenty of water, drain well, and divide among 4 individual heated bowls.

7. Bring the stock to a boil quickly, adding 1 tablespoon salt and $\frac{1}{4}$ cup rice wine. Pour the boiling stock into the bowls and top each with a portion of the shrimp-leek-and-egg mixture.

Sichuan noodles with pork

a small piece of ginger root
2 tablespoons peanut oil
7 ounces ground pork
2 tablespoons soy sauce
2 tablespoons rice wine
1 leek
1 large piece of Chinese pickled, salted mustard top (za-zai)
4 bundles fresh Chinese egg noodles
8 cups stock (see recipe on page 296)
To flavor:
8 tablespoons soy sauce
2 tablespoons vinegar
2 tablespoons ground sesame seeds
1⅓ teaspoons chili oil
2 teaspoons sesame oil
714 calories; 22.5g protein; 26.7g fat; 94.7g sugar

1. Chop the ginger finely.

2. Heat the peanut oil in the wok and stir-fry the ginger; as soon as it starts to release its aroma, add the ground pork, stirring and turning while frying to keep the meat from lumping.

3. When the pork is cooked, flavor with the soy sauce and the rice wine.

4. Wash the leek and chop finely.

5. Wash the mustard top throughly and chop.

6. Heat plenty of water in a wok or large saucepan and boil the noodles, untangling them as they cook.

7. Stir the noodles with chopsticks so that they do not stick to each other. As soon as the water boils add ½ cup cold water and then continue cooking until the noodles are tender. Drain well.

8. Mix the flavoring and pour an equal quantity into 4 bowls; pour in the boiling stock and stir.

9. Add the noodles and top with the leek, mustard top, and pork.

Noodles in broth with beef and green peppers

3½ ounces thinly sliced beef
¼ leek
2 green peppers
2 ounces boiled fresh or canned bamboo shoots
2 tablespoons peanut oil
1 teaspoon hot soybean paste
1 cup stock (see recipe on page 296)
1 tablespoon soy sauce
1 tablespoon rice wine
½ teaspoon sugar
2 teaspoons cornstarch
4 bundles fresh Chinese egg noodles
For the marinade:
½ teaspoon ginger juice
1 teaspoon soy sauce
1 teaspoon cornstarch
For the sauce:
7 cups stock
6 tablespoons soy sauce
4 tablespoons rice wine
½ teaspoon salt
536 calories: 15.8 g: 9.2 g fat: 93.8 g sugar

1. Cut the beef into thin strips and mix with the marinade of ginger juice, soy sauce, and cornstarch.

2. Shred the leek, peppers, and bamboo shoots the same size as the beef strips.

3. Heat the peanut oil in a wok and stir-fry the beef and leek strips. Drain and set aside.

4. In the remaining oil lightly stir-fry the peppers and bamboo shoots and then return the beef and leek to the wok.

5. Add the hot soybean paste; stir in 1 cup stock and cook rapidly over a high heat.

6. When the soybean paste has dissolved in the stock, add the soy sauce, rice wine, and sugar. Stir in the cornstarch mixed with 4 teaspoons water to thicken.

7. Boil the noodles in plenty of water, stirring so that they separate. When tender, drain and divide among 4 heated bowls.

8. Bring the sauce ingredients to a boil, pour into the bowls, and top each with a quarter of the beef-and-vegetable mixture from the wok.

Egg noodles with pork and soybean paste

1 leek
3½ ounces boiled fresh or canned bamboo shoots
a small piece of ginger root
⅓ cup peanut oil
7 ounces ground pork
7 ounces soybean sprouts
a few drops of vinegar
3 small or 1 large cucumber
2 eggs
⅓ teaspoon salt
4 bundles fresh Chinese egg noodles
For the sauce:
4 tablespoons soybean paste sweetened with a little sugar
⅓ cup soy sauce
⅔ cup stock (see recipe on page 296)
2 tablespoons sugar
786 calories; 26.7 protein; 29.6 fat; 103.3 sugar

1. Chop the leek, bamboo shoots, and peeled ginger finely.

2. Heat the peanut oil in the wok; stir-fry the pork, keeping the grains of meat separate.

3. Add the leek and ginger and stir-fry until they release their aromas; add the bamboo shoots and continue frying.

4. Mix the sauce ingredients, blending them well, and add to the wok. Cook over a low heat for 15 to 20 minutes, stirring and turning now and then.

5. Wash the bean sprouts thoroughly (remove the little dark seed coverings, as these can make the sprout a little bitter); put in a large pan of boiling water with a few drops of vinegar; when still crisp rinse with cold water and drain.

6. Pare off any small bumps on the cucumber skins, shred the cucumber into strips, and soak in cold water.

7. Beat the eggs with the salt.

8. Heat a little peanut oil in a wok, pour in ¼ of the egg mixture and make a small omelet; set aside and repeat three more times. Cut the omelets into long, thin strips.

9. Boil the noodles in plenty of water until tender but firm, drain well, and divide among four bowls.

10. Top the noodles with the bean sprouts, cucumber and omelet strips, and the pork mixture as illustrated below.

Chinese noodles with chicken and mushrooms in broth

An extremely easy recipe which is tasty and digestible.

½ spring chicken
10 cups water
⅓ leek
a small piece of ginger root
⅓ cup rice wine
½ bamboo shoot, boiled fresh or canned
4 fresh or dried Chinese mushrooms
1 leek
2 tablespoons lard or cooking fat
a pinch of salt
a pinch of pepper
1 tablespoon soy sauce
10 ounces Chinese dried wheat flour noodles, parboiled
parsley
4 bunches Chinese greens or chard
363 calories; 11.9g protein; 7.6g fat; 59g sugar

1. Wash the chicken well. Place in a large saucepan with 10 cups water and the lightly crushed ⅓ leek and ginger. Bring to a boil over a high heat.

2. Once the water has boiled, lower the heat, skim, and boil gently for about 20 minutes; skim frequently.

1

2

3

4

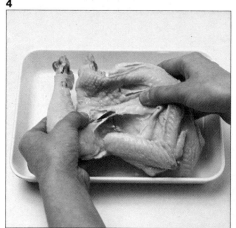

5

6

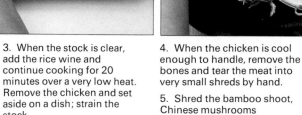

3. When the stock is clear, add the rice wine and continue cooking for 20 minutes over a very low heat. Remove the chicken and set aside on a dish; strain the stock.

4. When the chicken is cool enough to handle, remove the bones and tear the meat into very small shreds by hand.

5. Shred the bamboo shoot, Chinese mushrooms (presoaked for 20 minutes if dried), and the leek; stir-fry in the lard and season with a little salt and pepper. Pour in 6 cups stock.

6. Add the soy sauce, the chicken, and the parboiled noodles; cook for about 5 minutes or until the noodles are tender; and then transfer to a heated serving dish, topping with the parsley and Chinese greens or chard.

Crispy fried noodles

4 bundles Chinese egg noodles, steamed until tender
2 cups lard or cooking fat
3 ounces carrot
3 ounces celery
2 fresh Chinese mushrooms
2 leaves Chinese cabbage
1 clove garlic
3½ ounces very fresh chicken gizzards

1 tablespoon soy sauce
1 tablespoon rice wine or dry sherry
4 ounces raw or cooked shrimp
1 teaspoon ginger juice
1 teaspoon rice wine
1 teaspoon cornstarch
3 ounces pork
2 tablespoons soy sauce
1 teaspoon rice wine or dry sherry
1 teaspoon cornstarch
1 small squid
½ tablespoon cornstarch
4 tablespoons peanut oil
For the sauce:
3 cups stock (see recipe on page 296)
4 tablespoons soy sauce
2 tablespoons sugar
2 tablespoons rice wine
a pinch of salt
To thicken:
2 tablespoons cornstarch
819 calories; 33.1 g protein; 29.8 g fat; 98.8 g sugar

1. Place the steamed noodles in a colander and pour plenty of boiling water over them; drain well. Heat the lard or cooking fat in a wok and stir-fry the noodles until crisp and golden, stirring and turning to prevent burning. Drain. Leave the fat in the wok.

2. Cut the carrot and celery into rectangular pieces; shred the mushrooms; and cut the cabbage into pieces diagonally, working from the base upward. Pound the garlic with the cleaver.

3. Wash the gizzards well; cut open, trim, and score the pieces all over. Marinate in 1 tablespoon each soy sauce and rice wine.

4. Shell and devein the shrimp, removing the heads. Marinate in 1 teaspoon each ginger juice, rice wine, and cornstarch. Mix gently.

5. Cut the pork into small, thin pieces; add 2 tablespoons soy sauce and 1 teaspoon each rice wine and cornstarch. Clean the squid, remove the skin, and open up the body; score the inside surface with a trellis pattern (oblique cuts with the knife at 45 degrees to the working surface) and cut into bite-size pieces. Coat with ½ tablespoon cornstarch.

6. Reheat the fat in the wok up to 350°F. (180°C.) and stir-fry the squid, shrimp, pork, and gizzards, adding them to the fat in this order. Take care that they do not overcook or burn. Set aside when cooked and clean the wok.

7. Heat 4 tablespoons oil in the wok; stir-fry the garlic and, when it starts to release its aroma, add the vegetables prepared in step 2 followed by the ingredients of step 6. Mix the sauce ingredients and pour in. Stir-fry over a high heat.

8. When the mixture is cooked and the vegetables are quite tender, stir in 2 tablespoons cornstarch dissolved in 2 tablespoons water to thicken the sauce. Place the crispy noodles on a warmed serving dish and top with the contents of the wok.

Crispy noodles with chicken

5 ounces chicken breast
1 tablespoon ginger juice
1 tablespoon rice wine
1 teaspoon cornstarch
3 slices cooked ham
$3\frac{1}{2}$ ounces boiled fresh or canned bamboo shoots
4 dried Chinese mushrooms
1 leek
4 tablespoons peanut oil
4 bundles fresh Chinese egg noodles
8 tablespoons lard
For the sauce:
3 cups stock (see recipe on page 296)
$\frac{1}{2}$ tablespoon salt
2 teaspoons sugar
2 tablespoons rice wine
To thicken:
$1\frac{1}{2}$ tablespoons cornstarch
707 calories; 20.8 g protein; 25.1 g fat; 96 g sugar

1. Slice the chicken obliquely into thin strips and mix well with the ginger juice, rice wine and cornstarch.

2. Cut the ham into rectangles $\frac{1}{4}$ inch wide. Slice the bamboo shoots thinly and soak the dried mushrooms in water; when soft cut into thin strips.

3. Cut the leek into 1-inch lengths.

4. Heat 2 tablespoons oil in the wok and stir-fry the chicken; when done, drain and set aside on a plate.

5. Pour 2 tablespoons fresh peanut oil into the wok and stir-fry the mushrooms, bamboo shoots, and leek. Stir in the ham, add the chicken, and stir-fry over a high heat.

6. Mix the sauce ingredients together and pour into the wok; cook for 1 to 2 minutes. Stir in $1\frac{1}{2}$ tablespoons cornstarch mixed with an equal amount of water, to thicken.

7. Boil the noodles in plenty of water until just tender but still firm. Drain and place in a clean wok or skillet containing the melted lard. Stir-fry over a high heat, stirring and turning, until the noodles are crisp and golden.

8. Place the noodles on a serving platter and top with the sauce and vegetables and meat from the wok.

Crispy fried noodles and mixed vegetables

⏱ 20' 🍲 🍴

a 3½-ounce scallop of lean pork
6 leaves Chinese cabbage
1 onion
7 ounces soybean sprouts
½ carrot
2 green peppers
6 cloud-ear fungus
a large piece of ginger root
4 bundles Chinese egg noodles, steamed until tender
6 tablespoons lard or cooking fat
3 tablespoons peanut oil
3 tablespoons Worcestershire sauce
2 tablespoons soy sauce
a pinch of salt
a pinch of pepper
627 calories; 15.6 g protein; 19.7 g fat; 96.8 g sugar

1. Cut the scallop of pork into thin strips diagonally across the grain.

2. Cut the cabbage leaves into small pieces (ordinary cabbage may be used) and the onion into narrow strips.

3. Wash the bean sprouts well and drain.

4. Cut the carrot in half lengthwise, then in pieces, and finally into thin rectangular slivers. Remove seeds, stem, and pith from the peppers and slice into narrow rings or strips.

5. Soak the cloud-ear fungus in water, wash well, trim off any tough sections, and chop.

6. Slice the ginger into thin strips.

7. Place the noodles in a bowl, cover with boiling water, and drain. Heat the lard or cooking fat in a wok and stir-fry the noodles over a high heat.

8. Heat the peanut oil in a skillet, stir-fry the ginger, and as soon as it starts to give off its aroma, add the pork, cabbage, onion, bean sprouts, carrot, peppers, and mushrooms in that order. Stir-fry.

9. When the ingredients are tender, season with the Worcestershire sauce, soy sauce, salt, and pepper; add the noodles; mix; and serve.

Fried rice noodles

1 h 30'

10 ounces rice noodles
1 ounce Chinese dried shrimp
2 dried Chinese mushrooms
$3\frac{1}{2}$ ounces pork
2 medium-size leeks
3 ounces boiled fresh or canned bamboo shoots
$\frac{1}{3}$ carrot
2 green peppers
7 ounces soybean sprouts
7 tablespoons peanut oil
For the sauce:
4 tablespoons rice wine
2 teaspoons salt
$\frac{1}{3}-\frac{1}{2}$ teaspoon sugar
1 tablespoon soy sauce
$\frac{1}{3}$ cup water reserved from soaking the shrimp
524 calories; 13.8g protein; 16.9g fat; 75.5g sugar

1. Place the rice noodles carefully in a large bowl, breaking them as little as possible, cover with plenty of boiling water, leave to stand for 10 minutes, and then drain.

2. Wash the dried shrimp and soak them in warm water for about 1 hour. Reserve the liquid. Soak the mushrooms in water, remove the stems, and cut the caps into thin strips. Cut the pork into bite-size pieces.

3. Slice the leeks into $\frac{1}{4}$-inch rings; cut the bamboo shoots and carrot into rectangles; cut the peppers vertically in half, remove the seeds, and cut into strips.

4. Wash the bean sprouts, pick off the seed covers and thread-like roots, and drain.

5. Heat 3 tablespoons peanut oil in a wok; stir-fry the drained shrimp. Add the pork and continue frying over a moderate heat.

6. When the pork has changed color, add the leek, carrot, and soybean sprouts and stir-fry; add the bamboo shoots, mushrooms, and peppers, and cook briefly.

7. Mix the sauce ingredients and pour into the wok; cook for 1 to 2 minutes, stirring and turning, and then turn off the heat.

8. In another wok, heat 4 tablespoons peanut oil; add the rice noodles and stir-fry until they are well-coated with oil. Add the contents of the other wok and stir-fry briefly over a high heat before serving.

Curried egg noodles and vegetables

7 ounces thinly sliced pork
a pinch of salt
a pinch of pepper
1 rounded teaspoon Chinese curry powder
4½ tablespoons cornstarch
1 onion
4 fresh or canned Chinese mushrooms
7 ounces soybean sprouts
½ carrot
a small piece of ginger root
6 green beans
2 tablespoons lard or cooking fat
2 generous tablespoons Chinese curry powder
2 tablespoons peanut oil
4 bundles fresh Chinese egg noodles
For the sauce:
4 cups stock (see recipe on page 296)
3 tablespoons soy sauce
2 tablespoons Worcestershire sauce
2 tablespoons sugar
1 teaspoon salt
748 calories; 21.5g protein; 26.2g fat; 111.8g sugar

1. Cut the pork into bite-size pieces, add a little salt and pepper, a rounded teaspoon curry powder and ½ tablespoon cornstarch and mix well with the fingers.

2. Cut the onion in half and then into slices ½ inch wide. Cut the stems off the mushrooms and slice the caps into strips ½ in wide.

3. Wash the bean sprouts and drain well. Cut the carrot into rectangles and shred the ginger.

4. String the beans and boil fast until tender but crisp.

5. Heat the lard or cooking fat in a wok, add the ginger and pork, and stir-fry lightly; drain and set aside on a plate.

6. Add the onion, carrot, bean sprouts, and mushrooms to the wok and stir-fry quickly; return the ginger and pork to the wok with 2 tablespoons curry powder. Stir and turn and, when the curry is evenly distributed, pour in the sauce and cook, mixing occasionally.

7. When the vegetables are tender, stir in the remaining 4 tablespoons of cornstarch mixed with 6 tablespoons water to thicken the sauce.

8. Boil the noodles until just tender, rinse quickly with cold water and drain. Heat the oil in a skillet and stir-fry the noodles quickly.

9. Add the noodles to the other ingredients, mix, and serve.

Suzhou sugared noodle cake

An enjoyable dessert which is ready in minutes.

2 bundles dry Chinese egg noodles
½–1 cup lard or fresh cooking fat
confectioner's sugar as required
309 calories; 6.8g protein; 1.3g fat; 55g sugar

1. When buying the noodles, be sure they are within their date-stamp time limit; if too old they will have dried out too much and will be too stale for this recipe. Boil the noodles in plenty of water; drain when not quite cooked through.

2. Heat the lard or cooking fat in the wok and stir-fry the noodles lightly, stirring and turning.

3. When the noodles are well-coated with fat, shape and press into a firm cake, pushing them down into the wok with a wooden spatula.

4. Turn the noodle cake over carefully and fry on the other side until crisp and crunchy, again pressing down to shape. Transfer to a serving plate.

5. Use a fine strainer to dust the top of the cake with the sugar and serve.

Desserts

Soy, that ubiquitous ingredient in Chinese cookery, also plays its part in the preparation of many desserts and sweets, either as one of the main ingredients or in the form of jam or jelly for fillings.

The Chinese make a sweet soup, which is traditionally served between two of the many courses of a banquet celebrating one of their many festivals. The soup is made by skimming off the surface of soybean milk whey, one of the many by-products extracted during the making of bean curd; this substance is then boiled and sweetened with brown sugar. Although their cuisine boasts an infinite number of sweet dishes, solid, liquid, hot, and cold, the Chinese rarely confine them to the end of a meal as we do in the West. They are eaten at festival time or as everyday snacks or to provide a contrast between the courses of an elaborate meal; they may even be served as relishes.

Much the same is true of fruit, which China with her favorable climate produces in great quantity and variety. It is something to be enjoyed at any time of day and is not necessarily limited to rounding off a meal like a Western dessert.

Fried sesame seed balls

It is considered auspicious to serve these fried sweets to guests when celebrating the Chinese New Year.

4–6 servings:
3½ ounces powdered red soybeans
about 1 cup water
2 cups sugar
2 tablespoons vegetable shortening
5 ounces rice flour
scant 1 cup all-purpose flour
1½ cups water
rice flour for dusting
2½ ounces white sesame seeds
oil for frying
797 calories; 14.9 g protein; 26.3 g fat; 126.7 g sugar

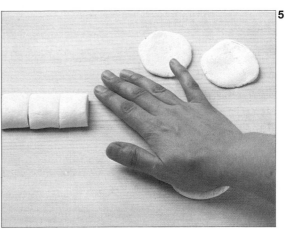

1. Place the powdered red soybeans in a saucepan, add enough water to make a fairly thick paste, and mix well over a low heat, using a wooden spoon. Stir in the sugar, adding a little more water if the mixture is too thick to work with the spoon.

2. Set aside to cool. Melt the vegetable shortening in a fairly large saucepan, add the cold red soy paste and cook over a low heat, mixing well with a wooden spoon.

3. Sift the rice flour and all-purpose flour together into a bowl and mix well. Gradually add up to $1\frac{1}{2}$ cups water, working the mixture by hand into a smooth dough.

4. When the mixture is firm and homogeneous, shape into a large ball; dust the pastry board with rice flour and gradually roll the ball into a long cylindrical sausage $1\frac{1}{4}$ inch in diameter.

5. Cut the roll of dough into slices $\frac{3}{4}$ inch thick, yielding about 30 portions; flatten with the heel of the palm and then press out each piece into a circle with the thumbs and fingers.

6. Shape the cold red soy paste into small balls $\frac{1}{2}$ inch in diameter. Enclose in the circles of dough, seal well, and roll between the hands to form smooth, round balls.

7. Pour the sesame seeds into a pie plate or other rimmed container and roll each ball in the seeds, covering liberally. If the seeds do not stick, moisten the surface of each ball with wet fingers before rolling.

8. Heat the oil in a wok or deep-fryer to about 300°F. (150°C.) or less; the oil must not be too hot since the balls must cook through without burning or browning too much on the outside. When the balls rise to the surface of the oil, the heat may be increased slightly to brown them.

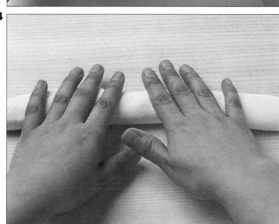

289

Fruit on the merry-go-round of happiness

This delicately flavored lemon jelly is particularly refreshing in hot weather.

Quantities for an 8-inch ring mold – about 6 servings:
1 strip agar-agar (3 ounces) or 4 tablespoons gelatin
3½ cups water
1 cup sugar
juice of ½ lemon
a few drops of lemon extract
1 small water melon
1 can lychees
106 calories; 0.7 g protein; 0.1 g fat; 28.5 g sugar

1. Divide the agar-agar into 2–3 pieces. Soak in cold, lightly salted water for at least 1 hour. Change the water once or twice (see Ingredients, page 302).

2. Squeeze to remove as much water as possible. Place in a saucepan, add the water, and bring to a boil; reduce the heat, and cook gently.

3. When the agar-agar has completely melted, add the sugar and stir over the heat until dissolved. Remove from heat and stir in the lemon juice and extract.

4. Strain the liquid through a piece of cheesecloth or a very fine strainer.

5. Rinse the ring mold with cold water. Fill with the hot liquid (agar-agar sets quickly once cool and should not be stirred or disturbed when it has started to set). Leave to stand until cool and then transfer carefully to the refrigerator.

6. Use a melon-baller to shape the melon balls (remove the seeds with a toothpick or cocktail stick); drain the canned lychees.

7. Just before serving, turn the mold out onto a plate and decorate with the fruit as illustrated.

Two-color lake dessert

This pudding can be served hot or cold. The small colored balls bobbing on the surface give it its name.

2 tablespoons white sesame seeds
5 tablespoons all-purpose flour
approximately 1½ cups water
5 tablespoons sugar
⅔ cup rice flour
⅓ cup water
a pinch of red food coloring powder or a few drops of liquid food color
187 calories; 3.2g protein; 3.1g fat; 36.5g sugar

1. Toast the sesame seeds, taking care not to burn or color them too much; place in the blender and grind fairly finely.

2. Sift the all-purpose flour and place in a saucepan over a low heat; cook the flour, stirring constantly until it turns a golden, light-nut brown. Do not overcook or it will not thicken when the water is added.

3. Pour 1½ cups water into the flour, a very little at a time, stirring constantly over a gentle heat. Add the sugar and continue mixing until the mixture is quite thick.

4. Add the ground sesame seeds and stir well. Keep warm.

5. Place the rice flour in a bowl and gradually add ⅓ cup water; the mixture should be firm and smooth.

6. Divide this mixture in half and add a little red food coloring to one batch, turning it pale pink.

7. Shape the two batches of dough into pink and white balls, ½ inch in diameter. Boil in water until they rise to the surface; drain well.

8. Pour the hot custard prepared in step 3 into a heated dish, drop the colored balls onto the surface and serve at once.

Almond cream jelly

This is the famous *shilen tou-fu*, at its most attractive set in elegant sherbet glasses and topped with a thin layer of fruit purée.

1 strip agar or 1 ounce gelatin
3 cups water
1 cup sugar
1 cup milk
$\frac{1}{2}$ teaspoon almond extract
For the fruit purée topping:
$\frac{1}{4}$ melon
2 tablespoons sugar
1 can yellow (clingstone) peaches
187 calories; 1.9 g protein; 1.7 g fat; 44.7 g sugar

1. Break the agar-agar into 2–3 pieces, place in a bowl of water and soak for at least 1 hour, changing the water several times.

2. Squeeze the agar-agar to get rid of all excess water. Tear into smaller pieces so it will melt more quickly. Place in a saucepan with 3 cups water and heat over a moderate heat.

1

2

3

4

5

6

3. Make sure that the agar-agar has completely melted, stirring with a wooden spoon as it comes to a boil. Add the sugar and stir until dissolved.

4. Pour in the milk and stir; as soon as the mixture comes to a boil, turn off the heat.

5. Add the almond extract, whisk in quickly, and strain through cheesecloth or a very fine strainer.

6. Rinse the serving glasses in cold water and pour in the agar-agar mixture (allow it to cool very slightly first so it will not crack the glass, but make sure it is still quite warm; agar-agar sets at room temperature and must not be disturbed once it has started to set). The glasses should be approximately $\frac{2}{3}$ full. Chill in the refrigerator. Remove the seeds from the melon. Make a melon purée and a peach purée by adding 1 tablespoon sugar to each and liquidizing separately in a blender for a few seconds. Pour the topping over the jelly cream and serve.

Coconut snowballs

Made with glutinous rice, this sweetmeat has a pleasantly sticky consistency. In China these little cakes would be eaten in tea parlors at any time of day.

To make 12 snowballs:
1 cup soy jam
2 cups glutinous rice flour
6¾ cups water
½ cup dried or freshly grated coconut
a few candied (glacé or crystallized) cherries
230 calories; 4.2 g protein; 3.1 g fat; 38.5 g sugar

1. Divide the soy jam into 12 portions.

2. Mix the rice flour with enough water (about ¾ cup) to make a soft paste, divide into 4 portions, and flatten into disks.

3. Bring 6 cups water to a boil and boil the four disks until they rise to the surface. Drain and leave to dry out somewhat on paper towels.

4. Place the cooked rice mixture in a bowl and beat very well with a wooden spoon for 5 minutes. Lightly oil the palms of your hands and shape the mixture into 12 round portions.

5. Flatten these portions, pushing them out into disks with your fingers and thumbs, and place a portion of jam in the center of each. Enclose the jam and shape into balls once more.

6. Roll the balls in the coconut and top each one with a piece of candied cherry. These little cakes can also be steamed for 5 minutes and served hot, or they can be deep-fried in oil.

Cinnamon-flavored sweet potato cakes

Fried sweet potatoes dusted with cinnamon, which go very well with strong tea, such as the classic black tea from Yunnan called p'u-erh.

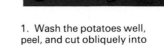

4 – 6 servings:
2 – 3 medium-size sweet potatoes
3 – 5 tablespoons sugar
$\frac{1}{2}$ – 3 teaspoons powdered cinnamon
peanut oil for frying
252 calories; 1.2 g protein; 10.2 g fat; 36.2 g sugar

1. Wash the potatoes well, peel, and cut obliquely into irregular-shaped pieces.

2. Place the potatoes in a bowl of cold water and leave to stand for a while to remove the bitter taste, drain, and dry well with a cloth.

3. Mix the sugar with the cinnamon and sift (confectioner's sugar can be used, if you prefer).

4. Heat plenty of oil to 350°F. (180°C.) and lower the dried potatoes into the oil carefully. When they are golden brown on the outside, lower the heat and fry until tender and completely cooked.

5. Place the sifted sugar and cinnamon in a large rimmed dish or bowl and roll the sweet potato pieces in the coating mixture. Serve hot.

Basic Recipes

CHICKEN STOCK

To yield 6 – 8 cups stock:
bones and carcass of 1 chicken
½ leek
2 small pieces of ginger root
1 light stock cube
1 tablespoon rice wine
Preparation time: 1½ hours

1. Bring plenty of water to a boil and add the chicken bones and carcass; remove the carcass and bones after 1 minute.

2. Pour 12 cups water into a large heavy pot, add the chicken carcass and bones together with the lightly pounded leek and ginger, the stock cube, and the rice wine. Bring to a boil.

3. Once the water has reached the boiling point, lower the heat and skim.

4. Simmer over a low heat for about 1 hour; do not cover the cooking pot if a clear stock is desired.

5. Strain the stock through a piece of cheesecloth or a fine sieve.

GENERAL PURPOSE STOCK

To yield 10 cups:
bones from 2 chickens
approximately ¼ pound pork belly, unboned
5 – 6 chicken wings
1 leek
2 small pieces of ginger root
Preparation time: 2 hours 40 minutes

1. Chop each chicken bone in 3 pieces and rinse in cold water.

2. Cut the pork, slicing between the bones.

3. Chop the chicken wings in half, place in a strainer, and pour plenty of boiling water all over them.

4. Slice the leek in 3 pieces, peel the ginger, and bruise both with the flat of the cleaver blade.

5. Place the bones, wings, and pork in a large, heavy saucepan or kettle, add 15 cups of water, and bring to a boil over a high heat.

6. Once the water has boiled, turn down the heat and skim. Simmer for 20 minutes.

7. Add the leek and the ginger and continue cooking for about 2 hours. If a clear stock is desired, leave the cooking pot uncovered and skim frequently.

8. When the stock has reduced by about ⅓, turn off the heat and strain through a very fine strainer.

MANDARIN PANCAKES FOR PEKING DUCK

For 12 servings:
2 cups sifted all-purpose flour
sesame oil
Preparation time: 30 minutes

1. Sift the flour into a large bowl and make a well in the center. Pour ½ cup of boiling water into the well and work into the flour. Add ½ cup of cold water a little at a time and blend into the flour, using a wooden spoon, until the dough is smooth and soft. Work the dough for a further 5 minutes, cover with a damp cotton cloth, and leave to stand for 20 minutes.

2. Roll the ball of dough into a long, cylindrical sausage shape and cut into 24 pieces. Roll each piece into a small ball between the palms of your hands. Lightly flour a pastry board and rolling pin and roll the balls out into thin, circular pancakes about 5 inches in diameter.

3. Place a skillet on the hob and brush the bottom with sesame oil, add one of the pancakes, and cook briefly on both sides; if brown spots appear, the pancake is overcooked.

4. Continue until all the pancakes are cooked. Fold them into quarters once they are cooked and wrap them in a cloth until they are served.

PANCAKES FOR SPRING ROLLS

Shanghai spring roll skins can be purchased at most Chinese food stores, but this recipe provides an alternative.

2 parts sifted all-purpose flour to one part water
pinch of salt
oil
Preparation time: 30 minutes

1. Mix the flour with the water and salt to make a thick batter. Leave to stand for 1 hour.

2. Heat a griddle and brush very lightly with oil or rub with an oiled cloth.

3. Take up a handful of the mixture, which should be quite elastic in consistency, and spread out on the griddle, shaping a pancake approximately 6 inches in diameter. As the mixture cooks (the heat should not be too high) a thin skin will form. Carefully peel it off the griddle, taking care not to tear.

4. Clean the griddle between pancakes with a cloth dipped in oil and repeat the procedure until the required number of pancakes or spring roll skins have been prepared. These spring roll skins can be kept in the refrigerator, covered with a damp cloth.

HSAO MAI DUMPLING CASES

Quantities for 36 casings:
2 cups all-purpose flour
a pinch of salt
Preparation time: 1 hour

1. Sift the flour with the salt into a bowl; form a well in the center and add scant 1 cup of boiling water, stirring quickly until a smooth, fairly thick dough is obtained.

2. Knead the dough for 3 minutes and then roll into a long, cylindrical sausage shape.

3. Cut the roll into 36 portions and roll each portion into a ball; flour the pastry board lightly and, using a lightly floured rolling pin, roll each ball out into a circle about 2¾ inches in diameter.

4. The dough sheets can be kept in the refrigerator, covered with a damp cloth.

IN THE KITCHEN AND AT THE TABLE

In the kitchen: the Ingredients

SAUCES AND FLAVORINGS

Chili oil: Powdered chili pepper is cooked in sesame oil to produce a very hot sauce. Tabasco can be substituted, but it does not have the same taste or consistency.

Cornstarch: This is the very fine starch extracted from grains of corn, which is valued for its lightness and for the fact that it is also very digestible. When used as a coating for foods before cooking, it gives an attractive sheen. Used for thickening sauces, it should be added sparingly at the end of the cooking process dissolved in a little cold water. Rice starch and wheat starch are equivalents, and potato flour can be substituted for cornstarch.

Fermented salted black beans: Small salted beans which are used to add a distinct flavor to food and will keep indefinitely in the refrigerator in a tightly closed jar. Always soak in cold water for 10 minutes before use to remove excess salt.

Hoisin sauce: Used for marinating or as a barbecue sauce or dip for poultry, pork, or duck. Made from yellow and sometimes red soybeans, sugar, and spices, it is dark red in color with a delicate, slightly sweet, spicy flavor.

Monosodium glutamate (M.S.G.): A neutral salt of glutamic acid in the form of small crystals. For hundreds of years the Chinese extracted the substance from seaweed and used it to heighten the taste of food; nowadays it is derived from wheat, beets, and corn. M.S.G. is manufactured in various countries under different names: Accent throughout the USA; Aji No Moto in Japan; Ve Tsin in Hong Kong. It should be used extremely sparingly and is often not necessary if very good quality, fresh ingredients are selected.

Oyster sauce: A velvety, golden brown thickish sauce made from the cooking liquid of oysters with added salt. It has a decided flavor of oysters but marries with other – sometimes unexpected – tastes extremely well. It is sold in bottles.

Rendered chicken fat or oil: Solid raw fat from the inside of a chicken is placed in a bowl in a steamer, covered and cooked until all the oil is rendered – about 1 hour depending on how much fat is treated. It is then strained, all solids are discarded, and it is stored in a covered container in the refrigerator. Usually added at the end of the cooking process to give extra flavor.

Sesame oil: A reddish-brown oil (the more refined, light yellow oil which is also found is not a satisfactory substitute). The oil has a strong flavor and a tendency to burn; it is therefore used as a condiment and not as a cooking oil.

Sesame seed paste: White sesame seeds are ground to make a paste which has a very pleasant and distinctive flavor; it is usually sold in jars and can also be found in Middle Eastern grocery stores under the name of *tahini*, but the Chinese variety should be used whenever possible as it has a better flavor. As the paste is thick, it is usually diluted with stock or with soy sauce mixed with vinegar. It is often used as a sauce for boiled pork.

Rice wine (Shao Shing): This straw-colored rice wine (sometimes known as Yellow Wine) tastes rather like a dry sherry or Japanese sake and is used a great deal in Chinese cooking. There is also a sweet variety.

Shrimp sauce: Made from tiny salted shrimp. A very salty sauce which is used to flavor vegetable dishes, squid, fried shrimp, and soups.

1.2.3. Soy sauce – 4. Shao Shing rice wine – 5. Sake – 6. Hoisin (barbecue) sauce – 7. Sesame oil – 8. Oyster sauce – 9. Sesame seed paste – 10. Shrimp sauce – 11. Monosodium glutamate – 12. Cornstarch – 13. Fermented salted black beans – 14. Fermented soybean paste.

Soy sauce: Soybeans, salt, roasted wheat, and yeast mold are fermented and the resulting sauce is produced in three varieties: red soy sauce, dark or black soy sauce, and light soy sauce. The dark, dense type has more color than flavor and is used for long, slow cooking. The lighter sauce is delicately flavored, and is best-suited for all-round Chinese cooking.

Soybean paste: A mixture of fermented black beans, flour, salt, and a particular type of mold which aids the fermentation process. Each region of China produces its own variety. The most widely known variety is seasoned with chili peppers.

Sweet soybean paste: A mixture of fermented or preserved soybeans, white flour, sugar, and spices. Hoisin sauce can be substituted.

Vinegar: Chinese vinegar is made from rice by a method similar to that used in making wine vinegar. There are several types: *black vinegar*, very strong; *red vinegar*, best suited to the preparation of fish dishes; *mild vinegar*, a by-product of black vinegar and usually included in braised dishes and stews; *white vinegar*, a delicately flavored mild vinegar (white wine vinegar can be substituted, using smaller quantities, since the Western product is stronger).

SPICES

Apricot kernels: Almonds are usually substituted for these by Western cooks, though the taste is not quite the same. There are two kinds: one slightly sweet and the other a little bitter.

The sweeter variety is used in a wide range of dishes, imparting a very pleasant, distinctive flavor. It may be often salted and eaten as an appetizer or ground, mixed with evaporated or condensed milk and agar-agar, and made into a dessert.

Chili peppers: These small, hot peppers add zest to dishes but must be used in moderation as they are very strong. They also stimulate the stomach and aid digestion. They may be used as a preservative with salted or pickled vegetables. Chili peppers are available fresh, pickled, fermented, dried, and ground in oil.

Chinese parsley or coriander leaves: Lacy-leafed with a distinctive flavor and paler color than ordinary parsley, the plant can easily be grown indoors. The flavor is slightly bitter but it

is a good seasoning for soups and provides an attractive garnish for fried foods.

Chinese pepper: Used in the whole grain form when cooking meat or in the powdered form for fried foods.

Dried mandarin peel: Dried mandarin peel stimulates the appetite and is put to many other uses by Chinese herbalists. It is also added to beef dishes to mask the smell (which most Chinese find offensive). The peel can also be specially treated and eaten as a snack.

Five-spice powder: Available in small packets or jars, this is a mixture of five spices: star anise, cloves, cinnamon, pepper, fennel seeds, and dried mandarin peel. This spice mixture is very strong both in taste and aroma and should therefore be used very sparingly. It is used in slowly cooked foods and in certain sauces. Mixed with salt, it is placed on the table as a condiment and sprinkled on fried foods.

Ginger: Throughout this book, unless otherwise stated, the fresh ginger root is to be used. At no time can powdered ginger be substituted. The fresh ginger root has a very strong, distinctive taste and, together with leek and garlic, is indispensable in Chinese cooking. Its main functions are to flavor a dish, mask strong or unpleasant odors (fish, etc.), and add an accent of extra aroma to a recipe.

For stir-fried dishes the ginger is chopped, whereas for those dishes which need longer cooking the ginger is bruised or pounded with the flat of the cleaver before it is added to the other ingredients. Generous amounts of ginger are used for tripe and duck dishes. Shredded or chopped ginger is also incorporated in sauces for pork or steamed fish. When cooked, ginger releases a very strong but pleasant flavor and when fried imparts a sharp, lemony fragrance. Refrigerate but do not freeze.

Ginger juice: Mix finely chopped or grated ginger with an equal quantity of water and pour through a damp cheesecloth, twist the cheesecloth tightly to extract the juice. Alternatively, crush the ginger in a garlic press.

1. Pepper – 2. Five-spice powder – 3. Whole, dried chili peppers – 4. Cinnamon sticks – 5. Cloves – 6. Fennel seeds – 7. Dried mandarin peel – 8. Garlic – 9. Leek – 10. Ginger root – 11. Star anise – 12. Apricot kernels.

Gingko nuts: These have a hard shell and cream-colored flesh. Used in soups, stews, and fillings. Available canned or dried.

Scallions: Half way between garlic and onion, these are used in much the same way. They can be replaced by leeks or shallots if necessary.

Sesame seeds: *White*: used for decoration, for sweets and fillings, and for sesame seed paste. *Black*: to impart a distinctive flavor to sweet soups; sometimes used for decoration.

Star anise: Also called "badiane," star anise is a spice obtained by drying the star-shaped fruit of anise. Widely used in Chinese cooking.

Used to impart a very subtle, slightly sweetish taste and flavor to stewed and steamed dishes, the spice is a strong one and should be used in moderation—$\frac{1}{2}$–1 piece usually suffices.

BASIC AND SPECIAL INGREDIENTS

Anything edible can be included in a Chinese meal; the basic requirement is that each ingredient must be chosen and prepared with an overall aim of harmony in taste, texture, fragrance, and color. The various components of a dish must complement each other and the freshest, best-quality goods should always be chosen.

It is necessary always to chose the method of preparation which best lends itself to the particular raw materials being cooked. Some ingredients are better cooked as simply as possible without any masking of their intrinsic flavors, in which case their own juices, flavored lightly with salt and soy sauce, will suffice. Some foods, however, need the contrasting and complementary presence of other ingredients. Such white, nonoily fish as trout, hake, bass, and sole all taste their best cooked in their own juices and are particularly good when steamed. Oily fish are best served with a sweet and sour sauce or braised with bamboo shoots and mushrooms; these last two ingredients belong to the category of foods whose role is to lend their flavors to the ingredients with which they are cooked. Then there are those foods which have no flavor of their own but rely totally on being impregnated with the tastes of added ingredients. Examples of these foods happen to be among the most highly prized of all Chinese delicacies: shark's fin and bird's nests. Tasteless, without aroma or color, and gelatinous in consistency, they must be sub-jected to long and complicated cooking processes before being served as the most exotic and extravagant soups in the world.

Abalone: A favorite delicacy of the Chinese, abalone is a mollusk with firm, smooth flesh also known as St. Peter's ear. It is sold in cans or dried. The canned variety is easier to prepare and will keep for several days in the refrigerator after the can is opened if the water is changed every day. The dried variety will keep almost indefinitely stored in a cool, dry place.

Agar-agar: A natural gelatin which is extracted from various seaweeds. It is sold in the form of long, dry translucent ribbons, in thin leaves, or in strips about 1 foot long. It should be soaked in cold water for at least 30 minutes before using. It is usually used for desserts, such as almond jelly cream, or for making jelly.

Bamboo shoots: The tender shoots which appear at the base of the bamboo are gathered at the end of the rainy season. They are sold fresh, canned, or dried. The thick foliage on the fresh variety must be removed before use. The dried shoots must be soaked in water for 12 to 24 hours before cooking. The canned variety are parboiled and will keep for up to a month in the refrigerator after the can is opened if placed in a bowl of water which is changed every day.

Winter bamboo shoots are more difficult to come by and therefore more expensive, but they are more tender and have a particularly delicate taste.

Bean curd: This product is obtained from the liquid or milk extracted from ground soybeans to which a small quantity of gypsum powder is added. If the water in which it should be kept is changed every day, it can be kept for up to 1 week in the refrigerator. Instant soybean curd powder is also available. *Fried bean curds*: cakes of fresh bean curd which have been fried. They keep well for several weeks in a dry place. *Dried bean curd*: sediment of soybean milk dried into stiff sheets, which are usually broken in pieces and soaked before cooking. Dried bean curd sheets, which are very thin and quite easily torn, are used to wrap certain foods for cooking and can be dissolved in warm water to produce soybean milk.

Chinese mushrooms: *Straw mushrooms*: among the best known Chinese mushrooms, they are also called egg mushrooms. They have a rather gelatinous but pleasant texture and very little taste. They are used whole or cut in half and are available fresh or in cans. *Edible fungus*: a dried mushroom-like fungus which on soaking swells to a soft brown gelatinous shape like a tiny ear. Must be carefully washed as they sometimes retain grit. Soak in warm water for 20 minutes before use. Do not use water used for soaking the fungus for cooking. Their flavor is mild and faintly musky. Used a great deal in vegetarian dishes and stews. There are several varieties, such as cloud-ear fungus and wood-ear fungus; though similar, they vary in size and texture. Cloud ears are the thinnest and most delicate.

Chinese okra: This is an oval-shaped vegetable of the mallow family. Its texture is rather like that of zucchini, which can be used as a substitute, as can cucumber and bitter melon.

Chinese or celery cabbage: Long pale green leaves with wide white ribs. There are two varieties: *pai t'sai* and the more tender *t'sai tum*. Both are nearly always sold fresh. Ordinary cabbage can be substituted but will not have the same taste or texture.

Flour: *High-gluten flour*: This should be used for dough sheets for such preparations as *won ton* since the flour gives the mixture greater elasticity, allowing it to be rolled out into extremely thin sheets. *Rice flour*: produced from ground polished rice, it is used to thicken and add body to certain sweet molds, puddings, etc. *Glutinous rice flour*: when cooked it has a sticky, elastic texture. *Low-gluten flour*: when cooked it becomes almost transparent; it is used for desserts and sweets.

Lotus leaves: The fresh or dried leaves of the lotus plant are used as a wrapping in which to cook foods to which they impart a distinctive flavor. If dried, they must be soaked before use.

Lotus root: This is a rhizome which is used in soups, vegetarian dishes and is also candied and eaten as a sweet or dessert. Its crisp texture, mild, slightly sweet flavor, and attractive appearance make it a great favorite. Available fresh, canned, sliced, dried, or candied. Fresh lotus root will keep well in a perforated plastic bag in the refrigerator for up to three weeks. Once the canned variety has been opened, it will keep for a week, placed in the refrigerator in a bowl of water that is changed daily.

Noodles: The most commonly used varieties are: *Egg noodles* made from wheat flour. These may be fresh, homemade noodles and some Chinese cooks are able to produce very fine, delicate egg noodles with a minimum of utensils and no special gadgets. *Rice noodles* come in many different widths and lengths. *Soy or mung bean flour noodles* are also called bean thread (transparent noodles). These must be softened in cold water for about 30 minutes before using and, whereas egg noodles can be replaced by Italian egg noodles, there is no substitute for soybean noodles.

Rice: *Chinese long-grain rice*: polished grains of rice with a low starch content. *Glutinous rice*: short, round grains which are creamy white and have an opaque, pearly look; they become translucent and sticky when cooked and are used for puddings and fillings for sweets and cakes.

Seaweed: The most commonly used are green seaweed (a thick, substantial variety, dried and sold in strips) which must be soaked in cold water overnight or in lukewarm water for $\frac{1}{2}$ hour before cooking, and dark purple (*nori*) seaweed (sold in dried sheets), which is also soaked and often placed on or added to the food when it is cooked or ready to serve, since it loses its taste and texture if cooked for any length of time.

Shark's fin: The main ingredient in the famous gourmet soup. Shark's fin should be bought in semi-processed form which shortens the cooking time. Possesses a very high vitamin content.

Taro root: An edible, starchy tuberous rhizome. Belonging to the arum lily family, it looks a little like a potato, with a darker, rougher skin. The flesh is firm and white with red streaks and is slightly sticky. Its taste is more delicate than the ordinary potato, but the latter can be substituted.

Tiger lilies or bud stems: Sometimes called golden needles, the lilies are dried and are used for flavoring vegetable dishes and steamed chicken. They must be soaked before use and will keep indefinitely in a dry place

Za-zai: A green leaf pickled vegetable, crisp, slightly bitter and pungent. Used in soups and certain fried dishes, it is sometimes known as Chinese mustard top.

In the kitchen: Cutting and Chopping Techniques

Chinese cookery is extremely flexible and versatile when it comes to the types and quantities of ingredients. Of the total preparation time for a great many dishes, 80 percent is usually taken up getting the ingredients ready for cooking:

Both dried and salted foods must be washed and soaked in water. Some salt will be removed and what remains will add flavor to the other ingredients in the recipe.

Meat, pork in particular, must be trimmed carefully to remove fat and gristle.

Fish are gutted and, where necessary, scales are removed, although often their heads and tails are left intact.

Shellfish sometimes have their shells removed, sometimes not, depending on the recipe.

Vegetables are washed and trimmed with great care – perhaps the most impressive example of this is when bean sprouts are painstakingly picked over to remove the thread-like root and the little seed cover.

Poultry is plucked and cleaned and usually jointed.

Of paramount importance is the careful cutting of all the ingredients into pieces of the same size; this helps ensure that they will all be evenly cooked and therefore have more flavor, and of course it gives an attractive appearance to the resulting dish.

SLICING

Since so many Chinese dishes are cooked only briefly, it is imperative that the ingredients should be very thinly sliced. The ingredients can be held vertically, horizontally, or at an oblique angle; and the Chinese cleaver or knife can be held in one of several positions depending on the cut desired: straight up and down for a vertical downward cut; at a 45-degree angle either toward or away from the hand for an oblique cut; or almost parallel to the chopping board for a horizontal cut.

One of the most commonly used cutting methods is of course to cut vertically down through the ingredients, cutting them into slices which are usually only $\frac{1}{8}$ inch thick.

In order to cut ingredients into diamond-shaped pieces, cut the food obliquely into diagonal pieces and then, holding these pieces vertically, cut into $\frac{1}{8}$ inch-thick slices.

For even thinner slices, hold the knife almost parallel to the chopping board and cut horizontally.

CUTTING INTO THIN STRIPS

Start by cutting the ingredient into 2½-inch pieces; cut vertically into thin slices, then cut each slice into thin strips. If the ingredient is very firm or hard, cut across the fibers; if soft cut along the grain.

It is most common to cut the ingredients in strips about the size and thickness of a match; the ingredient should therefore be sliced $\frac{1}{10}$ inch thick before shredding. Stack several of these slices, overlapping them in a stepped formation, and cut off the strips $\frac{1}{10}$ inch wide.

When shredding such ingredients as green peppers, which are thin to start with, simply cut downward into thin strips $\frac{1}{8}$ inch wide.

CUTTING INTO THIN RECTANGLES

These small pieces are usually about $\frac{1}{4}-\frac{1}{2}$ inch wide and 1–2 inches long. The technique is much the same as for cutting strips: The ingredient is first cut into pieces of the length desired, then cut to the desired thickness and finally sliced to the required width, to produce rectangles or approximate rectangles, depending on the ingredient used.

When cutting such ingredients as mushrooms, which are already of a determined thickness, into rectangles, simply make the width of the rectangle the same as the thickness of the ingredient.

If the ingredient is of an irregular shape, the most important requirement is that the slices should be of even size to ensure even cooking times.

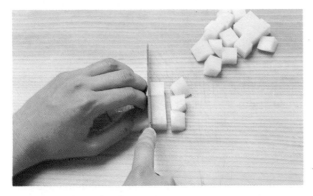

DICING OR CUBING

The dice usually measures between $\frac{1}{4}$ inch and $\frac{1}{2}$ inch cube, depending on the recipe and the ingredient used. If the ingredient is of an irregular shape, it can be cut into pyramids or other shapes, which will conform with the shape of the original.

For regular cubes of the most commonly used size, cut the ingredients into rectangles or strips $\frac{1}{2}$ inch thick and $\frac{1}{2}$ inch wide; then cut these rectangles across into $\frac{1}{2}$-inch cubes.

When dicing a cylindrical ingredient, such as cucumber, cut it lengthwise into quarters, sheer off the inner point of the triangle, and then cut the thick strips horizontally or diagonally into small pieces.

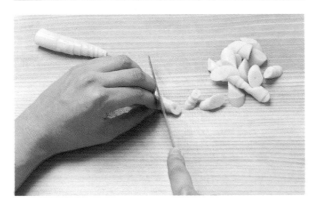

When thin cylindrical ingredients are to be cut, use the rolling cut technique: cut a diagonal slice from one end of the ingredient, roll it a $\frac{1}{4}$ turn toward you, and make a second diagonal slice slightly above the first. Continue rolling and slicing, keeping the pieces all the same size.

CHOPPING

This cutting method is used to reduce ingredients to very small pieces, less than $\frac{1}{10}$ inch cube. For the best results, cut the ingredient into very thin strips and then cut across the strips at very close intervals.

For example, when chopping a leek, slit it open with a knife, open the layers out flat, and cut into thin strips $\frac{1}{10}$ inch thick. Cut horizontally across these strips at $\frac{1}{10}$-inch intervals, and the leek will be fairly coarsely but neatly chopped.

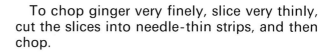

To chop ginger very finely, slice very thinly, cut the slices into needle-thin strips, and then chop.

CUTTING INTO VERY SMALL CUBES

To cut ingredients into very small cubes about $\frac{1}{10}$ inch square, follow the same procedure as for dicing and cubing above; simply adjust the thickness and width of the original rectangular slices.

When irregularly shaped ingredients such as za-zai are involved, there will obviously be a certain unevenness to the shape of the pieces.

CUTTING INTO ASYMETRICAL PIECES

Use essentially the same procedure as for dicing but on a larger scale. The ingredient should first be sliced into $\frac{3}{4}$-inch pieces and then cut to the required thickness.

The rolling cut technique can also be used. Slice the ingredient at an angle and roll it a $\frac{1}{4}$ turn between each slice. The pieces will vary in size depending on the angle at which the knife is held.

In the kitchen: Cooking Methods

As many as forty different techniques are involved in Chinese cooking, but only the most frequently used methods, which are needed for recipes in this book, are listed below:

Chu: Boiling in water.
Ch'ao: Pan frying and stir-frying.
Cha: Deep-frying.
Shao: Roasting or barbecuing.
Pao: Quick-frying whereby, in the second phase, the finely cut food is rapidly stir-fried over high heat. As a prefix it describes rapid cooking in oil or stock (it literally means explosion); it is the last stage in any cooking process which can include steaming, shallow-frying, or deep-frying.
Wei: Clear-simmering. Gentle, prolonged poaching in a clear stock or flavored sauce.
Men: Long, slow cooking over low heat. Braising or stewing. Food is first fried or seared in hot oil and then simmered in a little stock.
Lu: Soft food treatment, especially for fish or fragile foods, which are cooked in a thickened soy-flavored sauce without the usual stirring.
Tun: Food is placed in a closed container and cooked over, not in, boiling water, as in a double boiler.
Liu: Cooking in very little oil with a minimum of movement. A thickened sauce is added during or at the end of the cooking process.
Ch'eng: Open or wet steaming with the food being subjected to the direct action of steam.

Preparation of a dish often involves two or more of these processes. Food is often boiled before it is stir-fried or deep-fried and vice versa. Ingredients are often fried twice, once in their natural state and again when covered with a coating of flour, egg, or some other ingredient. Sometimes boiling oil or water is ladled or poured over raw foods.

Certain rules must be respected for successful cooking. The ingredients must be cut to the same size, the pan must be preheated, and the oil must reach the temperature given in the recipe. Only then can the prepared foods be lowered into the oil, beginning with those which take longest to cook, such as carrots, and leaving such tender vegetables as soybean sprouts and lettuce leaves until last.

Peanut oil is usually used for frying, since it can be heated to the high temperatures required in Chinese cooking. The oil can be given extra flavor by adding a slice of ginger or a clove of garlic. Other fats used are chicken and duck fat and lard, but these should not be heated to very high temperatures. Many ingredients are marinated or mixed with seasonings, flavorings, tenderizing agents, or coatings before cooking or between two cooking processes. Other ingredients are added at various stages, contributing to the flavor and balance of the finished dish. All these steps are clearly described in the recipes. The three most often used general cooking methods in this book can be broadly classified under three headings: Stir-frying, deep- or semi-deep-frying, and steaming.

Stir-frying: This can be done in two ways: The ingredients may be stir-fried raw – sautéed, but over a higher heat than would normally be used for sautéing – or they may first be semi-deep- or deep-fried. In both cases the pan must be placed over a high heat and enough oil poured in so that it can be swirled around the hot wok or pan to cover almost all the inside surface; it is then poured off and reserved. The amount of oil listed in each recipe is then poured into the wok and heated and used for cooking. This procedure helps to ensure that the food does not stick and burn.

A few tips are worth remembering:

1. Cut the ingredients into pieces of the same size and add those which take longest to cook to the wok first.

When being cooked briefly over high heat, each ingredient must receive an equal and even amount of heat on all sides, and if all ingredients are cut to the same dimensions and shapes the finished dish will also look much more attractive.

Shredding into thin strips, thin slicing, dicing, cutting into rectangles, and chopping are the most suitable preparations for stir-frying.

It does not matter if the ingredients differ in consistency and texture or if they vary in heat-resistance or change color when exposed to heat; if the tougher, more heat-resistant foods are first to go in the pan, followed by the others, all will be well, and very delicate, tender green, leafy vegetables can be added at the last minute so that they do not lose their color and become soggy. The stir-fry method should ensure that the ingredients are cooked evenly; the shape of a wok is particularly well adapted to satisfy the requirements of this technique, and the best heat to use is gas. Wok rings should be used with care as they can be a hazard when placed over certain types of gas burners.

2. Prepare all the ingredients and place within easy reach before starting to cook.

All ingredients and seasonings must be at hand, since the cooking process, once begun, must proceed uninterruptedly over a high heat. When the ingredients are $\frac{2}{3}$ cooked, they should be transferred to a serving dish, preferably all at once to avoid any of the pieces being over-cooked. The food will finish cooking in its own heat in the serving dish.

Frying: The aim is to cook the food evenly and to have it crisp and crunchy on the outside. This is best achieved by frying the food in two or even three stages, thus ensuring that the oil is always at the correct temperature.

If the food is fried once and left in the hot oil until it is finally cooked through, the outside coating or batter will be overdone. When a large piece of meat or fish is fried this way, the batter will turn very brown and be far too hard.

If ingredients are twice-fried, they are first $\frac{2}{3}$ cooked in moderately hot oil, drained, and then fried again in hotter oil.

Frying three times involves an initial short immersion in the hot oil, enough to set the batter, seal in the food, and cook it $\frac{1}{3}$ done. The food is then drained, the oil is heated again to the original frying temperature, and the food is lowered into the oil again to fry until $\frac{2}{3}$ done; at this point it should be very lightly colored on the outside. Finally, after removing and draining the food once more, the temperature of the oil is raised to very hot, and the final frying is completed; after this the outside of the food should be crisp and an attractive golden brown.

This procedure allows for accurate checking on the temperature of the oil each time the ingredients are removed and drained. The food is sealed and what oil does penetrate will do so evenly, while any liquid released by the food can drain away when the food is removed from the fryer between immersions.

To fry food without dipping it in batter, coat it with flour and cornstarch. A beaten white of egg or a few drops of oil can be added to the batter to make it lighter.

Each method will have a different effect on the appearance and texture of the food. It is usually felt that the paler and more delicate the batter, the more refined the dish; in this case the food will have to be fried at a relatively low temperature. But even if frying at a low temperature is considered the proper treatment for a particular ingredient, the final touch will be quick frying in very hot oil to seal and crisp the fried food. The same applies to foods given most of their cooking in moderately hot oil. Food cooked in very hot oil for any length of time becomes slightly bitter. Never deep-fry too many pieces of food at one time.

Oil used for frying at low temperatures will tend to retain odors and moisture. In order to reuse it, heat it very hot, drop in 1 piece each of leek and ginger, and once they have turned brown remove them, and turn off the heat. The oil can now be strained and reused. Oil used for frying fish should not be reused more than once.

Steaming: Fish, meat, poultry, and stuffed pastries are steamed over a high heat. Eggs and bean curd need a more gentle heat. See Typical Chinese Utensils (page 13) for the correct way to assemble and use the bamboo steamer.

At table: drinks and Chinese table manners

BEVERAGES

Everyone knows that tea is China's national drink and visitors to China relate how, on every social occasion, they are offered tea in tall, lidded, beautifully decorated porcelain cups. Indeed, this refreshing and stimulating infusion has been considered an integral and indispensable part of everyday life in China from time immemorial, and the fact that the famous Venetian traveler, Marco Polo, makes no mention of it in his writings is adduced by some rather questionable authorities as proof that he never actually set foot in China.

A description of tea is to be found in an ancient Chinese encyclopedia written when Constantine ruled the Roman Empire; just over three centuries later the first manual on tea was compiled. Tea was already subject to taxation, an indication of how popular it had become. In 1610 or thereabouts, Dutch travelers and merchants introduced tea into Europe, together with its name, *t'e* (from the dialect of the region surrounding the port of Amoy); this word survived, hardly changed, in English, French, German, Spanish, and Italian, whereas the Japanese, Indian, Persian, and Russian words for tea are all derived from the Cantonese word *ch'a*.

There are three types of tea: black, or fermented; green, unfermented; and oolong, which is semifermented. There are an infinite variety of blends, fragrances, and brands. In infusing the tea leaves, the aim is to extract as much caffeine as possible and a certain amount of tannin while capturing the fugitive aroma and taste. The quality of the water used for steeping the leaves is of critical importance, and the water must be boiling when it is added to the tea. But it should never be boiled for any length of time or boiled more than once because it will lose its precious oxygen content. The Chinese maintain that the kettle should always be earthenware and the teapot and cups porcelain (a Chinese invention, hence *china*). Tea must always be drunk while it is very hot, and the Chinese never add sugar, milk, or lemon, since these adulterate the true flavor.

Westerners mistakenly believe that tea is drunk with every meal in China just as we drink water, wine, beer, or soft drinks. The Chinese do not observe any hard and fast rules as to what goes with what, unlike Westerners who insist that certain wines accompany particular dishes and select a red or white, dry or sweet wine, in accordance with rigid guidelines in which each wine is allotted its proper place. This accounts for the somewhat surprising and sometimes incongruous variety of drinks one sees clustered on the tables of Chinese restaurants outside of China. Some patrons choose Chinese alcoholic beverages, some tea, and others their usual beer or favorite wine. These beverages may be excellent but are rather out of place at a Chinese meal. With the exception of some parts of China, tea plays a distinct role: it is used as a toast, as a symbol of hospitality and good fellowship, and as an inseparable part of polite social intercourse. It is served at the beginning and end of a meal and occasionally during a pause between courses to cleanse and refresh the palate, but it is not served with the food, since it does not go well with oil.

Instead, a light, usually vegetable, broth which sometimes contains a few shreds of meat, is drunk as a thirst quencher during meals. Alcoholic drinks may also be served in small delicate cups to toast the health of the other guests and generally add to the gaiety of the occasion.

The versatile seventeenth-century writer Lorenzo Magalotti in his *Account of China* (*Relazione della Cina*), 1672, tells of a meeting with the Jesuit priest, Johann Grueber, who had spent three years in China (1664–1666) and who had told him that liquid refreshment was served at certain intervals during the meal, when everyone raised their cups to their lips at the same time with the customary toast of *zin zin zin*, after which their cups had to be seen to be empty. This little ceremony spread to the

1. Ginseng – 2. Fen Chiew – 3. Mei Kwẹi Lu – 4. Chu Yeh Ching – 5. Ginseng – 6. Finest Green Tea – 7. Shao Shing rice wine – 8. Mao Tai – 9. "White" Pai Mu Tan tea – 10. Compressed tea (p'u-erh) – 11. Black Yunnan tea (p'u-erh) – 12. Medicinal tea – 13. Jasmine tea – 14. Oolong.

West and survived to a certain extent in the now rather dated expression "chin-chin" (zin was the seventeenth-century transcription of the Chinese expression "ch'ing"), when clinking glasses. It was incorrectly assumed that the origin of the saying was onomatopoeic.

The Chinese character for alcoholic drink comprises an ideogram signifying water and another that was formerly the name for the eighth month of the year (equivalent to September in the Western calender, since the Chinese year starts in February) and refers to millet, which was harvested in that month and was used to make the oldest type of "strong drink" in China. Fen Chiew, which originated in the provinces of Shansi, has been distilled from millet and sorghum for more than fourteen hundred years. Another drink, which comes from Shanxi, Kaoliang, is also distilled from sorghum. In common with most northern Chinese spirits distilled from sorghum, Fen Chiew and Kaoliang have a high alcoholic content, whereas in southern China the alcoholic beverages made with rice – the staple crop of that area – are not so strong. The most famous Chinese spirit, Mai Tai, has much in common with Kaoliang; Mai Tai is strong, colorless, and just the thing for warming people up in the freezing Peking winters. It has a rather strange smell and is sold in fascinating milky white opaque bottles. Although it is believed by some Westerners to date back to ancient times, it is of comparatively recent origin. The story goes that at the beginning of the eighteenth century, a merchant from Shanxi settled in the city of Maio Tai in the province of Guizhou (southwestern China) and started to distill this spirit in the same way as his native province's Kaoliang. As in the case of Fen Chiew, the character and taste of the spirit depends on the quality of the local water.

Apart from these strong cereal-based spirits, there are many sweet liqueurs, such as Chu Yeh Ching, Mei Kwei Lu, and Wu Chia Pi. The first, Chu Yeh Ching, or bamboo liqueur, is made from Fen Chiew (distilled, as previously noted, from sorghum and millet) and is given an added flavor and aroma, imparted by twelve different substances, of which dried orange peel and bamboo leaves are only two. The second, Mei Kwei Lu (poetically named Rose Dew), is sweeter and is made from a blend of sorghum and other cereals, which are distilled and then flavored, using a mixture of aromatic herbs and rose petals. This liqueur is used a good deal in cooking as well as for drinking. The third, Wu Chia Pi, is also distilled from sorghum and is given its distinctive taste and appearance (which are slightly reminiscent of Madeira) by the addition of caramelized barley sugar. In common with all alcoholic drinks, Wu Chia Pi is said to aid digestion and circulation and is used in cooking in much the same way as Madeira and brandy for certain gourmet meat dishes.

The wide variety of Chinese "medicinal" wines must not be forgotten. We in the West are familiar with the famous ginseng, made from the root of Panax Schinseng (the Latin word stems from the Greek panacea, or "remedy for all ills"). The root grows in Manchuria and Korea and is credited with phenomenal aphrodisiacal properties, which stimulate a lucrative and colorful trade in the root. But the Encyclopaedia Britannica states: "There is no evidence to suggest that ginseng has any value, either as a drug or as an aphrodisiac." There are countless other medicinal wines, including a liqueur distilled from snakes and another from tiger bones.

Although many of the alcoholic drinks we have mentioned are called wines and are served during Chinese meals, none of them corresponds to the Western conception of a table wine, although they marry well with food. (Mai Tai, for example, is the perfect accompaniment to Peking duck.) The nearest equivalent to our table wines would be what the Chinese call yellow wine. To quote Magalotti: "Their rice wine is pale and clear with amber glints, a very beautiful golden yellow in color: it has a very delicate taste and is sometimes so strong that we Europeans would mistake it for a Spanish wine. The common people drink from earthenware receptacles, the nobles from very curiously chased gold and silver cups, while important dignitaries drink from polished and carved rhinoceros horns with richly jewelled gold mountings." This description conjures up the exotic and luxurious ways of Imperial China and the rice wine to which Magalotti refers is Shao Shing, which originated from the town of the same name in the province of Zhejiang and is still considered the best of the "yellow wines" to this day. It can be as strong as eighteen degrees and is made from glutinous rice, millet, and ordinary rice; it resembles the Japanese rice wine sake and is usually drunk in the same way – warmed and served in delicate porcelain cups. It is usually aged for ten years, but sometimes for more than forty years, to produce a very rare wine of exceptional quality. It used to be the custom to put aside some Shao

Shing when a baby girl was born; this was to be opened and drunk on her wedding day.

Finally, we come to wine made from grapes. Today vines are grown in various parts of China, but the total area given over to viticulture is only $\frac{1}{45}$ of the total area devoted to growing vines in Italy. Very little wine is produced from grapes in China, the white wine being usually too acid and the red too sweet for Western tastes. Indigenous vines are known to have been cultivated four thousand years ago, and the wine was used for medicinal purposes. The European vine was introduced to China via the silk route under the Han dynasty in 130 B.C., and Marco Polo referred to wine made from grapes. Toward the end of the Ming dynasty in the seventeenth century new varieties of vine were introduced from Turkestan. Later, however, viticulture declined. Nevertheless, Chinese wine is celebrated in Chinese classical literature in the works of Li Po, who is considered the greatest Chinese lyric poet and who belonged to a group of poets called the Six Idlers of the Bamboo Stream. Li Po was admitted to the imperial academy by the Emperor Hsuan-tsung of the Tang dynasty and enjoyed a certain favor despite his tendency to drunkenness. He wrote a great deal of poetry, some of which survives, and from which the following lines are taken:

Amidst the flowers a jug of wine
I pour alone lacking companionship,
So raising the cup I invite the moon,
Then turn to my shadow which makes three of us.
Because the moon does not know how to drink
My shadow merely follows my body.
The moon has brought the shadow to keep me company awhile,
The practice of mirth should keep pace with spring.*

* From Cyril Birch, ed., *Anthology of Chinese Literature*, 2 vol., 1961–72.

SERVING A MEAL: CHINESE TABLE MANNERS AND ETIQUETTE

There is no rigid system of etiquette to be observed when being entertained in China; the main thing is to relax and savor the food with obvious enjoyment. Usually the table is round, and the food is arranged in the center.

The guest should always sit in the place indicated by the host; to decline the place of honor or to ask to change might appear ill-mannered. It is considered good etiquette to wait until the host invites everyone to start the meal before eating.

The seat farthest away from the entrance and facing the entrance is the place of honor while those on either side of it are the least important; this is the basis on which the table seating is planned. If eating informally, people sit down without ceremony as they arrive.

The use of a circular revolving food tray in the middle of the table enables everyone to reach dishes and serve himself without stretching over or getting up which would be thought impolite. The dishes are served first to important guests, and after that it matters little whether the revolving centerpiece is turned from left to right or vice versa.

It is also a mistake to try to be too finicky and refined when eating foods on the bone or in their shells; anything that is too difficult to cope with using chopsticks is best eaten with both hands. When shrimp have to be removed from their shells at the table, a finger bowl is usually provided, and the shells can be peeled off using both hands or using chopsticks and one hand. When meat has been chopped into small, bite-size pieces on the bone, simply place the morsel in your mouth and as the meat is eaten, remove the bones; usually the meat is so well-cooked and tender that it falls off the bone once in the mouth, so there is no problem.

In Hong Kong it is customary to drop the bones and shells onto the tablecloth, since the dirtier the tablecloth after the meal, the more relaxed and enjoyable the meal is thought to have been. Often, however, plates are provided for this purpose, or scraps can always be pushed to the side of one's plate and will be removed before the next course.

In China plates are not changed for each course, but only when someone's bowl or plate is full of bones or other leftovers. When helping yourself to a dish with sauce, hold your bowl close to the serving dish to avoid spills.

Some people might consider it unhygienic for all the diners to help themselves with their own chopsticks, but this follows from the underlying philosophy that everyone is gathered together around the table, and the bonds of fellowship make such a consideration of secondary importance. Indeed, it is considered very good form and a friendly gesture for a host to select a particularly choice morsel and to place it in his guest's bowl with his own chopsticks. Obviously, on formal occasions each serving dish has its own set of utensils, so that each guest can transfer the food to his bowl and then eat with his or her chopsticks.

SELECTING A CHINESE MENU

It is best to start the meal with light and delicate dishes, progressing toward full-flavored, richer fare, or the palate will be blunted by stronger tastes and fail to appreciate the more subtle flavors.

The Chinese maintain that a menu should start with Yang foods — solid yet light — and finish with Yin foods — dishes with sauces and liquids. By beginning the meal with the accent on Yang, the stomach is suitably prepared for all the food which is to follow. These foods should, however, be eaten slowly, and sudden contrast of hot and cold foods should be avoided. The meal will end with tea, since liquid is the epitome of Yin nourishment. The menu should include a variety of foods cooked by different methods, such as stir-fried, fried, stewed, or braised dishes and should incorporate a wide range of ingredients, tastes, and textures.

The age and sex of those present must also be borne in mind: if there is a preponderance of elderly people, then the food should be light and not too strongly or richly flavored. The menu could include a starter of some kind; shark's fin soup; one or two stir-fried dishes with fairly delicate ingredients, such as shrimp or other seafood; a dish of bean curd and ground pork; and a more strongly flavored dish of shrimp in chili sauce. This could be followed by Cantonese rice or fried noodles, but only if the preceding dishes were not accompanied by boiled rice; a dessert would then round the meal off suitably.

An old Chinese saying should be remembered when planning a meal: "There is no need to strive for perfection in combining the five flavors or to take inordinate pains to mingle the aromas or to go to great lengths to seek out rare ingredients from far-off lands."

Drawing on the wide selection of recipes given in this book and using a little flair and imagination it should be easy to plan some delicious Chinese meals. The following menus are merely suggestions.

Southern Chinese menu:
Steamed chicken salad with noodles, page 40; Sweet and sour pork, page 72; Shrimp with fresh fava beans, page 153; Ch'ao tou ya (stir-fried bean sprouts), page 204; Pai fan (boiled rice), page 254.

Light meal
Steamed fish, page 136; Bean curd with fermented black beans Sichuan style, page 206; Fried eggs, tomatoes, and mushrooms, page 186; Stir-fried green beans with mushrooms, page 190; Fish balls in broth, page 242; Pai fan (boiled rice), page 254.

Vegetarian meal
Green bean salad, page 44; Bean curd and shrimp salad, page 53; Fried eggplant with sweet and sour sauce, page 203; Mushroom soup, page 216; Pai fan (boiled rice), page 254; Suzhou sugared noodle cake, page 286.

Rich, full-flavored menu
Piquant cucumber salad, page 45; Stir-fried beef and onions, page 101; Fried chili scampi, page 160; Pai fan (boiled rice), page 254; Bamboo shoot soup, page 229.

Summer menu
Steamed chicken with mild garlic dressing, page 38; Bean curd and turnip tops with thousand-year-old eggs, page 54; Chinese chicken and ham salad with noodles, page 56; Lettuce and fillets of fish in broth, page 222; Almond cream jelly, page 292.

Winter dinner
Crispy fried shrimp snacks, page 28; Peking bean curd soup, page 228; Shizitou casserole (braised pork balls), page 84; Stir-fried snow peas with soybean paste, page 192; Congee rice with chicken, page 262.

An appetizing meal for children
Won ton soup, page 213; Fried eggs, tomatoes and mushrooms, page 186; Fried fish with peanuts, page 152; Sweet and sour chicken legs, page 115; Five-color fried rice, page 250; Two-color lake dessert, page 291.

Elaborate dinner party
Seven-color appetizer, page 20; Yu Ch'i (shark's fin soup), page 212; Hsiang su fei ya (classic spiced duck), page 130; Steamed bean curd and egg white, page 208; Cantonese fried scampi, page 156; Cucumbers and scallops with mushrooms, page 194; Yangzhou fried rice, page 248; Fruit on the merry-go-round of happiness, page 290.

Reception or party
Spring rolls, page 24; Bean sprout and noodle salad, page 46; Chiao tzu (stuffed dumplings),

page 60; Five-color hsao mai (steamed dumplings), page 64; Cha shao (roast pork), page 67; Tea eggs, page 187; Fried rice noodles, page 284; Coconut snowballs, page 294.

HOW TO USE CHOPSTICKS

The use of chopsticks dates back to the Shang dynasty (1766 – 1123 B.C.) but nobody knows when they began to take over from fingers, of which they can be considered an extension. They are a symbol of man's progressively more civilized eating habits, like the introduction of chairs to enable the diners to sit comfortably around the table.

Chopsticks used to be known by the name of *chu*, a word whose meaning is connected to the concept of "helping"; since, however, this word sounded a little like the word "finish" – an inauspicious word – there was a gradual change in favor of the expression *k'uai-tzu* meaning "that which is quick." But one is most likely to hear chopsticks referred to as *faai-tsi*, their name in Cantonese. This is another example of the Chinese people's superstitious attitude to those words in common use that sound like other words and acquire their significance by association. The ideograms which represent the word *k'uai-tzu* are pronounced in the same way as the good wish to newly married couples for "children soon" and ivory chopsticks are often given as a wedding present.

There is no strict rule as to how to hold chopsticks so long as they grasp the food firmly so that it can be carried safely from bowl to mouth. A few hints may be helpful:
1. The first chopstick should rest on the crook of the hand between thumb and forefinger, resting on the ring finger; this chopstick remains in a fixed position.
2. The second chopstick is gripped between the tip of the thumb and the tips of the index and the middle fingers, moving freely.
3. It should be easy to close the tips of the chopsticks together so that they touch.

The perceptive and imaginative Chinese have made an observation which shows how the individual travels the same road in his growth from infancy to maturity as all those who have come before him: a child naturally holds his chopsticks very close to their tips, so that his fingers almost touch the food, but gradually as he grows older, his fingers move up the chopsticks toward the other end, following a path which can be seen as a metaphor for his whole life.

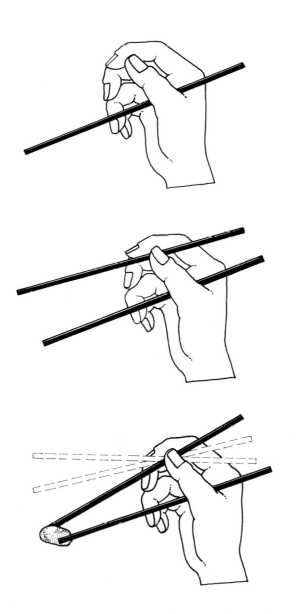

List of recipes

EGG DISHES

VEGETABLES

BEAN CURD DISHES

SOUPS

MONGOLIAN HOT POT COOKING

RICE DISHES

NOODLES

DESSERTS